PRICE GUIDE to the

Twentieth Century Dolls Series.

Presented by

Antiquarian and Historical
Society of St. Joseph on the Lake

Maud Preston Palenske Memorial Library
St. Joseph, Michigan

Carol Gast Glassmire 224 p.

Library of Congress
Catalog Number 80-54721

ISBN 0-87069-359-X

Published by

Wallace-Homestead Book Company
1912 Grand Avenue
Des Moines, Iowa 50305

Contents

120513

For Love or Money— Valuing Your Doll Collection

By Johana Gast Anderton

As a writer who has "spoken out" in print on more than one occasion concerning my views of price guides, the time has come to "eat my words." In the past, I have always stated my feelings that price guides were often out of date by the time they rolled off the presses. Since it often takes six months to a year or more from the time a manuscript is received until the book is released, my attitude was not unfounded.

From the time my first doll book, *Twentieth Century Dolls, From Bisque to Vinyl*, was released, we have been inundated with requests for a price guide to be used with the book. The clamor for such a guide increased after publication of the sequel, *More Twentieth Century Dolls*. Still I resisted the idea, feeling also that a number of worthy guides were already on the market and that I would rather work on several doll books presently in progress than spend time on a price guide.

After perhaps the tenth request from my publisher that I reconsider, I began to think of finding someone who could accomplish the task without pulling me away from the book I was working on. Being a part of a family of writers has its advantages. One Saturday morning, after having talked about a price guide with my editor on the preceding Friday, I called my sister in Florida. "Carol," I said, "how would you like to write a book for my publisher?" The rest is history, as they say. Carol agreed to put aside her own book for a period sufficient to accomplish the herculean task of assembling sufficient data for this guide. She also agreed to come to Kansas City for the final drafting of the manuscript and we spent a congenial, often jolly, two months together at the last of it. Her never-failing sense of humor carried us through some difficult periods and we renewed our relationship in a very special way. Carol's husband had been stationed on the East Coast, leaving us little opportunity over the past twenty-five years for in-depth communication. We talked and talked and talked. And worked and worked and worked.

Why did I change my mind about doing a price guide keyed to my doll books? There was, of course, the demand both from my publisher and from my readers. Then, too, there seemed to be an opportunity to make a statement about dolls and their values — a realistic statement.

4

When I first began to collect dolls as a serious hobby, German bisque dolls could be had for $25, and a nice French bisque was a microscopic $100 or $150. That is, it was microscopic in comparison to the prices they are commanding now. I remember feeling guilty about spending several hundred dollars a few years later for a beautiful French doll. The market was already increasing in most areas of doll collecting by the time my first doll book was released, both because of inflation rates and because so many new collectors were being attracted to the hobby. Demand always influences prices.

Collectors of long standing have watched doll prices escalate to often unbelievable heights, and we have wondered how we might continue to add to our collections in such a market. Dolls have begun to be regarded as investments, a somewhat frightening idea to some of us. Can the market continue to climb? Do we dare hold on to such assets? Should we sell our holdings? We begin to sound as though we are referring to the stock market!

All of this, of course, misses the mark for dedicated doll collectors. We, most of us, that is, are not in this game for the money. We have a love of dolls often dating back to childhood. We have an artistic appreciation for these lovely creations of a bygone era. We like to restore them, to return the worn or broken to former glory. We even like to try making a doll ourselves now and then. But the fact remains that these lovely, delicate, artistic works *are* investments, *must* be protected and preserved, and are worth ever-growing sums on the market. And we must keep ourselves aware of these increasing values for several reasons.

First, there is the matter of insurance. If your collection is not insured, I urge you to re-think the matter. Your dolls are, for the most part, irreplaceable. That is not to say you would be unable to find and purchase another 27" Shirley Temple to replace one lost by fire or theft. Not at all, for there are probably a number of dealers nationwide who could supply you with such a doll at any given time. What is not replaceable is the particular doll you have nurtured for so many years as a vital part of your collection.

That doll you found in six pieces in a box on a lower shelf of a junk store, brought home, cleaned, and costumed can never be replaced. The time you spent gently combing out that matted mohair wig and recurling it to its original style, the time you took in researching just the right movie costume for this little star of your collection, can never be adequately recompensed by insurance. Nevertheless, you do need insurance and should have a full-value policy. Your doll collection is a part of your estate! It has value to your heirs; or it should have. But if you are not aware of the value of the collection, then how can a non-collector be expected to know?

One of the saddest stories I have heard over the years is of the husband of a deceased doll collector who put out all her dolls at a garage sale for a dollar each and was relieved when the last old piece of junk was carried out the door by a smiling woman customer. Keep your family apprised of the value of your collection!

Better still, using a good price guide such as this one, take a week or a month — whatever is required — and complete a collection inventory. There are several record books on the market especially designed for such purposes, with space for photographs of the dolls and complete descriptions, including purchase price and date. Then be sure to update the values of the dolls at least on an annual basis.

Keep this book in a location other than the place where your collection is housed. This is very important. A bank lock box is a good place to keep your record, or perhaps you can exchange records with a collector friend. Your attorney may agree to keep your record book with other legal papers in his files. If you are a person who wants such things at fingertip at all times, purchase a briefcase especially to hold your collection record. Include sales slips which record prices you paid for your dolls and any other pertinent data. You can keep this briefcase by your side at all times or store it in the trunk of your car. Be sure to keep your insurance policy in a safe place other than where your collection is stored.

The second reason for keeping up with doll values, touched on earlier, is estate reasons. When the time comes for someone else to dispose of our collections, it is to be hoped that fair value will be obtained. The example mentioned in a previous paragraph is not an uncommon occurrence. I have heard such stories time and again from members of families of deceased doll collectors who learned too late of the extraordinary value of "Mother's old dolls."

A third reason to consider is that doll collectors sometimes sell dolls in order to upgrade collections, or more mundanely, to pay the rent and utilities! For whatever reason a doll is being sold, a doll collector has the right to expect a reasonable return on her "investment." The responsibility for determining the value of a given doll is not, however, up to the prospective purchaser. A collector has no one but herself to blame if she undersells a valuable doll.

For all of these reasons, and probably a few more, I believe it imperative that each of us be aware of the constantly changing doll market and the way in which that market affects the value of our own collections. But how may one be knowledgeable in such matters without spending inordinate amounts of time reading every trade paper, attending every doll show and sale, subscribing to and reading every doll magazine, and tracking about to every doll shop within driving distance? My answer to this valid question is: Read the price guide of an author who has done just that in his or her research . . . and spend the money for the update of that price guide every year or two, counting it as a worthwhile investment in protecting your much larger investment — your doll collection.

It is with a great deal of sisterly pride that I introduce you to Carol. She is a conscientious and hard-working person with a great eye for detail. She is persevering and funny at the same time. (The book she abandoned temporarily is a hilarious account of her years of government service and her experience as the wife of a Navy career man.) I know you'll like her and hope that you will respond to her invitation to contribute to future editions of this work. Be a doll to someone today.

Behind the Scenes

When Wallace-Homestead first approached me about writing a price guide for *Twentieth Century Dolls* and *More Twentieth Century Dolls*, I hesitated more than a moment to consider my reply. After all, my sister, Johana, is the one with the great knowledge of dolls and their values. I felt a rank amateur in this field, although purchasing and pricing are not things unknown to me. I have spent a number of years in government service as a purchasing agent and am familiar with the marketplace.

Johana assured me that she would be available for consultation and could offer a shoulder to cry on should the need arise. And all through my long bout with the numbers that appear here, she had one foot on my backside a good deal of the time. Before the project was completed, I had returned the favor on a few occasions, and the work was finally done.

By the time the initial research was finished and we had settled down to sorting out all of the information we had gathered, I had become so saturated with the subject of dolls that they began to appear in my dreams at night, in mini-series form.

The first night I was in a huge hall and every person I had ever known was milling around, excitedly awaiting the start of a lecture. An orchestra was tuning up and a choir was moving into place in preparation for the main event. We were gathered there to hear a very famous speaker who would give us insight into the proper way to write about the famous dolls of *Chitty Chitty Bang Bang*.

These same people had turned into dolls the next night and were sitting or standing on shelves in a charming doll shop. They all smiled, flirted, or pouted at me as I recorded information from their price tags for the book.

The third night found me perched on a high judicial bench, wearing a powdered wig and black robe, and considering a decision on a federal case between Ginny and Patsy to determine which was of the higher value. Now I knew that I would, indeed, be capable of completing this book, with all of this great experience behind me!

My confidence rose when my brother flew in from California to appear as an expert witness in a real court trial. I mentioned my insecurities to him and he assured me that I had nothing to worry about.

"After all," he quipped, "what is an expert but someone who is more than fifty miles from home?"

As I pondered this, my spirits and my confidence soared, for I had been more than fifty miles from home for quite a long time. The rest would be all downhill!

Like most little girls, I have had an interest in dolls from early childhood, but in my case that interest was pushed aside for several years as I set out to find my path in life. I was saddened when my own childhood dolls were left behind on a closet shelf during one of the numerous moves I made as the wife of a career Navy man.

My interest was renewed, however, when we produced two lovely daughters. We began collecting dolls for them when they were still quite small, and, as they grew older, they clung to their love for dolls. Our passion was intensified when Johana began work on her first doll book and has increased as she has continued to delve into the history of the dolls of our century. I have read a great deal about dolls, looked for them in shops, at auctions, flea markets, garage sales, and even friends' homes. As a result I have become more knowledgeable, but still must consider myself an amateur when compared to the many "doll people" I have met in the long months of traveling and research for this book.

I am still learning and will continue to do so the rest of my life, but this should not detract from the value of the information in this Price Guide for it is based on actual prices, advertised or realized, and presents an honest evaluation of the market as I found it.

I sincerely hope you will benefit from this book and use it as a guide to help you as you travel through the world of dolls.

— *Carol Gast Glassmire*

How to Use This Book

A price guide, per se, is of little value unless it reflects reality. By surveying the market and reporting actual prices being asked and paid for dolls the author hopes to provide a practical key to the true market value of dolls. By keying the Price Guide to specific examples in *Twentieth Century Dolls, From Bisque to Vinyl* and *More Twentieth Century Dolls, From Bisque to Vinyl*, we hoped to make this a thoroughly useful little book.

The groundwork for this Price Guide included gathering information from doll shops, antique shops, and shows, auctions, collectors, and helpful dealers all over the country. Prices from trade papers and magazines as well as sales lists were added to this information and compiled to represent what we believe to be a good view of the market.

Entries in this book are keyed exactly as are the photographs and paragraphs in "TCD" and "MTCD." If a doll is shown in TCD with a key of ADV-C1, then the price guide entry for that doll will be keyed identically. If a doll is shown on page 364 of TCD, one simply scans down the left-hand column of the price guide to find that page number and the entries for all the dolls shown on page 364.

In most cases there are three prices shown for each entry. Prices were determined, as stated earlier, by compiling actual prices. The high price and the low price shown in this guide are the actual highest and lowest prices found during our survey. The average price shown represents a true average of all of the prices found for each doll, obtained by adding together all prices found for that doll and dividing by the number of examples used. (In this case we were most grateful for our electronic calculator!)

Because condition usually affects price, it is somewhat safe to assume that the higher prices shown reflect sales values of mint or near mint dolls. Conversely, the low price usually indicates that a doll is either nude or in poor condition. Rarity is also a factor, of course, as are current trends in popularity of certain dolls. Sometimes popularity overrides reason and the latest fad in collecting escalates a type or particular doll into higher brackets quite aside from its aesthetic or intrinsic value.

Some dolls are so rare that the example shown in TCD or MTCD is the only one we have seen or heard about in our research, making it nearly impossible to set a value on these particular dolls. In such cases, the price column indicates that these items have no price available and is marked

"NPA." In a few cases, we have used the single discovered price since we felt it represented a fairly true value.

In the case of some catalog illustrations, sufficient descriptive information was lacking to allow a cross-identification with known examples. The price column, therefore, carries merely a notation indicating the item is a Catalog Illustration. With other trade catalog listings where several sizes are given, we have shown a range of prices generally covering all the sizes of that model. This was necessary since there were so few examples to draw on and the prices given seemed to cut across size guidelines. In the future, as more and more examples of certain dolls are seen or reported, it will be possible to open up the category to include price spreads for individual sizes.

As in the case of Madame Alexander, whenever a manufacturer uses the same doll in many guises (costumes), we have inserted parenthetically, whenever possible, the name of the basic doll used.

Many of the dolls shown in TCD and MTCD are the property of known collectors. This Price Guide, by referring to these dolls, does not in fact or intent set an arbitrary value limit on these specific dolls. Rather, it refers to the overall production of that particular doll and reflects prices of actual dolls offered for sale across the country.

Since it is impossible for one person, in this case the author, to be everywhere, readers' letters reporting actual sales or verified advertised prices are welcomed. To qualify as a verified ad price, we must have the advertisement or a photocopy of it. A copy of the sales ticket giving date, doll description, and price paid will also be helpful. When writing please give all pertinent information such as name of doll, manufacturer, size, condition, materials, etc., as well as the related key in TCD or MTCD, the price advertised or realized from actual sale, and date of sale or advertisement.

Every effort has been made to make this an accurate and up-to-the-minute Price Guide. Updates were completed minutes before sending the manuscript off to the publisher. Please remember, however, that this little book is a guide, only, and has been designed to help the reader determine prices by using the information herein plus his or her own good judgment based on experience and knowledge of this fascinating world of dolls.

Key to Abbreviations

Every effort has been made to make this book as helpful and usable as possible for the collector. Its size and format were carefully considered before the design was completed. At first it was felt it would be possible to refrain from using any abbreviations; however, it soon became apparent that for size considerations alone it would be necessary to incorporate certain abbreviations into the entries.

Standard abbreviations familiar to most collectors have been used, with the addition of a few specially tailored letter combinations which seemed to fit our purpose. With a little practice, the reader soon will be able to interpret our hieroglyphics.

Adv	Advertisement	OL	Open Leg
BBsq	Black bisque	OCM	Open-closed mouth
BJ	Ball joints	OM	Open mouth
BL	Bent leg	OW	Otherwise
BSH	brush stroke hair	PBsq	Pink bisque
Bisq	Bisque	Ptd	Painted
c	Circa	ref:	Reference
Clo	Clothes	rp	Rigid plastic
cm	Centimeters	rv	Rigid vinyl
CM	Closed mouth	SBsq	Stone bisque
compo	Composition	SGE	Side glance eyes
e	Eye	SlpE	Sleep eyes
fea	Features	SL	Straight leg
GlsE	Glass eyes	sp	Soft plastic
HB	Hair bow	Std	Seated
HHr	Human hair	sv	Soft vinyl
hp	Hard Plastic	s/s	Shoes and socks
Hr	Hair	TM	Trademark
hv	Hard vinyl	Unmkd	Unmarked
Jtd	Jointed	WBsq	White Bisque
Jts	Joints	Wg	Wig
LAL	Look-alike	Wgd	Wigged
Mkd	Marked	1-pc	One-piece doll
MO	Molded-on	2-jts	Jointed at shoulders only
MoHr	Mohair	4-jts	Jointed at shoulders and hips
MP	Molded and painted	5-jts	Jointed at shoulders, hips,
NPA	No price available		and neck

Comprehensive Price Guide to the Twentieth Century Dolls Series

A

TCD Page	Key	Nomenclature	Size	Low	Avg.	High
17	A-1	Baby, A.B.C./TOYS	24″	35	50	78
	A-2	Boy, RAILROAD KING	15″	50	65	92
18	A-3	Colored Baby, 1961 ALTER	19″	25	30	42
	A-4	Mama Doll, AM DOLL CO.	25″	65	95	150
	A-5	Amberg Walking Doll	19½″		NPA	
			22½″		NPA	
			28½″		NPA	
19	A-6	American Beauty Dolls	13″		NPA	
			14″		NPA	
			15″		NPA	
			18″		NPA	
			19″		NPA	
			19½″		NPA	
	A-6a	American Beauty Dolls	14″		NPA	
			15½″		NPA	
			17″		NPA	
			20″		NPA	
	A-7	Girl, Unmarked, hp	19″	25	40	78
	A-8	Lady, ARROW PLASTIC	25″	15	35	54
20	A-9	Baby, Arrow Rubber/Plastics	10″	5	10	27

ADVERTISING

TCD Page	Key	Nomenclature	Size	Low	Avg.	High
	ADV-A1	Aunt Jemima, litho/ cloth	12″	8	24	45
	ADV-A2	Aunt Jemima, litho on muslin	15″	25	36	54
	ADV-A3	Aunt Jemima			Adv.	
21	ADV-A4	Aunt Jemima, compo/cloth	18½″	45	55	78
22	ADV-A5	Harriet Hubbard Ayer Make-up Doll	14-14½″	20	40	92
			16″	25	45	78
			20″	30	47	78
23	ADV-B1	Billie-Whipple	6½″	2	3	8
	ADV-B2	Buster Brown			Adv.	
24	ADV-CK1	Campbell Kid, Compo/cloth	10½″	85	135	178
	ADV-CK2	Campbell Kid, cloth/ compo	11″	85	135	195
	ADV-CK3	Campbell Kid, cloth/ compo	12″	85	135	195

TCD Page	Key	Nomenclature	Size	Low	Avg.	High
	ADV-CK4	Campbell Kid, compo	12½"	38	90	210
25	ADV-CK5	Campbell Kid, compo	12½"	38	90	210
	ADV-CK6	Campbell Kid, compo	11½"	95	131	270
26	ADV-CK7	Campbell Kids, vinyl	13"	20	45	92
	ADV-CK8	Campbell Kid, vinyl	8"	8	16	30
	ADV-CK9	Campbell Kid, vinyl	10"	20	35	54
27	ADV-CL1	Miss Clairol Doll, Glamour Misty	12"	7	10	18
	ADV-CL2	Miss Clairol Doll, Glamour Misty	12"	7	10	18
	ADV-CL3	Clicquot Club Eskimo, compo/cloth		30	65	115
	ADV-CR1	Rastus, the Cream of Wheat Chef	18"	30	35	78
	ADV-CR2	Cream of Wheat		Adv.		
28	ADV-CR1	Crackerjack Sailor boy		Adv.		
29	ADV-CU1	Cubeb Smoking Doll, compo	25"	150	165	270
	ADV-CU2	Miss Curity, plastic/vinyl	14½"	40	55	92
	ADV-E1	Eskimo Pie Boy, litho/cloth	15"	2	4	8
30	ADV-F1	Flossie Flirt	20"	65	80	115
	ADV-G1	Gerber Baby, rubber	11"	12	24	42
	ADV-G2	Gerber Baby, vinyl	14"	10	12	30
31	ADV-G3	Jolly Green Giant, cloth	16"	3	5	10
	ADV-G4	Green Giant Trademark		(TM)		
	ADV-K1	Kellogg's Snap, Crackle, Pop		15	20	30
	ADV-K2	Kodak Display Dolls	10"	NPA		
32	ADV-L1	Buddy Lee, plaster compo	13"	35	65	100
	ADV-L2	Buddy Lee Cowboy Doll	13"	85	110	215
	ADV-L3	Buddy Lee Engineer Doll	13"	85	110	215
33	ADV-L4	Buddy Lee Industrial Doll (Allow higher price for Coca-Cola uniform)	13"	85	110	215
	ADV-L5	Composition, Buddy Lee type	13½"	20	33	54
	ADV-M1	Mr. Magoo, vinyl/cloth	16"	5	20	42

TCD Page	Key	Nomenclature	Size	Low	Price Avg.	High
	ADV-M2	Modern Priscilla			Adv.	
34	ADV-Mc1	Betsy McCall, hp/ vinyl	8″	20	48	115
	ADV-Mc2	Betsy McCall	22″	135	168	240
	ADV-Mc3	Betsy McCall, hp/ vinyl	14″	35	50	92
			20″	135	168	240
	ADV-Mc4	Betsy McCall, hp/ vinyl	14″	35	50	92
	ADV-Mc5	Betsy McCall, hp/ vinyl	14″	35	50	92
35	ADV-Mc6	McCall—Peggy the Modern Fashion Model	13″	25	30	44
36	ADV-MU1	Arthur Murray Dancing Doll	14″	65	75	100
	ADV-N1	Nestle Little Hans, rag	13″	8	12	18
	ADV-N2	Nestle Little Hans, vinyl	13½″	10	23	54
37	ADV-N3	Nickerson Farms Honey Bee	13″	3	3	6
	ADV-N4	Cuddles, Needlecraft Magazine			NPA	
38	ADV-P1	Phillip Morris "Johnny", compo/ cloth	15″	65	75	195
	ADV-P2	Mr. Peanut, litho/ cloth	22″	2	5	10
	ADV-P3	Pillsbury Poppin Fresh Dough Boy	14″	2	4	6
39	ADV-Q1	Quaker Crackels Boy, litho/cloth	17″	35	81	180
	ADV-P4	Purina Scarecrow, vinyl/cloth	22″	8	16	27
40	ADV-R1	Little Miss Revlon, plastic/vinyl	10½″	10	23	54
	ADV-R2	Miss Revlon, plastic/ vinyl	18″	22	48	100
			20″	30	52	115
			22″	25	55	132
41	ADV-S1	"Fresh Up Freddie" Seven-Up	9″	5	10	15
	ADV-S2	Singer Mannikin Doll Set	13″	25	49	96
	ADV-S3	Smokey The Bear, cloth	16″	6	9	15
42	ADV-S4	Stuffed Rabbit	18″		NPA	
	ADV-T1	Toni, hp	14″	23	30	72
	ADV-T2	Toni Walker, hp	20″	28	64	180

TCD Page	Key	Nomenclature	Size	Low	Price Avg.	High
43	ADV-T3	Toni, vinyl	10½"	23	25	65
			14"	25	30	70
			20"	25	64	150
			25"	50	65	85
	ADV-T4	Thumbs-Up Victory Doll	8"		NPA	
	ADV-T5	Teddy Snow Crop Hand Puppet		6	7	10
44	ADV-T6	Tintair Glamour Girl, plastic	14"	65	75	100
	ADV-V1	Vanta Baby, compo/ cloth	14"	65	74	145
			19"	50	108	175
			21½"	65	115	189

ALEXANDER DOLL CO

TCD Page	Key	Nomenclature	Size	Low	Price Avg.	High
46	ALEX-1	Girl, Little Betty, compo	8½"	55	94	150
	ALEX-2	Alice in Wonderland, compo	7"	75	167	390
	ALEX-3	Baby, Little Genius, compo/cloth	17"	85	93	120
	ALEX-4	Little Genius, (hd. circ.)	14"	85	97	132
	ALEX-5	Baby, Princess Alexandria, compo/cloth	24"	95	130	195
48	ALEX-6	Scarlett O'Hara, compo	18½"	165	251	420
	ALEX-7	McGuffey Ana, compo	21"	225	238	300
	ALEX-8	Flora McFlimsey, compo	18"	135	275	540
49	ALEX-9	Flora McFlimsey, compo	13"	145	206	360
	ALEX-10	Princess Elizabeth, compo	24"	125	182	495
	ALEX-10a	Princess Elizabeth, compo	15"	85	161	360
50	ALEX-11	Wendy-Ann, compo	13"	85	132	270
	ALEX-12	Wendy-Ann, compo	13"	85	132	270
51	ALEX-13	Wendy-Ann, compo	13"	85	132	270
	ALEX-14	Alice in Wonderland, compo	13"	85	132	270
	ALEX-15	Alice in Wonderland, compo	13"	85	132	270
52	ALEX-16	Karen Ballerina, compo	21"	225	248	270
	ALEX-17	Princess Flavia, compo	22"	400	440	480

TCD Page	Key	Nomenclature	Size	Low	Avg.	High
53	ALEX-18	Kitty Baby, compo/ rubber	21″	90	95	100
	ALEX-19	Jeannie Walker, compo	14″	90	135	210
			19″	110	145	225
54	ALEX-20	The Wedding Party				
	ALEX-20a	Bride, compo	17″	180	195	230
			22″	225	285	300
	ALEX-20b	Bridesmaid, compo	15″	165	182	220
			18″	185	200	240
			21½″	200	260	300
	ALEX-20c	Flower Girl, compo	16″	145	175	210
			20″	170	225	270
			24″	170	225	270
55	ALEX-21	Bride, hp	17″	120	170	225
			21½″	150	185	270
	ALEX-22	Fairy Queen, compo	14½″	210	250	280
			17½″	250	275	360
	ALEX-23	Babs, The Ice-Skating Girl, hp	15″	150	180	240
			18″	150	188	270
56	ALEX-24	Fairy Queen, hp	14½″	150	194	270
			17½″	200	208	270
	ALEX-25	Nina Ballerina, hp	14½″	150	175	240
			17½″	150	181	270
	ALEX-26a	Polly Pigtails, hp	14½″	145	190	270
			17½″	150	169	210
	ALEX-26b	Cinderella, hp	14″	125	180	300
57	ALEX-26-1	Slumbermate, vinyl/ cloth	14″	75	95	150
	ALEX-26-2	Bunny-Baby, vinyl/ cloth	18½″	125	175	270
	ALEX-27	Violet, hp	17″	135	149	162
58	ALEX-28	Cissy, plastic/vinyl	20″	75	137	342
	ALEX-29	Active Miss, plastic	18″	135	149	162
	ALEX-30	Cynthia, hp	14″	450	475	600
	ALEX-31	Margot Ballerina, plastic/vinyl	15″	85	130	240
59	ALEX-32	Boy, hp	12″	85	89	92
	ALEX-33	McGuffey Ana, hp	17½″	175	208	240
	ALEX-34	Kathy, vinyl	21″	35	63	102
	ALEX-35	Marybel, The doll that gets well, vinyl	15″	35	95	198
61	ALEX-36a	Sleeping Beauty, compo	16″	250	275	300
	ALEX-36b	Sleeping Beauty, hp/ vinyl	17″	250	275	300
			21″	120	307	540
62	ALEX-37	Ballerina Elise, hp/ vinyl	17″	175	193	210

TCD Page	Key	Nomenclature	Size	Low	Price Avg.	High
	ALEX-38	Chatterbox, hp/vinyl	24″	55	84	168
	ALEX-39a	Caroline, plastic/ vinyl	14″	125	169	270
63	ALEX-39b	Caroline, plastic/ vinyl	14″	160	199	300
	ALEX-40	Jacqueline, plastic	10″	125	318	420
			21″	600	675	900
	ALEX-40-1	Kitten, vinyl/cloth	14″	22	36	60
			18″	50	65	114
64	ALEX-41	Leslie, plastic/vinyl, Bride	17″	125	135	174
		Ballerina	17″	125	128	162
		Debutante	17″	125	145	210
	ALEX-42	So Big, vinyl/cloth	22″	25	70	138
65	ALEX-43	Little Huggums, vinyl/cloth	12″	10	30	42
		Big Huggums, vinyl/ cloth	25″	15	32	45
	ALEX-44	Pumpkin, vinyl/cloth	22″	30	48	78
	ALEX-45	Puddin', vinyl/cloth	21″	40	56	90
	ALEX-46	Happy, vinyl/cloth	20″	85	94	103
	ALEX-47	Marry Cassett Baby, vinyl/cloth	14″	80	88	100
			20″	95	105	132
66	ALEX-48	Pussycat, vinyl/cloth	14″	14	29	36
			20″	30	50	66
			24″	30	48	70
	ALEX-49	Victoria, vinyl/cloth	20″	30	40	60
	ALEX-50	Lucinda, vinyl/plastic	12″	135	158	210
67	ALEX-51	Suzy, vinyl/plastic	12″	125	138	150
	ALEX-52	Madame Doll, plastic/vinyl	14″	95	127	162
			21″	1000	1100	1200
	ALEX-53	Heidi, plastic/vinyl	14″		NPA	
	ALEX-54	Rebecca, plastic/ vinyl	14″	30	88	200
	ALEX-55	Alice in Wonderland, plastic/vinyl	14″	50	63	90
68	ALEX-56	Jenny Lind and Her Listening Cat	14″	85	168	300
	ALEX-57	Degas Girl	14″	32	34	42
	ALEX-58	Renoir Girl	14″	100	110	120
	ALEX-59	Grandma Jane	14″	150	167	252
	ALEX-60	Cinderella, vinyl/ plastic	14″	18	39	78
69	ALEX-61	Sound of Music Dolls, Brigette	11″	125	165	225
			14″	150	170	180
		Frederich	8″	85	96	107
			11″	125	165	225
		Gretl	8″	85	96	107

TCD Page	Key	Nomenclature	Size	Low	Avg.	High
			11″	125	165	225
		Liesl	11″	150	165	180
			14″	150	195	240
		Louisa	12″	250	275	300
			14″	200	220	240
		Maria	12″	150	170	180
			17″	175	193	210
		Marta	8″	85	96	120
			11″	125	165	225
	ALEX-62	Peter Pan Dolls,				
		Peter Pan	14″	225	250	270
		Tinker Bell	11″	225	250	270
		Wendy	14″	250	280	300
		Michael	14″	225	250	270

AMERICAN CHARACTER

TCD Page	Key	Nomenclature	Size	Low	Avg.	High
70	AMER-1	Mama Doll, compo/ cloth	17″		NPA	
	AMER-2	Baby, Bent Leg, compo	23″	65	80	95
71	AMER-3	Sally, compo/cloth	16″	85	91	95
	AMER-3-1	Bottletot, compo/ cloth	13″	75	80	85
72	AMER-4	Toddle-Tot, compo/ cloth	18″		NPA	
			21″		NPA	
			24″		NPA	
	AMER-5	Perfect Beauty, compo/cloth	24″		NPA	
	AMER-5-1	Happytot, rubber	10½″		NPA	
73	AMER-6	Mama Doll, compo/ cloth	19″	45	70	95
	AMER-6-1	Child, vinyl	16″	25	35	45
	AMER-7	Toodles, compo/vinyl		35	42	60
74	AMER-8	Toodles Toddler, vinyl	23″	35	43	60
	AMER-9	Toodles, vinyl	21″	50	77	125
75	AMER-10	Toodles Toddlers, vinyl	25″	50	77	125
			30″	50	90	165
	AMER-10a	Toodles, vinyl			Adv.	
	AMER-11	Toodles, vinyl	21″	50	66	95
	AMER-12	Tiny Tears, hp/ rubber	13″	20	33	45
76	AMER-13a	Tiny Tears, hp/ rubber	11″	18	39	65
	AMER-13b	Tiny Tears, hp/vinyl	19″	30	48	85
	AMER-13c	Tiny Tears, hp/ rubber	13″	20	43	75
	AMER-13d	Tiny Tears			Adv.	

TCD Page	Key	Nomenclature	Size	Low	Avg.	High
	AMER-14	New Tiny Tears, vinyl	8½"	8	10	15
			12"	12	13	16
77	AMER-14a	Teeny Tiny Tears, vinyl	8½"	9	12	15
			12"	5	6	10
	AMER-15	Sweet Sue Sophis-ticate, plastic	18"	45	49	54
			20"	50	85	150
			22"	45	49	54
			25"	38	45	60
		Dressed as Annie Oakley			NPA	
	AMER-15-1	Sweet Sue Sophisticate			Adv.	
	AMER-15-2	Besty McCall, hp/vinyl	8"	40	45	60
79	AMER-16	Tressy, plastic/vinyl	12"	6	17	22
	AMER-17	Cricket, plastic/vinyl	9"	12	14	18
80	AMER-18	Teenie Weenie			Adv.	
	AMER-19	Pretty Baby			Adv.	
	AMER-20	Whimsies, vinyl	21"	18	44	60

ARMAND MARSEILLE

TCD Page	Key	Nomenclature	Size	Low	Avg.	High
81	AM-1	Kiddie Joy, bisq/compo/cloth	10"	225	250	325
	AM-2	Baby, GERMANY/327/A.9 M. bisq/pm	17"	325	350	450
82	AM-3	Dream Baby, bisque head/cloth	10"	225	250	330
	AM-4	Dream Baby bisque head/cloth	12"	275	300	390
83	AM-5	Baby, 351.14K, bisq/pm	17"	325	350	450
	AM-6	Baby, 351, bisq/compo/cloth	17"	325	350	450
84	AM-7	Baby, 352, bisq/compo/cloth	12"	200	225	300
85	AM-8	Bisque Shoulder Head Girl, 370	22"	225	240	300
	AM-9	Bisque Shoulder Head Girl, 370	20"	225	238	300
	AM-10	Bisque Shoulder Head Girl, 370	24"	275	287	360
	AM-11	Bisque Socket Head Girl, 390	21"	250	287	390
86	AM-12	Girl, 390, bisq, socket head	17"	200	215	270

TCD Page	Key	Nomenclature	Size	Low	Price Avg.	High
	AM-13	Girl, 390, bisq/ compo/pm	15½"	180	190	240
	AM-14L	Boy, 390, bisq socket head	13½"	180	201	270
	AM-14R	Boy, 971, bisq/pm	10"	225	237	300
87	AM-15L	Young Lady, 390, bisq/kid	13"	180	190	240
	AM-15R	Boy, A.M. 8/0/ Germany, bisq/pm	9"	150	216	325
	AM-16	Rosebud, bisq/kid	23"	275	300	390
88	AM-17	Miss Columbia, bisq/ wood/compo	22"	325	338	425
	AM-18	Baby Betty, bisq/kid	20"	325	338	435
89	AM-19	Florodora, bisq/ compo/pm	22"	225	250	330
	AM-20	Florodora, bisq/kid/ cloth	19"	200	215	270

ARRANBEE

TCD Page	Key	Nomenclature	Size	Low	Price Avg.	High
90	R&B-1	Baby, compo/cloth	22"		NPA	
	R&B-2	Debu Teen, compo/ cloth	17"	85	103	165
91	R&B-3R	Girl, hp	17"	65	96	135
	R&B-3L	Girl, hp	17"	75	100	150
	R&B-4	Baby, compo/cloth	17"	35	50	65
92	R&B-5L	Girl, compo	16"	65	91	105
	R&B-5C	Girl, compo	17"	75	100	150
	R&B-5R	Girl, compo	14"	65	80	115
	R&B-6	Nancy, compo	12"	55	71	115
			17"	75	125	180
94	R&B-7	Girl, compo	21"	65	112	180
	R&B-8	Littlest Angel, vinyl/ hp	10"	8	34	65
	R&B-9	Unmarked Nancy, compo	11½"	30	48	95
	R&B-10	Child, compo/cloth	20"		NPA	
95	R&B-11	Dream Baby, compo/cloth	26"	45	70	95
	R&B-12	Dream Baby, compo	16"	35	50	65
		compo/cloth	21"		NPA	

AVERILL

TCD Page	Key	Nomenclature	Size	Low	Price Avg.	High
96	AVRL-1	Dolly Record, compo/cloth	26"	300	350	425
97	AVRL-2	Baby, MADAM HENDREN/12	12"	65	95	135
	AVRL-3	Baby, MADAM HENDREN/818M	14"		NPA	
	AVRL-4	Whistling Sailor, compo/cloth	13½"	85	110	145
98	AVRL-5	Cowboy Whistler, compo/cloth	13½"	85	110	145

TCD Page	Key	Nomenclature	Size	Low	Avg.	High
	AVRL-6	Rock-a-Bye Baby, compo/cloth	18"	75	88	125
99	AVRL-7	Sunny Girl, cell/ compo/cloth	14"	100	115	150

B

TCD Page	Key	Nomenclature	Size	Low	Avg.	High
	B-1	Baby Ruth, compo/ cloth	22"	65	113	150
100	B-2	Bannister Baby, vinyl	18"	25	30	55
	B-3	B. D. Co. Compo Baby	18"	55	95	135
	B-4	Bed Doll, French Dandy, cloth	32"	40	80	135
	B-5	Bed Doll, French Girls, cloth	24"	40	80	135
102	B-6	Bed Doll Melissa, compo/cloth	28"	95	140	175

BISQUE DOLLS

TCD Page	Key	Nomenclature	Size	Low	Avg.	High
103	BISQ-1	CM German Bisque	15"	600	750	900
	BISQ-2	CM German Bisque Child	15"	425	580	675
104	BISQ-3	S&H Bisque	20"	750	1500	2250
105	BISQ-4	Boy, Franz Schmidt	17"	425	450	475
	BISQ-5	OM German Child	25"	375	425	475
106	BISQ-6	SFBJ Child	19"	350	630	850
	BISQ-7	SFBJ Head		NPA		
107	BISQ-8	OM German Bisque	24"	375	450	525
108	BISQ-9	OM Paul Schmidt	14"	100	155	225
	BISQ-10	Kestner 136	23"	225	406	500
109	BISQ-11	Mellita/11	20"	NPA		
	BISQ-12	OM German	23"	400	425	450
	BISQ-13	Handwerck type	23"	400	450	540
110	BISQ-14	Dollar Princess	25"	250	341	480
	BISQ-15	Schuelzmeister & Quenat bisque	22"	275	300	390
111	BISQ-16a	Heubach-Koppelsdorf 275	15"	195	205	252
	BISQ-16b	Florodora	15"	200	231	270
	BISQ-16c	Gbr. K. Child	15"	225	276	330
112	BISQ-17	Herm. Steiner New Born Babe 240	10"	175	223	270
	BISQ-18	Tynie Baby-type	6½"	225	370	450
	BISQ-19	R. A. 127 Baby	6½"	250	362	450
113	BISQ-20	Head, Jutta/1914/ 8½	3"	NPA		
	BISQ-21	Baby, Complete Doll	20"	400	425	480
	BISQ-22	Nancy Ann Story Book Dolls	8"	20	31	60
	BISQ-23	ABC Sugar Bisque	9¼"	35	50	65

TCD Page	Key	Nomenclature	Size	Low	Price Avg.	High
114	BISQ-24	Baby, Germany			NPA	
	BISQ-25	German All-bisque Baby	4″	55	91	135
	BISQ-26a	Pink bisque, Child, German	6″	175	231	275
	BISQ-26b	Pale Pink bisque, German child	3½″	125	151	180
	BISQ-26c	All-bisque German child	4¼″	125	151	180
115	BISQ-27	Sugar Bisque Girl	6½″	25	35	47
	BISQ-28	German Doll House Dolls	1⅜″-3½″	85	150	275
	BISQ-29	Nodder Girl, 758/ BB/GERMANY	3″	125	187	250

BYE-LO BABY

116	BLB-1	Bye-lo Baby (13″c)	14″	380	492	625
	BLB-2	Bye-lo Baby (11¾″c)	13″	135	337	540
117	BLB-3	Bye-lo Baby (12″c)	14″	200	370	550
	BLB-4	Bye-lo Baby (10¼″c)	11″	150	383	540
118	BLB-5	Fly-lo Baby (10¼″c)	12″		NPA	
119	BLB-6	Bye-lo Baby, Reproduction	12″		NPA	
	BLB-7	Bye-lo Baby Salt	2½″		NPA	
	BLB-8	Bye-10 Baby, box			NPA	

CAMEO DOLL PRODUCTS

121	CAM-1	Joseph L. Kallus			*Portrait*	
	CAM-2	Sitting Kewpies, bisque		225	245	270
	CAM-3	Kewpies, 1947			*Catalog Illus.*	
	CAM-4	Kewpies, Floppy			*Catalog Illus.*	
	CAM-5	Kewpie, bisque	5″	85	97	135
122	CAM-6	Kewpie, compo	14″	100	152	275
	CAM-7L	Kewpie, bisque	5¼″	85	98	115
	CAM-7R	Kewpie, Vinyl	9″	20	53	75
	CAM-8L	Kewpie, Vinyl	3¾″	5	7	9
	CAM-8R	Kewpie, cell	2¼″	25	38	65
123	CAM-9	Kewpie, Compo	11″	100	165	275
	CAM-10	Kewpie, modern vinyl	13″	20	39	55
	CAM-11	Kewpie Gal, vinyl			NPA	
124	CAM-12	Kewpie, vinyl		20	53	75
	CAM-13	Ragsy Kewpie, vinyl	8″	12	29	42
	CAM-14	Scootles, Comp.				
		White	12″	200	230	255
		Black	12″	300	358	425
		White	15″	100	160	215
		Black	15″	200	318	425

TCD Page	Key	Nomenclature	Size	Low	Price Avg.	High
125	CAM-15	Scootles, Vinyl	19"	65	155	215
	CAM-16	Scootles, Wood pulp compo		200	283	325
126	CAM-17	Baby "Bo-Kaye," bisque	5½"	1200	1250	1500
		Celluloid		250	400	500
		Bisque-Head	16"-20"		1650	
	CAM-18	Little Annie Rooney	16"	375	541	650
128	CAM-18-1	Giggles, compo	11"	300	430	540
	CAM-19	Betty Boop, segmented wood/compo	12"	200	375	450
	CAM-20	Ho-Ho, soft vinyl			NPA	
129	CAM-21	Disney Dolls			NPA	
	CAM-22	Pinkie, wood pulp compo			NPA	
130	CAM-23	Champ, wood pulp compo	16"		NPA	
	CAM-24	Dyp-a-Babe, vinyl	24"		45	
131	CAM-25	Affectionately Peanut			NPA	
	CAM-26	Margie, Segmented wood/compo	9½"	125	153	185
	CAM-26b	Margie, vinyl	17"		NPA	
132	CAM-26a	Margie, vinyl	17"		NPA	
	CAM-27	Miss Peep, vinyl	18½"	25	36	55
	CAM-28	Baby Mine, vinyl	20"		NPA	
134	CAM-29	Landscape			*Painting*	
	CAM-30	Portrait of a Child			*Portrait*	
	CAM-31	Portrait of an Old Man			*Portrait*	

C

TCD Page	Key	Nomenclature	Size	Low	Price Avg.	High
135	C-1	Little Lady of Fashion, vinyl	12"	10	17	25
	C-2	Miss Century, compo/cloth	22"		NPA	
136	C-3	Century girl, compo/cloth	16"	35	74	102
	C-4	Century Shoulder head, only	6"	15	31	45
	C-5a	Grace Corry Boy, compo/cloth	13½"	95	135	185
	C-5b	Grace Corry Boy, compo/cloth	15"	100	145	225

CELLULOID

TCD Page	Key	Nomenclature	Size	Low	Price Avg.	High
138	CEL-1	Girl, Diamond Turtle Mark	8"	40	48	63
		Boy, Diamond Turtle Mark	8½"	40	48	63

TCD Page	Key	Nomenclature	Size	Low	Avg.	High
	CEL-2	Child, Diamond Turtle Mark	13½"	100	111	125
	CEL-3	Boy, Diamond Turtle Mark	22"	110	152	265
	CEL-4	Girl, Turtle Mark	17"		NPA	
140	CEL-5	Babies, Parsons-Jackson	10½"	100	177	275
	CEL-6	Baby, Parsons-Jackson	12"	110	174	275
	CEL-7	Heads for hand puppets	2½"	6	15	25
141	CEL-8	Baby, unmarked	19½"	100	162	215
	CEL-9	Soldier, Germany	5"	10	13	15
	CEL-10	Clown, Japan	6"	25	32	40
			13"	25	30	35
142	CEL-11	Baby, Hong Kong	12¼"	10	23	35
	CEL-12a	Carnival type, FETHALITE	11"	25	30	35
	CEL-12b	Girl, HOLLYWOOD	5"	4	9	15
	CEL-12c	Kewpie, JAPAN	2¼"	25	38	65
	CEL-12d	Carnival type, OCCUPIED JAPAN	6"	30	35	40
	CEL-12e	Girl, JAPAN	3½"	3	4	7
	CEL-12f	Girl, KNICKER-BOCKER	6"	6	18	35
	CEL-12	Irwin, U.S.A.	6½"	9	18	30
	CEL-13	Boy, JAPAN	6"	6	19	40
143	CEL-14	Baby, U.S.A.	5"	25	30	35
	CEL-15	Baby, in pink metal buggy	2½"		NPA	
	CEL-16	Baby, YANOCO/ USA	8"	10	23	35
	CHINA					
144	CHI-1	Ruth, GERMANY	19"	105	180	275
	CHI-2a	Bertha, GERMANY	12"	105	148	200
145	CHI-2b	China Head, Civil War type	8½"	60	123	175
	CHI-3	1880's type	17"	275	336	525
	CHI-4a	Dresser doll, powder box	6"	25	45	65
	CHI-4b	Powder puff doll	7½"	25	45	65
	CHI-4c	Powder box doll	6½"	25	45	65
146	CHI-5	Blonde China	23"	300	350	395
	CHI-6	Miniature China	4¾"	65	75	95
	CHI-7	Blonde China	19"	175	275	350
147	CHI-8	Deep Shoulder China	25"	275	350	425
	CHI-9	Old China	23"	300	350	475
	CHI-10	Half-doll, 9493	4"		45	

TCD Page	Key	Nomenclature	Size	Low	Avg.	High
		COMICS				
148	COM-B1	Buttercup, cloth	15"		NPA	
	COM-B2	Charlie Brown, vinyl	7½"	7	9	12
149	COM-C1	Ella Cinders, Horsman	18"	125	177	235
	COM-D1	Dagwood, cloth	18"	85	87	95
	COM-D2	Dennis the Menace, vinyl/cloth	15"	20	37	55
150	COM-D3	Dennis the Menace, vinyl	13"	7	29	45
	COM-F1	Elmer Fudd, vinyl	8"	6	12	20
	COM-F2	Flintstones Characters, vinyl	12"	15	23	30
			8"	18	23	28
151	COM-F3	Felix, wood	8½"	75	185	355
	COM-G1	Gasoline Alley Figures, bisque		45	119	245
	COM-G2	Gasoline Alley Characters, cloth		45	60	75
152	COM-L1	Linus, vinyl	8¼"	6	8	9
	COM-L2	Little Lulu, cloth	15"	15	32	55
153	COM-L3	Little Orphan Annie, oilcloth	13½"		NPA	
		Sandy, oilcloth	9"		NPA	
	COM-L4	Little Orphan Annie, wood	5½"		35	
	COM-L5	Little Orphan Annie, rag	18"	52	80	105
154	COM-L6	Little Orphan Annie, compo	12"	35	85	125
	COM-L7	Little Orphan Annie dishes			NPA	
	COM-L8	Little Orphan Annie, compo	10"	32	70	145
155	COM-M1	Mighty Mouse, vinyl	9½"	6	10	14
	COM-N1	Nize Baby, cloth	15½"		NPA	
	COM-01	Olive Oyl, vinyl/cloth	10"		20	
156	COM-P1	Joan Palooka, stuffed vinyl	14"	35	81	125
	COM-P2	Pogo and Friends, vinyl		2	3	5
157	COM-P3	Popeye, wood/compo	10½"	165	195	225
	COM-P4	Popeye, wood	5"		35	
	COM-P5	Popeye, soft vinyl	13"		65	
158	COM-P6	Porky Pig, vinyl	7"	5	7	10
		Elmer Fudd, vinyl	8"	5	7	10
	COM-S1	Sad Sack, vinyl	16"		NPA	
	COM-S2	Brenda Starr, vinyl	11½"	85	103	165
159	COM-T1	Bonnie Braids, rubber	14"	20	32	55

TCD Page	Key	Nomenclature	Size	Low	Price Avg.	High
	COM-T2	Bonnie Braids, vinyl/ compo/cloth	15″	20	32	55
	COM-T3	Bonnie Braids, stuffed vinyl	12″	20	32	55
160	COM-T4	Sparkle Plenty, hp head/vinyl	14″	25	61	90
	COM-T5	Honey Moon, vinyl/ cotton	15″	23	38	55
	COM-T6	Moon Maid, plastic/ vinyl	13″	23	32	45

D

DELUXE READING CORP.

TCD Page	Key	Nomenclature	Size	Low	Price Avg.	High
161	D-1	Baby Magic	18″	15	25	40
	D-2	Suzy Homemaker	21″	15	27	45
162	D-3	Nancy Nurse	21″	15	21	28
	D-4	Penny Brite	8″	5	8	12
	D-5	Suzy Cute	7″	6	10	18
163	D-6	Child, compo/cloth	16″		NPA	

DISNEY

TCD Page	Key	Nomenclature	Size	Low	Price Avg.	High
164	DIS-1a	Donald Duck, hp	11″	15	18	22
	1b	Donald Duck, bisque, JAPAN	3″		8	
	1c	Donald Duck, soft vinyl, flexible	2⅜″		3	
	1d	Donald Duck, vinyl, sqeeze toy	7″		3	
	1e	Donald Duck, candy dispenser	4¼″		2	
	DIS-2	Sleepy, cloth	12½″	75	98	145
	DIS-3	Grumpy, cloth	12½″	75	98	145
165	DIS-4	Dopey, compo/cloth	11″		NPA	
	DIS-5	Christopher Robin, plastic	12″		NPA	
		Winnie the Pooh, plastic	8″		NPA	
	DIS-6	Christopher Robin, vinyl	11″		24	
		Winnie the Pooh, vinyl	3½″		NPA	
166	DIS-7	Christopher Robin, vinyl/cloth	19″		26	
	DIS-8	Jiminy Cricket, cloth	9″		3	
	DIS-9	Tinker Bell, vinyl	12″	30	38	45
	DIS-10	Minnie Mouse, plaster	3″	15	25	30
		Orphan Annie, bisque, JAPAN	3½″	15	25	30
167	DIS-11	Character Hand Puppets	4″		2	

TCD Page	Key	Nomenclature	Size	Low	Avg.	High
	DIS-12	Mickey Mouse, vinyl	10"	30	40	45
		Mouseketeer Girl, vinyl	12"	16	29	50
168	DIS-13	"Famous Movie Stars," rubber				
		Big Bad Wolf	9½"		NPA	
		Three Little Pigs	6"		NPA	
		Mickey Mouse	6"		NPA	
	DIS-14	Pinocchio, wood	8"	100	120	175
		Jiminy Cricket, wood	8"	100	120	175

E

TCD Page	Key	Nomenclature	Size	Low	Avg.	High
	E-1	Eugenia, compo	7"		20	
	E-2	English plastic girl, Roddy	12"		10	

EEGEE (GOLDBERGER DOLL MFG.)

TCD Page	Key	Nomenclature	Size	Low	Avg.	High
169	EG-1	Composition baby	29"		35	
	EG-2	Composition Girl, S. Temple LAL	18"	45	50	65
170	EG-3a	Susan Stroller, hp/vinyl	23"		45	
	EG-3b	Susan Stroller, hp/vinyl	19½"		40	
			23"		45	
			26"		50	
171	EG-4a	Walker, rigid plastic/soft vinyl	27"		NPA	
	EG-4b	Walker	19½"		NPA	
			23"		NPA	
			26"		NPA	
172	EG-5	Boy, vinyl	13"	18	23	35
	EG-6	Sugar Kandi, vinyl			10	
	EG-7	Baby Care, vinyl	18"		12	
173	EG-8	Baby Carrie, vinyl	14"		10	
			18"		12	
			24"		15	
	EG-9	Camilla, foam	16"		12	
	EG-10	Carol, vinyl	22"	9	12	15
174	EG-11	Annette, vinyl	16"		NPA	
			32"		25	
			36"	35	46	75
	EG-12	Posi Playmate, foam body	12"		10	
	EG-13	Bundle of Joy, foam/vinyl	16"		10	
			19"		15	
			25"		18	
	EG-14	Softina, foam/vinyl	18"		6	
	EG-15	Flowerkins		12	15	18

TCD Page	Key	Nomenclature	Size	Low	Price Avg.	High
	EG-16	Babette, vinyl/cloth	15″		6	
			25″		18	
	EG-17	Puppetrina, vinyl		15	31	50
EFFANBEE DOLLS (F & B)						
176	F&B-1	Baby Dainty, compo/cloth	14″		75	
177	F&B-2	Mary Jane			Adv.	
	F&B-3	Baby Grumpy, compo/cloth	12″	100	128	150
	F&B-3a	Baby Grumpy, compo/cloth	11″	100	128	150
178	F&B-4	Baby, compo/cloth	16″		65	
	F&B-4-1	Baby, compo/rubber	13½″		NPA	
179	F&B-5	Colored baby, 1-pc, compo	12″		65	
	F&B-6	Chubby Boy, compo	7″		25	
	F&B-7	Baby, compo/cloth	19″		75	
180	F&B-8	Baby, compo/cloth	24″		45	
	F&B-9	Baby, compo/cloth	20″		40	
181	F&B-10	Baby, compo/cloth	20″		NPA	
	F&B-11	Bubbles Twins, compo/cloth	22″	90	96	150
182	F&B-12	Bubbles, compo/cloth	14″	75	105	150
183	F&B-13	Mama Doll, compo/cloth	29″	45	92	175
	F&B-14	Rosemary, compo/cloth	18″	40	68	105
184	F&B-15	Rosemary, compo/cloth	18″	40	68	105
	F&B-16	Rosemary, compo/cloth	22″	45	78	150
185	F&B-17	Marilee, compo/cloth	22″	75	88	150
	F&B-18	Marilee, compo/cloth	22″	75	88	150
186	F&B-19	Pat-o-Pat, compo/cloth	14″		50	
	F&B-20	Lovums, compo/cloth	20″	75	90	120
	F&B-21	Lovums, compo/cloth	17½″	75	86	120
187	F&B-22	Patsy Baby-ette, compo	8½″	20	52	115
	F&B-23	Patsy Ann, compo	19″	45	107	227
188	F&B-24	Patsy Lou, compo	22″	45	133	275
	F&B-24a	Patsy Lou	22″	45	133	275
	F&B-25	Patsyette, compo	9″	30	55	115
189	F&B-26	Patsy Jr., compo	11″	25	64	185
	F&B-27	Patsyette, compo	9″	30	55	115
	F&B-28	Patsy-Baby, compo/cloth	13″	40	78	120
191	F&B-29	Patsy Ruth, compo	27″	50	141	285
	F&B-30	Patsy-Mae, compo/cloth	30″	65	166	350

TCD Page	Key	Nomenclature	Size	Low	Price Avg.	High
	F&B-31	Patsy-Joan, compo	16"	40	92	185
	F&B-32	Patsy Type, compo	12"		95	
192	F&B-33	Patsy, compo	13½"	30	80	160
	F&B-34	Patsy Type, compo	14"		85	
	F&B-35	Patsy Ann, vinyl	15"	20	32	42
193	F&B-35a	Yes-No Patsy Ann, vinyl	10½"		8	
			11"		18	
	F&B-36	Baby, compo/cloth	17"		NPA	
194	F&B-37	Mary Ann, compo	20"		NPA	
	F&B-38	Mary Ann, compo	20"		NPA	
195	F&B-39	Candy Kid, compo	13"	50	71	115
	F&B-40	Suzanne, compo	14"	45	66	110
	F&B-41	Majorette, compo	18"	45	74	125
196	F&B-42	Dewees Cochran, compo	20"	295	415	695
	F&B-43	Baby, compo/cloth	16"		78	
	F&B-44	Mickey, compo/cloth	20"	35	106	165
197	F&B-45	Sister, compo/cloth	12"	40	48	65
		Brother, compo/cloth	16"	40	48	65
	F&B-46	Honey Walker, plastic	14¼"	25	46	115
			18"	35	58	150
	F&B-47	Dy-Dee Baby, hp/ rubber	16"	35	55	82
198	F&B-48	Dy-Dee Darlin', vinyl	18"	11	17	32
	F&B-49	Mickey, All-American Boy, vinyl	11"	6	15	30
	F&B-50	Mickey, All-American Boy, vinyl	11"	6	15	30
	F&B-51	Mickey, All-American Boy, vinyl	11"	6	15	30
200	F&B-51-1	Girl Scout, vinyl/ plastic	15"	17	19	22
	F&B-52	Half Pint, vinyl	12½"	15	18	30
	F&B-53	Lil Sweetie, vinyl	16"	16	39	65
	F&B-54	Dy-Dee Baby, vinyl	16"	10	21	30

ETHNIC DOLLS

TCD Page	Key	Nomenclature	Size	Low	Price Avg.	High
201	ETH-1	Man, Woman w/babies	16"		35 set	
	ETH-2	Skookum, compo	6½"	15	31	55
	ETH-3	Baby, bisque-like compo	10"	10	45	85
	ETH-4	Chief, seated, cell/ cloth	9½"	10	15	18
202	ETH-5	Navajo, cloth	12"		25	
	ETH-6	Chinese Girl, compo/ cloth	9"	30	98	175

TCD Page	Key	Nomenclature	Size	Low	Price Avg.	High
	ETH-7	Indians, Seminole, cypress fibre	10"	20	39	68
	ETH-8	Hula Girl, cloth	13½"		25	
	ETH-9	Sioux Indians, doeskin	8½"		65 Pr	
204	ETH-10	Guatamalean Dolls, sticks/cloth	3"		5	
	ETH-11	Guatamalean Woman, seated	5"		8	
	ETH-12	Korean Girl, compo/ cloth	14"	38	51	75
	ETH-13	Swedish Girl, hp	13"	10	15	18
	ETH-14	Alaskan, plastic	8"	10	15	20
	ETH-15	Chinese Baby, compo	8"	24	29	40

F

TCD Page	Key	Nomenclature	Size	Low	Price Avg.	High
206	F-1	Baby, compo/cloth	21"		65	
	F-2	Flapper Head, pm	4½"		25	
207	F-3	Flapper Bed Doll, compo/cloth	28"	35	50	78
	F-4	Flapper Cigarette Smoker, compo	21"	55	243	450
	F-5	Flapper Vamp, compo/cloth	24"		NPA	
			30"		NPA	

FRENCH MODERNS

TCD Page	Key	Nomenclature	Size	Low	Price Avg.	High
208	FR-1	Clodrey Toddler, vinyl/foam	18"		NPA	
	FR-2	Raynal Child, hp	20"	65	110	165
	FR-3	French, compo/cloth	19½"		200	
	FR-4	French Child, compo/cloth	24"		135	
210	FR-5	Pettitcollin, vinyl	20"		65	

G

TCD Page	Key	Nomenclature	Size	Low	Price Avg.	High
	G-1	German, compo/ cloth	15"		65	
	G-2	German, Hansel, hp	16"		35	
		Gretel, hp	16"		35	
	G-3	German Girl, compo/pm #150	9½"		65	
211	G-4	Poor Pitiful Pearl, stuffed vinyl	17"	40	43	55
		jointed vinyl	12"	10	25	40
	G-5	Poor Pitiful Pearl	17"	40	43	55
	G-6	Billy Boy, compo	11"		165	
212	G-7	GEM 5-In-One-Doll, compo/cloth	16"		NPA	

GOLDBERGER — See EEGEE

TCD Page	Key	Nomenclature	Size	Low	Price Avg.	High
		H				
	H-1	Girl, Hansi, compo/ cloth	10″	65	80	115
	H-2	Bonnie Blue Bell, compo	5¼″	7	12	18
213	H-3	Mary Hoyer, hp	14″	45	85	165
214	H-4	Hummels, Peterle, vinyl	11½″	20	69	150
		Rosl, vinyl	11″	20	69	150
	H-5	Baby Hungerford, vinyl	12″		15	

HANDMADE DOLLS

TCD Page	Key	Nomenclature	Size	Low	Price Avg.	High
215	HMD-1	Uncle Pink and Aunt Jenny, wood			NPA	
	HMD-2	Portrait of artist Polly Page			*Portrait*	
	HMD-3	Huck Finn, artist's compo	4″		35	
	HMD-4	Ozark Woman, cloth	11″		35	
216	HMD-5	Irvin Wallace, wood/ cloth			NPA	
	HMD-6	Bride, wood/cloth	12″		NPA	
	HMD-7	Virginia Mae, wood/ cloth			NPA	
217	HMD-8	Spanish Lady, wood	6″		NPA	
	HMD-9	Hitty, wood	6″		NPA	
218	HMD-10	Ped-a-Dolls, artists' compo			NPA	
	HMD-10a	Queen Elizabeth I, artists' compo			NPA	
	HMD-11	Helen Young Dolls, china/cloth			NPA	
	HMD-12	Mammy, cloth		25	35	45
219	HMD-13	Peddlar	2¾″		65	

HANDWERCK DOLLS

TCD Page	Key	Nomenclature	Size	Low	Price Avg.	High
	HWK-1	Child, bisque, #109	21″	275	330	375
	HWK-2	Child, bisque	32″	495	750	795
220	HWK-3	Nurse, bisque	21″	150	280	395
	HWK-4	Walker, bisque	23″	325	450	575

HASBRO

TCD Page	Key	Nomenclature	Size	Low	Price Avg.	High
221	HAS-1	Little Miss No Name, vinyl	15″	16	29	45
	HAS-2	Sad Eyes, vinyl	8″		6	
	HAS-3	GI Joe, vinyl/plastic	11½″	4	13	25
		Talking	11½″	8	17	30
222	HAS-4	GI Joe, Action Nurse	12″		22	

TCD Page	Key	Nomenclature	Size	Low	Price Avg.	High
	HEUBACH DOLLS					
	HEU-1	Bisque Head Whistling Jim	12¾"	375	600	750
	HEU-2a	Herm Steiner #128 Child	9"	125	200	275
	HEU-2b	Heubach-Koppels-dorf #320 Child	9"	100	205	385
	HEU-2c	Handwerck #185 Child	7"	80	210	350
223	HEU-3	Heubach #7845 Boy	20"	250	316	390
	HEU-4	Heubach #60 Boy	9"	180	341	450
	HEU-5	Heubach #87 Boy	8"	180	341	450
	HEU-6	Heubach Daisy Mark Baby	15"	180	300	450
224	HEU-7	Bisque Head Girl	7½"	250	320	375
	HEU-7a	Heubach #189 Boy	8½"	400	623	695
	HEU-8	Heubach-Koppels-dorf #399, black	16"	365	555	700
	HEU-9	Bisque Boy			NPA	
	HORSMAN DOLLS					
225	HORS-1	Billiken, compo/cloth	11"	175	200	225
	HORS-2	Boy, compo/cloth	11"		225	
226	HORS-3	Baby Bumps, compo/cloth	12"	95	157	325
	HORS-3-1	Nurse Doll, compo/cloth			NPA	
227	HORS-4	Child, compo/cloth	20"		NPA	
228	HORS-4-1	HEbee-SHEbee, bisq	8"		475	
		compo	10½"		90	
	HORS-5	Child, compo shoulder head	17"		65	
229	HORS-6	Rosebud, compo/cloth	18½"	45	62	105
	HORS-6a	Dolly Rosebud, compo/cloth	17"	45	64	115
			20"	55	77	125
	HORS-6-1	Tynie Baby, compo/cloth	11"		NPA	
			18"		NPA	
			20"		95	
230	HORS-7	Baby Dimples, compo/cloth	14½"	95	120	150
			17½"		NPA	
			20"	100	125	185
			22"		NPA	
	HORS-8	Baby Dimples, compo/cloth	15"	100	125	150
	HORS-9	Baby Dimples, compo/cloth	22"	60	95	150

TCD Page	Key	Nomenclature	Size	Low	Price Avg.	High
231	HORS-10-1	Gold Medal Baby, compo/cloth	18"		NPA	
			20"		NPA	
			22"	65	120	175
	HORS-10-2	Buttercup, compo/ rubber	12"		30	
			16"		45	
232	HORS-11	Toddler, 1935, compo	13"	40	46	55
	HORS-12	JO-JO, compo	13"	45	70	90
	HORS-13	Toddler, 1937, compo	13"	40	46	55
233	HORS-14	Sister, 1937, compo/ cloth	22"		NPA	
	HORS-15	Girl, 1930s, compo/ cloth	17"		NPA	
	HORS-16	Composition head Baby, 1938-1942	6"		NPA	
234	HORS-16-1	Horsman dolls			Catalog Illus.	
	HORS-17	Baby, ca 1940, compo/cloth	25"		65	
	HORS-18	Chubby Baby, compo	17"	24	33	42
	HORS-19	Bi-bye Baby, vinyl hand puppet	12"		28	
236	HORS-19a	Squalling Baby, vinyl/cloth	20"		75	
	HORS-19b	Squalling Baby, stuffed vinyl	18"		60	
237	HORS-20	Yes-No Toddler, vinyl	10½"		7	
	HORS-20a	Yes-No Toddler, hp	11"		15	
	HORS-20b	Yes-No Toddler, hp	11"		13	
239	HORS-21	Sleepy, stuffed plastic/cloth	21"	12	27	35
	HORS-22	Sleepy, stuffed plastic/cloth	21"	12	27	35
	HORS-23	Child #96, stuffed vinyl	22"		21	
	HORS-24	Lady Doll, vinyl	25"	25	65	85
	HORS-25	Thirstie Baby, vinyl	18"	3	6	10
240	HORS-26	Floppy Baby, vinyl/cloth	22"		35	
	HORS-27	Thirstie Baby, vinyl	16"	3	5	7
	HORS-28	Kewpie Kin, vinyl	4¾"		NPA	
241	HORS-29	Baby, vinyl	16"		20	
	HORS-30	Lullabye Baby, vinyl	12"	14	16	18
	HORS-31	Crawling Baby, vinyl	14"		18	
242	HORS-32	Baby Tweaks, vinyl/cloth	20"		12	

I

TCD Page	Key	Nomenclature	Size	Low	Avg.	High
	IDEAL					
	IDL-1	Baby, compo/cloth	18″		65	
243	IDL-2	Flossie Flirt,				
		compo/cloth	18″	65	95	185
			22½″	100	125	150
			26″		125	
	IDL-3	Tickle Toes, comp/-				
		rubber/cloth	14½″		85	
			16½″	45	57	75
			18½″		NPA	
			20½″	50	69	85
			22½″	25	65	95
		Ticklette, compo/-				
		rubber/cloth	13″	32	38	65
244	IDL-4	Honeysuckle "Ducky" compo/-				
		rubber/cloth	14″		85	
	IDL-5	Honeysuckle "Ducky"				
		compo/rubber	10″		NPA	
			12″	32	38	65
			14″		85	
			16″	35	69	115
245	IDL-6	Honeysuckle "Snoozie," compo/rubber/- cloth			*Catalog Illus.*	
	IDL-7	Pinocchio, wood/compo	11″	100	120	175
	IDL-8	Girl, compo, 1930s	13″		22	
246	IDL-9	Nancy Lee, compo.	13″		25	
	IDL-10	Nancy Lee, compo.	13″		25	
247	IDL-11	Betsy Wetsy, wardrobe and case	12″		125	
	IDL-12	Snow White, cloth	15″		65	
	IDL-13	Snow White, compo/cloth	19″	50	60	78
248	IDL-14	Girl, compo	14″		23	
	IDL-15	Poppa-Mamma Baby Doll, compo/cloth	16″		NPA	
			19″		NPA	
	IDL-16	Teen Star, compo	21″	185	267	425
249	IDL-17	Teen Star, compo	21″	185	267	425
	IDL-18	Magic Skin Baby, compo/rubber	20″		55	
	IDL-19	Magic Skin Baby, compo/rubber	13″	35	40	45
251	IDL-21	Sleepy Time Twins, compo/cloth	15″		24 ea.	

TCD Page	Key	Nomenclature	Size	Low	Price Avg.	High
	IDL-22	Magic Skin Babies, hp/cloth	14″	20	28	42
			16″	32	35	45
			18″	38	43	55
			20″	39	50	65
	IDL-23	Plassie, hp/rubber	16″	32	35	45
			18″	38	43	55
252	IDL-24	Kiss Me, "Blessed Event," vinyl/cloth	21″	18	36	45
	IDL-25	Musical Snoozie, vinyl/cloth	16″		45	
	IDL-26	Tickletoes, hp/latex	15″	20	29	41
			19″	29	42	56
			23″	31	52	67
253	IDL-27	Sara Lee, vinyl/cloth	17″		85	
	IDL-28	Brother Coos, hp/cloth/compo	30″		95	
254	IDL-29	Brother Coos, hp/cloth/compo	30″		95	
	IDL-30	Baby Coos		*Catalog Illus.*		
	IDL-31	Baby Coos		*Catalog Illus.*		
255	IDL-32	Pete and Repete		*Catalog Illus.*		
	IDL-33	Saucy Walker, hp	23″	20	34	65
	IDL-34	Saucy Walker, hp	19″	38	45	60
256	IDL-35	Colored Saucy Walker, hp	19″	40	57	70
	IDL-36	Baby Big Eyes, vinyl/cloth	23″	25	38	45
	IDL-37	Posie, hp	24″	28	39	55
257	IDL-38	Magic Lips, vinyl/cloth	24″	45	48	52
	IDL-39	Girl, stuffed vinyl	17″		NPA	
258	IDL-40	Betsy Wetsy, vinyl	12″	12	18	32
			13½″	15	26	45
			16″	15	29	45
	IDL-41	Cream Puff, vinyl	19″	18	27	35
			21″	25	34	45
			24″	45	48	55
	IDL-42	Miss Ideal, plastic	25″	20	36	65
			30″	40	53	90
259	IDL-43	Tammy, vinyl	12″	4	7	15
	IDL-44	Tammy's Family, Dad, vinyl	13″	8	12	18
		Mom, vinyl	12″	8	11	18
	IDL-45	Tammy's Brother, Ted, vinyl	13″	6	13	18
260	IDL-46	Tammy's Sister, Pepper, vinyl	9″	6	12	18
	IDL-47	Tammy's Little Brother, Pete and his Pony	8″	5	12	18

TCD Page	Key	Nomenclature	Size	Low	Price Avg.	High
	IDL-48	Kissy, vinyl	22"	18	33	65
261	IDL-49	Kissy Baby, vinyl/cloth	16"	20	24	35
262	IDL-50	Thumbelina, vinyl/cloth	14"	12	15	22
			17"	14	16	25
			20"	15	18	29
	IDL-50-1	Goody Two-Shoes plastic/vinyl	18"	25	52	95
263	IDL-51	Baby Lu, vinyl	13"		15	
	IDL-52	Giggles, vinyl/plastic	18"	12	35	65
	IDL-52a	Baby Giggles, vinyl, plastic	16"	15	29	75
	IDL-53	Little Lost Baby, vinyl/cloth	22"	25	32	45
264	IDL-54	Betsy Wetsy, vinyl/poly	9"		25	
	IDL-55	Beautiful Crissy, vinyl	18"	5	12	45
	IDL-56	Tressy, vinyl	18"	9	15	29
	IDL-57	Velvet, vinyl	15"	5	12	35

ITALIAN MODERNS

265	IT-1	Bettina by Sebino, vinyl	16"		50	
	IT-2	Ratti, vinyl/plastic	16"		50	
266	IT-3	Furga Baby, vinyl/poly	22"		45	
	IT-4	Bonomi Boy, vinyl	17"		52	
	IT-5	Bonomi Girl, vinyl	15"		50	

J

JAPANESE DOLLS

267	JAPA-1	Traditional Baby, pm/cloth	23"		NPA	
268	JAPA-2	Traditional Baby, pm/cloth	23"		NPA	
	JAPA-3	Traditional Baby, pm/cloth	9"		NPA	
	JAPA-3-1	Thomas Nast Cartoon				
	JAPA-4	Nippon Bisque Head (only)	12"c.		NPA	
	JAPA-5	Morimura Bisque Head Baby	12"	150	183	235
271	JAPA-6	Nippon Bisque Head Baby	10"	65	120	140
	JAPA-7	Lady "Maiko"	9½"	35	105	150
	JAPA-8	Traditional Doll	5½"	65	115	150
	JAPA-9	Japanese Wooden Dolls, nodders	2¼-4¼"	15	25	50

TCD Page	Key	Nomenclature	Size	Price Low	Avg.	High
	JAPA-10	All Bisque Hawaiian Souvenir	7½"	65	75	90
272	JAPA-11	Baby, Nippon, bisq/pm	11"	85	90	165
	JAPA-12	Baby, painted bisque	7½"		95	
273	JAPA-13	Baby, bisque	4"		45	
	JAPA-14	Girl, painted bisque	7"		25	
	JOL-1	Imp, plastic/vinyl "Small Stuff"	14"	3	7	14

K

KAMMER & REINHARDT

TCD Page	Key	Nomenclature	Size	Price Low	Avg.	High
274	KR-1	Baby, bisque/compo	10"	395	564	800
275	KR-2	Baby, bisque/compo	21"	775	800	950
	KR-3	Lady, K*R 255, Turtle Mark, cell	24"	200	288	400
	KR-4	Lady, K*R 255 Turtle Mark, cell	17"	145	237	375
		Man, K*R 255 Turtle Mark, cell	18"	165	246	375
276	KR-5	Bisque Head Baby, K*R Simon Halbig 126	15"	350	485	600
	KR-6	Child, K*R 255, cell	28½"		NPA	

K AND K

TCD Page	Key	Nomenclature	Size	Price Low	Avg.	High
277	K&K-1	Child, compo/cloth	7½"		25	

KATHE KRUSE PUPPEN

TCD Page	Key	Nomenclature	Size	Price Low	Avg.	High
	KK-1	Kathe Kruse Child, cloth	18"	350	581	800
278	KK-2	Kathe Kruse Boy, cloth	15"	150	428	800
	KK-3	Kathe Kruse Jettchen, 1969	14"	175	230	250
			18"	200	239	275
279	KK-4	Mimerle and Dorette, 1969	14"	175	230	250
			18"	200	239	275
	KK-5	Helene and Riekchen, 1969	14"	175	230	250
			18"	200	239	275
	KK-6	Kay and Jim, 1969	10"	85	97	155

J. D. KESTNER DOLLS

TCD Page	Key	Nomenclature	Size	Price Low	Avg.	High
280	KEST-1	Character Baby, J.D.K. #211	14"	300	362	450
	KEST-2	Hilda, #1070	16"	745	1304	1900
281	KEST-3a	Girl, bisque #140	4½"	65	170	245
	KEST-3b	Kestner Girl, bisque	6"	95	210	295

TCD Page	Key	Nomenclature	Size	Low	Avg.	High
	KEST-3c	Soldier Boy, bisq/pm #117	6″	95	174	225
	KEST-3d	Monkey	2½″		NPA	
	KEST-4	Kestner type, bisque/cloth	18″	95	152	198
282	KEST-5	Kestner type, bisque/kid	15″	195	278	350
	KEST-6	Baby, bisq/pm	17″	210	445	625
	KEST-7	Bisque Shoulder Head, #154	21″	275	375	550
	KEST-8	Baby, #152	13″	300	346	450

L

284	L-1	Girl, Lil Sis Toy, 1920s, compo	13″		45	

M

285	M-1	Miss Marie, compo/cloth	22″		45	
	M-2	Miss Marie, compo	21″		45	
	M-3	Baby Marie, compo/cloth	14″		38	
			18″		45	
286	M-4	Australian Aborigine, vinyl	13″		28	
	M-5	Musical Baby, vinyl/cloth	11″		15	
287	M-6	Metropolitan compo/cloth	15″		38	
	M-7	Mama Doll, compo/cloth	26″		40	
288	MAG-1	Magic Skin Baby, compo/rubber	18″	38	46	56

MARX & CO. INC.

289	MARX-1	Johnny West & Horse, plastic	11½″		20	
	MARX-2	Miss Toddler, plastic	21″		25	

MATTEL

290	MATT-1 to 5	Chatty Cathy				
		Black doll	20″	95	115	135
		Blonde hair, brown eyes	20″		NPA	
		Blonde hair, blue eyes	20″	10	20	35
		Brown hair, brown eyes	20″	25	40	65
		Brown hair, blue eyes	20″	15	25	45
		Red hair, brown eyes	20″		85	
		Red hair, blue eyes	20″		45	

TCD Page	Key	Nomenclature	Size	Low	Price Avg.	High
291	MATT-6	Charmin' Chatty	25"	15	30	65
	MATT-6a	Charmin' Chatty	25"	15	30	65
292	MATT-7	Matty Mattel	18"	12	19	30
	MATT-8	Sister Belle	18"	6	22	35
	MATT-9a	Tiny Chatty Brother	15"	10	22	45
293	MATT-9b	Tiny Chatty Brother	15"	10	22	45
	MATT-9c	Colored Tiny Chatty Brother	15"	75	100	125
	MATT-10	Barbie Family Portrait:				
		Midge		7	14	19
		Midge		7	14	19
		Barbie #3		38	84	125
		Barbie, Fashion Queen		4	15	23
		Barbie		5	9	20
		Barbie, Pony Tail		6	18	30
		Ken, 1963		4	15	21
		Ken, 1960		4	10	16
		Midge		7	14	19
		Christie, Bendable		4	13	20
		Skipper		3	8	14
		Barbie, Bendable		5	15	23
	MATT-11	Skooter	9¼"	9	13	21
		Ricky	9¼"	5	12	16
294	MATT-12	Barbie		7	15	22
		Skipper		5	12	18
	MATT-13	Barbie		5	9	20
		Ken		4	10	16
	MATT-14	Midge		7	14	19
		Barbie, Fashion Queen		4	15	23
295	MATT-15	Scooba Doo, vinyl/cloth	20"	10	22	35
	MATT-16	Sister Look 'n Say, vinyl/plastic	19"		25	
	MATT-17	Dancerina, vinyl	24"	28	34	65
296	MATT-18	Cinderella, vinyl	11"		NPA	
	MATT-19	Cheerful Tearful, plastic/vinyl	13"	9	21	36
297	MATT-20	Baby's Hungry, vinyl	16"		14	
	MATT-21	Baby Cheryl, vinyl/cloth	18"		20	
298	MATT-22a	Tiny Chatty Brother, vinyl/plastic	15"	10	22	45
		Tiny Chatty Baby, vinyl/plastic	15"	10	22	45
	MATT-23	Baby Pattaburp, vinyl/cloth	16"		15	
299	MATT-24	Chatty Baby, vinyl/plastic	18"	25	34	42
	MATT-25	Dee Dee, vinyl	15"	16	23	30

TCD Page	Key	Nomenclature	Size	Low	Price Avg.	High
300	MATT-26	Baby Secret, vinyl/foam	18″	10	14	20
	MATT-27	Singin' Chatty, vinyl/plastic	17″	15	17	18
	MATT-28	Captain Lazer, vinyl/plastic	12″		NPA	

METAL DOLLS

301	MET-1	Baby, metal	16″	65	110	150
302	MET-2	Baby, metal shoulder head	13″	50	65	75
	MET-3	Minerva Tin Head, complete doll		85	93	115
303	MET-4	Contortionist, metal/compo	7½″	45	90	150
	METRO-1	Girl, compo/cloth	17″	55	85	115

MULTIFACE DOLLS

304	MULTI-1	Famlee Doll, compo/cloth	16″	175	350	425
	MULTI-2a-2b	Same as MULTI-1				
305	MULTI-3	Famlee Doll, compo/cloth	16″	175	350	425
	MULTI-4	Hedda Get Bedda, vinyl	21″	18	34	60
	MULTI-5	Three Face My-Toy Co., vinyl	7″		4	
306	MULTI-6	Soozie Smiles (Ideal)	16″		Adv.	
	MULTI-7	Soozie Smiles, 1923, compo/cloth	16″	50	105	165
	MULTI-8	Soozie Smiles	16″		Adv.	
	MULTI-9	Trudy, compo/cloth	15½″	65	140	250
308	MULTI-10	Double Doll, vinyl	16″		15	
	MULTI-11	Double Doll, vinyl/cloth	12″		12	

N

	N-1	NAJO Composition Head, wood/pm	19″		285	
	N-2	N.D.C. Composition shoulder head	15″		25	
310	N-4	Nancy Ann Storybook Dolls,				
		painted bisque	5½″	10	21	28
		compo	5½″	12	20	25
		hard plastic	5½″	8	17	24
		soft plastic	5½″	8	13	25

P

311	P-1	Plassie, hp/compo/cloth	17″	35	46	55

TCD Page	Key	Nomenclature	Size	Low	Avg.	High
			19"	35	46	55
			22"	35	46	55
	P-2	Baby, vinyl/foam	18"		10	
	P-3	Baby, vinyl/foam	18"		6	
312	P-4	Princess of Doll Land			NPA	
	PM-1	Papier mache/-compo/cloth	30"	325	350	425

PERSONALITY DOLLS

TCD Page	Key	Nomenclature	Size	Low	Avg.	High
313	PERS-A1	Amosandra, rubber	9½"	25	27	35
	PERS-B1	Baby Peggy of the Movies, compo/cloth	20"		165	
	PERS-B2	Talking Mrs. Beasley, vinyl/cloth	22"		25	
314	PERS-B2a	6" Buffy, 3½" Mrs. Beasley, Set		8	11	20
	PERS-C1	Clarabelle the Clown, head only, compo			NPA	
	PERS-C2	Clarabelle the Clown, mask face	19"		135	
315	PERS-D1	Debbie Drake, flexible plastic	11½"		12	
	PERS-D2	Patty Duke, vinyl	12"	10	12	18
	PERS-E1	Mr. Ed Talking Hand Puppet			15	
316	PERS-E2	Princess Elizabeth, compo	15"	85	161	300
	PERS-E3	Princess Elizabeth, compo	18"	90	172	300
	PERS-E4	Coronation Elizabeth, hp	10"		475	
	PERS-F1	The Flying Nun, vinyl	12"		25	
317	PERS-F2	Anne Francis as "Honey West"		12	15	18
	PERS-F3	Fairy Tale Characters, compo F&B	9¾"		175 ea	
	PERS-H1	Mary Hartline, early hp	8"		10	
318	PERS-H2	Mary Hartline, hp	16"	45	90	175
	PERS-H3	Howdy Doody, hp ventril.	24"		17	
	PERS-M1	Jerry Mahoney, compo ventril.	24"	15	24	35
319	PERS-M2	Mary Martin, hp	14½"	260	350	425
320	PERS-M3	Charlie McCarthy, compo/cloth	20½"		135	
	PERS-M4	Charlie McCarthy, compo/cloth	16"		125	

TCD Page	Key	Nomenclature	Size	Low	Price Avg.	High
322	PERS-M5	Carmen Miranda, compo	14″	250	275	325
	PERS-M6	Carmen Miranda, compo	21″	395	400	475
	PERS-M7	Carmen Miranda and Friend, compo	11″		10 *ea*	
	PERS-M8	Herman Munster, vinyl/cloth	21″		12	
323	PERS-O1	Margaret O'Brien, compo	21″	375	450	525
	PERS-O2	Our Gang Comedy Dancers, compo	12″		NPA	
	PERS-O3	Danny O'Day, vinyl/cloth	24″	8	12	15
			30″		10	
324	PERS-P1	Prince Phillip, hp	18″	365	400	475
	PERS-P2	Mary Poppins, Jane & Michael, vinyl	12″, 8″		60 set	
325	PERS-P3	Pollyana, vinyl	31″	20	34	52
	PERS-P4	Pollyana, vinyl	17″	25	37	55
326	PERS-R1	Little Rickey (Rickey, Jr.)	13″	30	42	55
			17″	18	49	90
			21″	20	56	95
	PERS-S1	Samantha the Witch, vinyl	12″	12	17	21
		Anne Francis (Honey West)	12″	12	15	18
327	PERS-S2	Anne Shirley, compo F&B	15″	38	45	65
	PERS-S3	Anne Shirley, compo F&B	17″		69	
	PERS-S4	Anne Shirley, compo F&B	21″	75	109	150
328	PERS-S5	Skippy, compo	15″	75	120	180
	PERS-S6	Skippy, compo swivel head	13½″	75	124	185
329	PERS-S7	Mortimer Snerd, Flexy	12½″	85	98	125
	PERS-S8	Swing and Sway Doll, Bobbie-Mae, compo	11″	85	91	100
330	PERS-S9	Judy Splinters, ventril.	17″	25	38	54
	PERS-W1	Linda Williams, vinyl	14″	10	19	35

PORTRAIT DOLLS

331	PORT-B1	Baby Sandy Henville, compo	16″	145	171	200
	PORT-B2	Baby Sandy Henville, compo	12″	125	150	185

TCD Page	Key	Nomenclature	Size	Low	Avg.	High
332	PORT-B3	Fanny Brice, Flexy	12½"	85	127	200
	PORT-C1	Ben Casey, vinyl	12"		23	
		Nurse, vinyl	11½"		23	
	PORT-C2	Charles Chaplain, compo/cloth	14"		NPA	
333	PORT-C3	Prince Charles of England, vinyl	9½"		NPA	
	PORT-C4	Dick Clark, vinyl/cloth	26"	85	145	195
334	PORT-C5	Loula Long Combs, artists' compo	24"		750	
335	PORT-C6	Jackie Coogan	13½"		NPA	
	PORT-C7	Hopalong Cassidy, vinyl/cloth	21"		NPA	
336	PORT-D1	Dionne Toddler, compo	11½"	150	225	245
	PORT-D2a	Dionne Baby, compo	10"		165	
	PORT-D2b	Dionne Child, compo/cloth	20"		325	
337	PORT-D3	Dionne Baby, compo	7½"	85	115	165
	PORT-D4	Dionne Toddler, compo	8"	70	95	135
338	PORT-D5	Dionne Toddler, compo	19"	250	283	325
	PORT-D6	Baby, compo Dionne-type	7½"	85	125	150
339	PORT-D7	Babies, Dionne copy, compo	5"		65 set	
	PORT-D8	Baby, compo Dionne-type	7½"		25 ea	
340	PORT-D9	Babies, Dionne-type, bisque	1⅜"		65 set	
	PORT D9-1	The Dionne Quintuplets – The World's Darlings			Adv.	
341	PORT-D10	Doctor Doolittle, vinyl/cloth	22"	20	30	45
	PORT-D11	Doctor Doolittle, vinyl	6"	5	9	18
342	PORT-D12	Deanna Durbin, compo	25"	350	400	425
	PORT-D13	Deanna Durbin, compo	21"	185	350	400
343	PORT-F1	W. C. Fields, compo/cloth, F&B	17½"		NPA	
	PORT-G1	Judy Garland, compo, Ideal	18"		850	
344	PORT-H1	Sonja Henie, compo	15"	60	144	225
345	PORT-H2	Sonja Henie, compo	14"	60	144	225
	PORT-H3	Sonja Henie, compo	14"	60	144	225

TCD Page	Key	Nomenclature	Size	Low	Price Avg.	High
346	PORT-J1	Jeannie (Barbara Eden) vinyl	20"		30	
		That Girl (Marlow Thomas) Alex.			425	
	PORT-J2	Julia (Diahanne Carroll) vinyl/plastic	11½"	9	17	30
347	PORT-J3	Julia (Diahanne Carrol) talking vinyl/plastic	11½"	9	17	30
	PORT-K1	Emmett Kelly (Willie the Clown) vinyl/cloth	24"	45	58	75
348	PORT-K2	Emmett Kelly (Willie the Clown) vinyl	13½"	40	48	55
		Johnny, Phillip Morris		65	75	165
	PORT-K3	John F. Kennedy, vinyl head	13½"		95	
349	PORT-L1	Pinky Lee, vinyl/cloth	25"		45	
	PORT-L2	Stan Laurel, Knickerbocker	10"		18	
		Oliver Hardy, Knickerbocker	8"		18	
350	PORT-L3	Shari Lewis, plastic/vinyl	21"	250	375	425
	PORT-M1	General Douglas MacArthur, compo	16"	150	175	225
	PORT-M2				Catalog Illus.	
	PORT-R1	Dianna Ross, vinyl, Ideal	20"		85	
352	PORT-ST1	Shirley Temple, compo	29"	365	450	650
	PORT-ST2	Shirley Temple, compo	18"	85	210	550
353	PORT-ST3	Shirley Temple, compo	27"	175	222	300
	PORT-ST4	Shirley Temple Baby, compo	19"		650	
354	PORT-ST5	Shirley Temple, compo	18"	85	210	550
	PORT-ST6	Shirley Temple, compo	13"	100	325	500
	PORT-ST6a	Shirley Temple knockoff, compo	13"		35	
355	PORT-ST7	Shirley Temple, plastic/vinyl 1957	17"	25	89	175
	PORT ST7a	1957 Catalog Illustration			Adv.	
	PORT-ST8	Shirley Temple, vinyl/plastic 1957	12"	38	57	95

TCD Page	Key	Nomenclature	Size	Low	Price Avg.	High
	PORT-ST9	Shirley Temple, compo	18″	85	214	550
356	PORT-ST10	Shirley Temple, unmarked	18″	85	214	550
	PORT-ST11	Shirley Temple knockoff, compo	15″	45	60	75
357	PORT-ST12	Shirley Temple look-alike, compo	20″	75	86	100
	PORT-ST13	Shirley Temple look-alike walker, compo	21″	85	156	275
358	PORT-TL1	Talking Terri Lee, hp/vinyl	16″	75	128	200
359	PORT-TL2	Terri Lee, compo., PAT. PEND.	16″	60	71	150
	PORT-TL3	Linda Baby, soft vinyl	10″	65	91	125
360	PORT-TL4	Connie Lynn, hp	18″	50	92	135
	PORT-TL5	Terri Lee, glued-on mohair wig	16″	35	63	125
	PORT-TL6	Tiny Terri Lee, glued-on mohair wig	10″	35	57	90
	PORT-TL7	So-Sleepy, vinyl	9½″		45	
361	PORT-TL8	Terri Lee Girl Scout	16″	35	63	125
	PORT-T1	Marlo Thomas, hp, ALEX	17″		425	
	PORT-T2	Twiggy, vinyl/plastic	11½″	15	35	50
362	PORT-V1	Dick Van Dyke (Mr. Potts) cloth	25″		25	
	PORT-W1	Jane Withers, compo, ALEX	17″	400	450	535
	PORT-W2	Jane Withers, compo, ALEX	20″	400	510	600

PUPPETS AND MARIONETTES

TCD Page	Key	Nomenclature	Size	Low	Price Avg.	High
364	PUPP-1	Famous Personality Hand Puppets			NPA	
	PUPP-2	Pelham Puppets, Pinnochio			NPA	
	PUPP-3	Pelham Puppets, Pop Singers			NPA	
	PUPP-4	Hand Puppet, "The Monkees"	11″	15	20	26
365	PUPP-5	Hazelle Thimble Puppets, vinyl			1 ea	
	PUPP-6	Hazelle Hand Puppets, vinyl heads		3	7	12
	PUPP-7	Hazelle Marionettes, vinyl or "Tenite" heads, various sizes		10	17	35

R

TCD Page	Key	Nomenclature	Size	Low	Avg.	High
	RAG DOLLS					
368	RAG-1	Dolly Dear, Catalog Illustration			25	
369	RAG-2	Shoebutton Sue			NPA	
	RAG-3	Raggedy Ann and Raggedy Andy			*Catalog Illus.*	
	RAG-4	Beloved Belindy			*Catalog Illus.*	
370	RAG-5	Raggedy Ann		30	35	42
		Friend		30	35	42
	RAG-6	Chase Boy, Stockinette fabric	18″	275	395	450
371	RAG-7	Lenci Girl, all felt	16″	195	430	750
	RAG-8	Lenci dolls, all felt	11″	225	366	450
			15″	165	341	525
372	RAG-9	Dean Rag Doll, mask face/velvet	14″		65	
	RAG-10	Football Player, Kruger	17″	9	16	25
373	RAG-11	Topsy, all black cloth	31″		85	
	RAG-12	Norah Wellings Sailor	14″	45	73	95
	RAG-13	Little Sister, mask face, compo arms	13½″		35	
		Big Sister, mask face, compo arms	15″		35	
374	RAG-14	Alabama Baby, hand-painted features	18″	400	483	500
	RAG-15	Gramma Rag Doll, Mattel	20″	10	15	18
	RAG-16	Captain Kangaroo, talker, Mattel	21″	6	13	22
	RAG-17	Laughing Rag Clown, Gund	20″		25	
375	RAG-18	Gepetto, litho cloth	15″		8	
	RAG-19	Muffin, ALEXANDER	14″		20	
		Funny, ALEXANDER	18″	15	19	25
377	R-1	Johnny Hero, Rosko-Steele, Inc.	13″		15	
	R-2	Raleigh Dolls, compo/cloth			*Magazine page*	
	REMCO					
378	REM-1	The Littlechap Family Set		60	95	135
	REM-2	Libby Littlechap	10½″		30	
		Judy Littlechap	13¼″	8	12	20

TCD Page	Key	Nomenclature	Size	Low	Avg.	High
	REM-3	Dr. John Littlechap	15″	10	18	27
		Lisa Littlechap	14″		10	
379	REM-4	Baby Crawl-Along, plastic/vinyl	20″	4	13	20
	RUBBER					
	RUB-1	Child, one-piece body, vinyl/latex	26″		*Catalog Illus.*	
	RUB-2	Sunbabe, Sun Rubber	11″	10	16	25
380	RUB-3	Sunbabe, Sun Rubber	13″	12	18	30
	RUB-4	Wendy and Billy Boy	18″		75 pr	
	RUB-5	Sleepy Baby, 1-pc, rubber	10″		15	
	RUB-6	Sun Rubber			*Catalog Illus.*	

S

TCD Page	Key	Nomenclature	Size	Low	Avg.	High
381	S-1	Dolly Sunshine, compo/cloth	16″		NPA	
			18″		36	
			19½″		45	
382	S-1a	Sunshine, Baby compo/cloth	14″		35	
			18″		48	
			23″		NPA	
	S-2	Miss Sunshine, compo/cloth	18″		45	
	S-3	Baby Sunshine, compo/cloth	26″		50	
383	S-4	Shackman Toys			NPA	
	S-4a	Girl, 9¼″ & Baby 4¾″, compo/felt			25 pr	
384	S-5	Girl, compo/cloth	24½″	45	65	95
	S-6	Girl, hp ALEXANDER	18″		125	
385	S-7	Sweetie Pie, hp	27″		45	
	SAYCO					
	S-8	Sayco Bed Doll, vinyl/plastic	26″		28	
	SHINDANA					
	S-9	Baby Janie, Shindana, vinyl	13″		15	
	S-10	Malaika, Shindana, vinyl	15″	20	24	30
386	S-11	Talking Tamu, Shindana, vinyl/cloth	16″		9	

TCD Page	Key	Nomenclature	Size	Low	Avg.	High
	SUN RUBBER					
	S-12	So-Wee, rubber, Sun Rubber		10	19	30
	SIMON & HALBIG					
387	S&H-1	Child, bisque head #1079	9″	175	235	275
	S&H-2	Girl, marked Germany	16″	350	400	600
	S&H-3	Santa, bisque socket head	34″	650	850	1100
388	S&H-4	Baby, bisque head #122	11″	275	432	550
	S&H-5	Child, bisque head #1079	19½″	375	430	500

T

TCD Page	Key	Nomenclature	Size	Low	Avg.	High
	TEDDY BEARS					
390	TED-1	Teddy Bear c. 1904	20″		175	
	TED-2	Old Ted, c. 1927	18″		85	
	TED-3	Teddy Bears			Adv.	

U

TCD Page	Key	Nomenclature	Size	Low	Avg.	High
	UNEEDA DOLLS					
391	UNEE-1	Mama Doll, compo/cloth	29″		65	
	UNEE-2	Baby, vinyl	16″		20	
392	UNEE-3	Princess Doll, plastic/vinyl, (Disney)	32″	14	40	55
	UNEE-4	Freckles, plastic/vinyl	32″	20	25	38
393	UNEE-5	Colored Girl (Princess type)	32″	30	42	55
	UNEE-6	Dollikin, hp/vinyl	19″	20	22	30
394	UNEE-7	Coquette, vinyl	16″		12	
	UNEE-8	Coquette, vinyl	16″		12	
395	UNEE-9	Colored Posy Pixie type, vinyl/foam	17″	10	15	19
	UNEE-10	Posy Pixies (Vogue) vinyl/foam	17″	10	18	25
	UNEE-11	Tiny Toddler, vinyl/plastic	11″		7	
396	UNEE-12	Pri-thilla, vinyl	12½″		16	
		Popeye, soft vinyl (Cameo)	13″		65	
	UNMARKED DOLLS					
	UNMKD-1	Baby, compo/cloth	13½″		35	
397	UNMKD-2	Baby, compo 1940s	11″		32	

TCD Page	Key	Nomenclature	Size	Low	Avg.	High
	UNMKD-3	Baby, compo/cloth 1910s	18"		65	
	UNMKD-3a	Baby Doll, compo/ cloth, 1917		*Catalog Illus.*		
398	UNMKD-4	Baby, compo/cloth	21"		65	
399	UNMKD-5	Baby, compo/cloth		*Catalog Illus.*		
	UNMKD-6	Baby, compo/cloth	25"		65	
400	UNMKD-7	Baby, compo/cloth, 1920s	13"		25	
	UNMKD-8	Baby, compo/cloth, 1920s	17"		25	
	UNMKD-9	Baby, compo/cloth, 1920s	17"		25	
401	UNMKD-10	Baby, compo/cloth, c-1940	18"		30	
	UNMKD-11	Mama Doll, compo/ cloth	21"		45	
402	UNMKD-12	Black "Topsy" Baby, compo	10"		25	
	UNMKD-13	Babies, compo	9"	12	18	26
	UNMKD-14	Chubby Kid, compo	14"		24	
403	UNMKD-15	Chubby Kid, compo	18"		20	
	UNMKD-16	Chubby Kid, compo	8"		15	
404	UNMKD-17	Girl, compo, c-1920-1930	14"		35	
	UNMKD-18	Black Mama Doll, compo/cloth c-1919	14"		35	
405	UNMKD-18a	Aunt Jemima, compo/cloth 1925		*Catalog Illus.*		
	UNMKD-19	Dutch Girl, compo/ cloth	10"		85	
406	UNMKD-20	Walker, brown hp, c-1953	27"		65	
	UNMKD-21	Colored Toddler, vinyl	12"	35	65	80
	UNMKD-22	Boy, compo/cloth, 1910s	17"		125	
407	UNMKD-23	Doughboy, compo/ cloth, 1916-18	17"		35	
	UNMKD-24	W.W.I. Doughboy, compo/cloth	29"		55	
408	UNMKD-25	Boy, compo/cloth, c-1918	30"		55	
	UNMKD-26	Googly-Eyed Boy, compo/cloth	10"	475	562	650
409	UNMKD-27	Chubby Boy, compo, 1930s	15½"		25	
	UNMKD-28	Boy, (Reliable) compo, 1942	12"		35	
410	UNMKD-29	W.W.II Sailor Boy, compo/cloth	15"		35	

TCD Page	Key	Nomenclature	Size	Low	Avg.	High
	UNMKD-30	Air Force Baby W.W.II vinyl/rubber	20"		45	
411	UNMKD-31	Googly-Eyed Boy, compo/cloth, 1945	20"		25	
	UNMKD-31-1	Rusty (Make Room for Daddy) vinyl	16"		25	
	UNMKD-32	Girl, compo/cloth, 1910s	20"		55	
412	UNMKD-33	Girl, compo/cloth, 1920s	25"		45	
	UNMKD-34	Baby, compo/cloth, 1920s	23½"		50	
413	UNMKD-35	Girl, compo/cloth, 1930s	23"		35	
	UNMKD-36	Girl, compo, c-1928	16"		45	
	UNMKD-37	Girl, compo/cloth, c-1930	26"		85	
414	UNMKD-38	Girl, compo/cloth, c-1930	24"		65	
	UNMKD-39	Smiling Girl, compo/cloth, c-1928	27"		125	
	UNMKD-40	Girl, compo/cloth, c-1930	26"		65	
415	UNMKD-41	Girl, compo/cloth, c-1930	24"		65	
	UNMKD-42	Girl, compo/cloth, 1930s	21"		65	
416	UNMKD-43	Brown Girl, compo/cloth, c-1939	22"		95	
417	UNMKD-44	Girl, compo/cloth, 1930s	24"		65	
	UNMKD-45	Girl, compo/cloth, c-1930	25"		65	
	UNMKD-46	Girl, compo, c-1936	18"		95	
418	UNMKD-47	Girl, compo, c-1939	20"		40	
	UNMKD-48	Girl, compo, 1930s	20"		35	
	UNMKD-49	Girl, compo, 1930s	20"		30	
419	UNMKD-50	Child, compo/cloth, c-1936	17"		95	
	UNMKD-51	Girl, compo, c-1940	18"		35	
420	UNMKD-52	Girl, hp, c-1948	15"		35	
	UNMKD-53	Girl, compo, c-1940	16"		30	
421	UNMKD-54	Chalk Cupid, Carnival Dolls	10"		10 ea	
	UNMKD-55	Brown Display Mannequin, compo	27"		NPA	
422	UNMKD-56	Walker, Early hp, c-1955	28"		20	
423	UNMKD-57	Friend of the Bride, c-1956	19"		20	

TCD Page	Key	Nomenclature	Size	Low	Price Avg.	High
	UNMKD-58	Bride, plastic/vinyl, c-1956	19″		20	
424	UNMKD-59	Grandma, vinyl, c-1960	19″	40	45	75
	UNMKD-60	Gumdrop, vinyl/ plastic, c-1962, F&B	15½″		25	
	UNMKD-60a	Gumdrop, vinyl/ plastic, c-1962, F&B	16″		25	

V

VOGUE DOLLS, INC.

TCD Page	Key	Nomenclature	Size	Low	Price Avg.	High
426	VOG-1	Ginny, Skating Girl, compo	8″	35	90	150
	VOG-2	WAC, W.W.II, compo	13″		NPA	
	VOG-3	Brickett, hp/vinyl	22″	35	46	65
	VOG-4	Brickett, hp/vinyl	19″	25	37	55
427	VOG-5	Brickett, vinyl/poly	16″	16	33	50
			22″	35	46	65
	VOG-6	Baby Two Dear, E. Wilkin, vinyl	17″	70	85	95
	VOG-7	Ginny, hp	8″	30	48	90

W

TCD Page	Key	Nomenclature	Size	Low	Price Avg.	High
428	W-1	Girl, compo, c-1947	18″	45	64	80
	W-2	Girl, hp/vinyl, mkd. W.J. WILSON	20″		45	

WALKING-TALKING DOLLS

TCD Page	Key	Nomenclature	Size	Low	Price Avg.	High
429	W-T-1	Coleman Dolly Walker, c-1917	29″		325	
430	W-T-2	Walkalon doll, hp, c-1949	21″		95	
	W-T-2a	Walkalon Walker, hp	20″		95	
431	W-T-3	Wanda, The Walking Doll, key-wind (Advance), c-1950	18″	20	37	60
	W-T-4	Happi-Time Walker, hp, 1950s	19″		50	
432	W-T-5	Baby Step, vinyl/ plastic	18″		18	
	W-T-6	Baby Walk Alone, plastic/vinyl REMCO	14½″		15	
	W-T-7	Crawler, tin/vinyl, JAPAN	6″		9	

TCD Page	Key	Nomenclature	Size	Low	Price Avg.	High
433	W-T-8	Crawler, metal/ plastic/vinyl, c-1967	16″		9	
	W-T-9	Mae Starr, compo/ cloth, c-1930	28″	295	345	425
434	W-T-10	Noma, Talking Doll, hp/cloth, F&B, c-1949	28″		NPA	
	W-T-10a	Noma New Electronic Talking Doll			*Catalog Illus.*	
435	W-T-11	Melodie, plastic, c-1946	30″		NPA	
	W-T-12	Little Miss Echo, vinyl/plastic	30″	20	46	75
	W-T-13	Little Miss Echo, vinyl/plastic	30″	20	46	75
	WOODEN (SCHOENHUT)					
436	WOOD-1	Boy, mohair wig, SL Toddler	16″	275	405	500
	WOOD-2	Girl, mold-carved hair ribbon	14″	450	783	1000
437	WOOD-3	Girl, mold-carved hair	16″	600	835	1000
	WOOD-4	Girl, mohair wig	16″	375	418	500
438	WOOD-5	Baby, bent-leg	12½″	235	311	425
	WOOD-6	Piano, Twenty-Two Keys		85	100	125
		Eighteen Keys			65	
		Fifteen Keys			55	
	WOOD-7	Humpty-Dumpty Circus:				
		Small set, tent and 22 pcs.		1000	1812	2750
		Large set, tent and 52 pcs.		3250	5000	6500
440	WOOD-8	Humpty-Dumpty Circus Figures				
		Animals:				
		Alligator, glass eyes		200	225	275
		painted eyes		150	175	225
		Bear, small brown, glass eyes		125	135	165
		large brown, glass eyes		195	200	250
		Bear, Polar, glass eyes		195	200	250
		Buffalo, glass eyes, cloth ruff		125	200	250
		early type		195	250	300
		Bulldog, painted brown eyes		185	225	275

TCD Page	Key	Nomenclature	Size	Low	Price Avg.	High
		Burro, glass eyes		180	225	275
		Camel, one hump, glass eyes		200	225	275
		small, double hump		150	175	225
		large, double hump		175	200	250
		Cat, painted eyes		175	200	250
		Deer, glass eyes		230	275	335
		painted eyes		165	200	250
		Donkey, large with blanket		95	110	135
		large, glass eyes		160	200	250
		small, painted eyes		30	45	65
		Elephant, small, glass eyes		70	95	125
		small, painted eyes		35	50	65
		large, glass eyes w/blanket		165	200	250
		large, painted eyes		95	150	200
		Elk, glass eyes		165	200	250
		Giraffe, small, painted eyes		165	200	250
		large, glass eyes		175	250	300
		large, painted eyes		155	200	250
		Goat, glass eyes		110	200	250
		Goose, painted eyes		135	200	250
		Hippo, glass eyes		165	250	300
		painted eyes		140	200	250
		Horse, small, carved mane, painted eyes		125	150	200
		large, platform, glass eyes		165	200	250
		large, riding, glass eyes		172	200	250
		Kangaroo, glass eyes		185	225	275
		Lamb, painted eyes		130	150	200
		Leopard, glass eyes		165	225	275
		painted eyes, OM		140	225	275
		Lion, small		95	125	150
		wide head, glass eyes		80	125	150
		large, carved mane		165	200	250
		Monkey, painted eyes		85	150	200

TCD Page	Key	Nomenclature	Size	Low	Avg.	High
		Ostrich, glass eyes		195	225	275
		painted eyes		165	200	250
		Pig, glass eyes		125	150	200
		Poodle, small, carved ruff		125	175	225
		small, cloth ruff		95	175	225
		small, glass eyes		175	200	250
		small, painted eyes		65	115	150
		Rhino, glass eyes		145	225	275
		Tiger, glass eyes		150	225	275
		painted eyes		85	150	200
		Zebra, glass eyes		165	200	250
		painted eyes		165	200	250
		Performers:				
		Acrobat, lady, bisque		165	225	275
		lady		145	150	200
		Oriental, large		160	175	225
		Bare Back Rider, bisque head		195	250	300
		Clown, large, cotton suit		65	95	115
		Dude, small, Negro		150	175	225
		large, Negro		175	200	250
		Lion Trainer, bisque head		195	250	300
		wood head		150	175	225
		Ring Master, bisque head		185	250	300
		bisque head, 8″		195	235	350
		Strong Man, bisque head		250	275	350
		Props:				
		Barrel		7	10	18
		Cage, wild animal wagon		95	150	185
		Chair		9	11	15
		Dirigible, 13″, c-1929		50	65	85
		Fire Plug		85	150	185
		Platform		8	10	16
		Sign, Humpty-Dumpty		50	75	90
		Tent, 25×35		250	400	650

WOOD, OTHER

TCD Page	Key	Nomenclature	Size	Low	Avg.	High
441	WOOD-9	Pinnochio, Poland	7″	45	60	70
	WOOD-10	All Wood Character	9″		10	
	WOOD-11	Mr. Muscles, Blind Industries	10″		4	
442	WOOD-12	Dutch Dolls, (Penny Wooden, Peg Wooden)	11½″	12	25	38

A

A.B.C. TOY

482	ABC-1	Anette Baby, compo/ cloth	18″	65	75	90

ACME TOY MFG

	ACME-1	Boy, compo/cloth, assorted sizes		65	82	115
	ACME-2	Baby, compo/cloth	17″	60	73	85
483	ACME-3	Grumpy-type, compo/cloth	15″	65	79	95
	ACME-4	Bye-lo-type, compo/ cloth	14″	65	83	95
	ACME-5	Baby, compo/cloth	19″	55	86	95

ADVANCE DOLL & TOY CO

484	ADVA-1	The Walking "Wabbit"	18″		NPA	

ADVERTISING

	ADV-A6	Allergy Annie, litho cloth	15″		13	
	ADV-A7	Dolls of the World, plastic	8″		2	
	ADV-B3	Babbitt Cleanser Boy, compo/cloth	15″		175	
	ADV-B4	Bakery Girl, litho cloth			5	
	ADV-B5	Bazooka Joe, litho cloth	18″		7	
485	ADV-B6	Beta, litho cloth	10½″		9	
	ADV-B7	Betty Blue Bonnet, PerfeKta	17″		30	
	ADV-B8	Jennie, litho cloth	22″		10	
486	ADV-B9	Bracho the Clown, litho cloth	18″		6	
	ADV-B10	Bonnie Breck, vinyl	9″		12	
	ADV-B11	Buster Brown Bed Doll, compo/cloth	27″		75	
	ADV-B12	Buster Brown Boy, compo.	26″		NPA	
487	ADV-B13	Buster Brown, bisque	4″	30	45	60
	ADV-C1	C & H Sugar Kids, litho. cloth	16″		7	
	ADV-C2	C & H Sugar Kids			Adv.	
	ADV-C3	Colored Campbell Kid, compo/cloth	11½″	90	125	165
	ADV-C4	Campbell Kid, rubber	7″		12	

MTCD Page	Key	Nomenclature	Size	Low	Price Avg.	High
488	ADV-C5	Campbell Kids, vinyl, c-1972	10″	9	10	12
	ADV-C6	Campbell Kids, litho cloth, c-1973	12″	5	8	12
	ADV-C7	Carnation Cry Baby, vinyl	18″	16	20	24
489	ADV-C8	Charlie Chocks, litho cloth	20″	5	6	8
	ADV-C9	Cheer Girl, vinyl/ plastic	10″	2	5	7
	ADV-C10	Chicken of the Sea Mermaid, vinyl/ cloth	20″	35	42	95
490	ADV-C11	Chore Girl, litho/ cloth	16″	6	8	11
	ADV-C12	Cooky, vinyl/hp	11″	7	10	15
491	ADV-C13	Colgate Baby Bunting, c-1917			Adv.	
	ADV-C13a	Colgate trademark drawing, c-1913			TM	
	ADV-C14	Golden Locks, litho cloth	14″	65	81	95
	ADV-C15	Cracker Jack Boy, compo/cloth			175	
	ADV-C15a	Cracker Jack Trademark			TM	
	ADV-C16	Rastus, the Cream of Wheat Chef, litho/ cloth, c-1920	18″	30	35	65
492	ADV-D1	Uncle Mose, stuffed plastic, c-1948	13½″	8	23	35
	ADV-D1a	Dolly Drake, compo/ cloth, 1917, (Reliance Novelty)	19″		NPA	
	ADV-D2	Dutch Boy Puppet, vinyl/cloth	12″		9	
	ADV-F2	Facit Business Machine Man, vinyl, (Germany)	24″		45	
	ADV-F2a	Facit Business Machine Man, vinyl, (Hong Kong)	4″		10	
493	ADV-F2-1	Sunny Jim, compo/ plush, 1909	12″		115	
	ADV-F3	Benjamin Franklin, litho cloth	13″	6	8	11
	ADV-F4	Friendlee, litho cloth, 1972, White Front, Inc.	16″		7	
	ADV-G5	Bandy, compo/wood, 1929	18″	65	90	135

MTCD Page	Key	Nomenclature	Size	Low	Avg.	High
	ADV-G6	Sugar Bear, litho cloth		5	9	12
	ADV-G7	Minx, litho cloth, 1953	10″	6	8	11
494	ADV-G8	Gerber Baby, soft vinyl	10″	7	12	18
	ADV-H1	Heinz Baby, vinyl	8½″	27	35	40
	ADV-H2	Hot Point Man, compo/wood	16″	65	90	135
	ADV-J1	Jolly Joan, compo, c-1940	12″		45	
	ADV-J2	Green Giant, litho cloth	28″	10	14	20
		Sprout, litho cloth	10¼″	5	7	8
495	ADV-J3	Li'l Miss Just Rite, vinyl, (Dakin)	6¾″	7	8	10
	ADV-K3	Karo Princess, Lignumn fibre, c-1919	10¼″	50	81	115
	ADV-K4	Keebler Elf, Chase, c-1974	6¾″	5	6	8
	ADV-K5	Goldylocks, litho cloth	13″		40	
		Papa Bear, litho cloth	13½″		40	
		Mama Bear, litho cloth	12″		40	
		Baby Bear, litho cloth	10″		40	
	ADV-K5-1	Toucan Sam, litho cloth, 1960s	8″	3	6	10
	ADV-K5-2	Tony the Tiger, stamped cloth face	13″	10	12	14
496	ADV-K6	Mini People from Many Lands, beechwood figures, Kellogg's, 1970	3″-4½″		2 ea	
	ADV-K7	Korn-Krisp, litho cloth	26″	32	44	65
	ADV-K8	Kresge Christmas Elf, vinyl/cloth	4″		5	
497	ADV-L6	Lion Uniform Doll, old heavy plastic	13″	35	65	85
		new thin plastic	13″	25	35	65
	ADV-L7	Lustre-Creme Starlet	7½″		25	
	ADV-L8	Lustre-Creme Movie Star Doll	9″		35	
498	ADV-M3	Ronald McDonald, litho cloth, 1971	16″	2	5	8
	ADV-M4	Patti Flip, (KAYSAM) vinyl	18″		10	
	ADV-M5	Marky Maypo, vinyl	10″	6	8	12

MTCD Page	Key	Nomenclature	Size	Low	Price Avg.	High
	ADV-M6	Betsy McCall, plastic/hard vinyl	30″	55	86	145
	ADV-M6a	Betsy McCall			Catalog Illus.	
499	ADV-M7	Betsy McCall, vinyl/plastic	22″	135	168	200
	ADV-M8	Besty McCall, vinyl/plastic	11½″	35	50	75
	ADV-M9	Besty McCall, soft vinyl/plastic, (American Character)	35″	125	160	240
	ADV-M10	Sandy McCall, soft vinyl/plastic	36″	135	185	300
	ADV-M11	Sandy McCall, soft vinyl/plastic	36″	135	185	300
500	ADV-M12	Wizard of Oz Characters, litho cloth				
		Strawman	18″		8	
		Tin Man	18″		8	
		Dorothy	16″		8	
		Cowardly Lion	9″		8	
	ADV-M13	Twins, Maisy & Daisy, litho cloth	17″		10 ea	
	ADV-M14	Priscilla, compo. 1929	14″		NPA	
	ADV-N3	Uneeda Kid, 1914			Catalog Illus.	
	ADV-N4	Uneeda Kid, compo/cloth, 1915	15″	150	175	235
	ADV-N5	Uneeda Kid, compo/cloth, 1915	11½″	150	175	225
501	ADV-N6	Dolly Strong, "The Naptha Soap Baby", compo/plush, 1910			165	
	ADV-N7	Baby Bobby, compo/cloth, c-1900-1915	18″		NPA	
502	ADV-N8	Baby Mae, compo/cloth, 1925	18″		65	
	ADV-N9	Neslings Baby and Crib Blanket, Heubach bisque doll			275	
	ADV-01	Oster Super Pan, litho cloth	18″		8	
	ADV-P5	Peter Pan, litho cloth	18″		7	
503	ADV-P6	Phillips '66 Man, compo	7″	13	24	32
	ADV-P7	Pickle Power, 1-pc vinyl, 1957			10	

MTCD Page	Key	Nomenclature	Size	Low	Avg.	High
	ADV-P8	Pizza Pete, hp	7″		6	
	ADV-P9	Storykins Cinderella and Coach, plastic	4″		3	
	ADV-P10	Mr. Clean, vinyl	8″	7	12	22
504	ADV-P11	Raisin Doll, litho cloth	15″	4	6	8
	ADV-R3	Roni Mac, litho. cloth	11″		25	
	ADV-S5	Speedy Alka Seltzer, 1-pc. vinyl	7½″	6	7	10
	ADV-S6	Selling Fool, compo/wooden, 1926	15½″	150	175	250
505	ADV-S7	Sandies Football Player, nodder, compo	7″		13	
	ADV-S8	Leprechaun, litho cloth	15″		6	
	ADV-S9	Skookum, compo	16″		90	
	ADV-S9a	Teddy Snow Crop, terry cloth, 1972	14″	5	6	9
506	ADV-S10	Sony Boy, vinyl	8″	7	9	12
	ADV-S11	Spic and Span, compo/cloth, c-1912			NPA	
	ADV-S12	Miss Sunbeam, vinyl/plastic	17″	16	24	30
	ADV-S13	Elephant, litho cloth	6½″	10	17	25
	ADV-S14	Miss Supreme, stamped oil cloth	15″		18	
	ADV-S15	Bugs Bunny, vinyl/plush	11″	9	12	18
	ADV-T7	Texaco Cheerleader, vinyl, c-1973	11½″	8	8	12
507	ADV-V2	Vermont Maid, vinyl, c-1964	15″	*Magazine Illus.*		
	ADV-V2a	Vermont Maid		18	28	50
	ADV-W1	Carol Brent, vinyl, c-1961	15″	20	32	40
508	ADV-W2	Dolly-Gram, litho/cloth/velvet	6″	3	5	8
	ADV-W3	Cozy Glo Kid, 1-pc compo	12″	150	200	250
	ADV-W4	The Spearmint Kid, compo/cloth, 1915		65	95	115
509	ADV-W5	The Spearmint Kiddo, compo/cloth, 1912	13″		135	

ALEXANDER, MADAME DOLL CO.

MTCD Page	Key	Nomenclature	Size	Low	Avg.	High
510	ALEX-63a	Oliver Twist, c-1925, cloth	16″	95	210	300

MTCD Page	Key	Nomenclature	Size	Low	Price Avg.	High
	ALEX-63b	Little Shaver	14″	150	210	275
	ALEX-64	Boy, cloth, mask face, c-1924	20″		NPA	
	ALEX-65	Tippy Toe, cloth	18½′	245	264	350
	ALEX-66	Little Dorrit, cloth	16″	225	291	350
512	ALEX-67	Beth of Little Women, cloth	16″	225	281	350
	ALEX-68	Lady, cloth	24″	225	316	425
513	ALEX-69	Alice in Wonderland, cloth	16″	200	287	350
	ALEX-70	Alice in Wonderland, cloth	22″	150	200	295
514	ALEX-71	Little Shaver, cloth, c-1937	16″	95	215	325
515	ALEX-72	Snow White, compo, c-1930	13″	150	200	245
	ALEX-73	Pollera, compo, c-1930	7″	125	170	220
	ALEX-74	Dr. Dafoe, compo.	14″	400	445	495
517	ALEX-75	Butch/McGuffey/ Genius, compo/ cloth, c-1938-1940	21″	85	120	150
	ALEX-76	Girl, w/teeth, compo, c-1936	19″	135	200	250
	ALEX-77	Betty, compo, c-1934	19″	150	158	195
	ALEX-78	Little Betty, compo, c-1934	13″	125	150	185
518	ALEX-79	Betty Jane, compo	16″	300	450	540
	ALEX-80	Cookie, compo/cloth	17″	135	205	275
519	ALEX-81	Jeannie Walker, compo/wood, c-1939	14″	65	140	225
	ALEX-82	Jeannie Walker, compo/wood, c-1939	14″	65	140	225
	ALEX-83	Jeannie Walker, compo/wood c-1939, in original box	14″		325	
521	ALEX-84	Pinky, compo/cloth, c-1940	20″	95	126	160
	ALEX-85	Crying Baby, rubber/ sp/cloth, c-1949-52	17″	85	95	115
	ALEX-86	Slumbermate, compo/cloth, c-1950	10″	65	85	100
	ALEX-87	Genius/McGuffey, hp/cloth	16″	85	125	150
	ALEX-88	Cherub, (Butch/ Little Genius), vinyl/magic skin	9½″	19	65	95

MTCD Page	Key	Nomenclature	Size	Low	Avg.	High
	ALEX-89	W.A.V.E., compo, W.W. II era	14"	125	175	225
	ALEX-90	W.A.A.C., compo. W.W. II era	14"	125	175	225
522	ALEX-91	Butch, vinyl/cloth, c-1940	14"	75	95	115
	ALEX-92	Toddler, Rosebud, vinyl/cloth	18" 24"	18 24	52 64	75 95
523	ALEX-93	Debbie, (Fleischaker), c-1951	22"	85	135	160
	ALEX-93a	Debbie, (Fleischaker), c-1951	22"	85	135	160
	ALEX-94	Lovey Dovey, hp/ magic skin, c-1950	15"	55	125	175
	ALEX-95	Honeybun, stuffed vinyl/cloth, c-1954	22"	50	85	100
524	ALEX-96	Barbara Jane, stuffed soft vinyl, rooted wig, c-1954	27"	200	236	250
	ALEX-96-1	Barbara Jane, stuffed soft vinyl, rooted wig, c-1954	27"	200	236	250
	ALEX-96-1a	Alice in Wonderland, glued-on wig	27"	300	345	375
525	ALEX-97	Barbara Jane, stuffed soft vinyl, glued-on wig, c-1952	27"	200	236	250
	ALEX-98	Barbara Jane, stuffed soft vinyl, glued-on wig, c-1952	27"	200	236	250
526	ALEX-99	Boy, stuffed vinyl, c-1952	33"	225	350	425
527	ALEX-100	Madelaine, sv/hp, c-1954	17"	150	275	300
	ALEX-101	Madelaine, sv/hp, c-1954	17"	150	275	300
	ALEX-102	Little Women, plastic	12"	200	235	265
	ALEX-103	Margaret Rose, plastic, c-1950	17"	150	265	325
528	ALEX-105	Nina Ballerina, hp, c-1951	14½"	150	175	225
529	ALEX-106	Alice in Wonderland, (Maggie/Margaret), plastic, c-1954	18"	165	229	325
	ALEX-107a	Muffie, (Nancy Ann) hp, c-1952	7½"	15	28	40
	ALEX-107b	Wendy Ann, hp, c-1964	8"	60	105	150

MTCD Page	Key	Nomenclature	Size	Low	Price Avg.	High
	ALEX-107c	Ginny, (Vogue), hp, c-1952	7″	30	48	90
	ALEX-108	Binnie Walker, hp, c-1954	18″	125	173	250
	ALEX-108a	Winnie Walker, hp, c-1954	18″	115	193	275
	ALEX-109	Maggie Walker, hp, c-1954	15″	65	119	300
531	ALEX-110	Cissette, vinyl/plastic, c-1950	9″	65	144	275
	ALEX-111	Beth of Little Women, hp, c-1955	15½″	65	175	245
	ALEX-112	Marmee of Little Women, hp, c-1955	15½″	65	175	245
	ALEX-113	Annabelle, hp, c-1955	20″	135	207	275
	ALEX-114	Nun, hp, Order of St. Joseph, c-1955	20½″		NPA	
	ALEX-115	Kathy, sv/hp, c-1955	20″	25	51	90
532	ALEX-116	Story Princess, hp, c-1956	15″	165	200	250
	ALEX-117	Sleeping Beauty, hp, c-1957	9″	195	250	300
533	ALEX-118	Kathy Baby, vinyl, c-1958	21½″	35	73	115
	ALEX-119	Kathy, vinyl/plastic, c-1958	20″	35	73	115
	ALEX-120	Kathleen, plastic c-1958	29″		165	
	ALEX-121	Kelly, vinyl, c-1958	11½″	250	300	350
	ALEX-122	Kelly, (Marybel face), vinyl, c-1958	15″	70	125	165
	ALEX-123	Kelly, (Marybel face), vinyl, c-1958	20½″	97	150	225
534	ALEX-124	Pollyanna, (Marybel face), vinyl, c-1958	15″	95	150	185
	ALEX-125	Edith, the Lonely Doll, vinyl, c-1958	15″	68	149	225
535	ALEX-126	Joanie, vinyl, c-1959	35″	125	274	475
	ALEX-127	Sleeping Beauty, hp/vinyl	21″	295	430	545
	ALEX-128	Kathleen, vinyl, c-1959	24″	95	125	185
	ALEX-129	Janie, rv, c-1959	36″	115	165	235
	ALEX-130	Mary Ellen Walker, hp, c-1959	32″	150	206	275
536	ALEX-131	Cissy Debutante/Queen, hp, c-1960	20″	225	280	325

Page	Key	Nomenclature	Size	Low	Avg.	High
537	ALEX-132	Baby Genius (Timmy), vinyl, c-1960	21″	45	88	125
	ALEX-133	Maggie Mixup, vinyl, c-1960	16″	195	231	275
	ALEX-134	Timmy, hv, c-1960	29″	55	115	165
	ALEX-135	Mimi, sv/hp, c-1961	30″	125	192	245
	ALEX-136	Mimi, dressed as Heidi, soft vinyl/ hp, c-1961	30″	155	233	275
538	ALEX-137	Little Mary Sun- shine, vinyl, c-1961	15″	150	163	200
	ALEX-138	Jacqueline, vinyl, c-1961	21″	600	700	900
	ALEX-139	Baby Sweetheart, vinyl, c-1961	21″		NPA	
539	ALEX-140	Smarty, vinyl/ plastic, c-1962	12″	50	73	165
	ALEX-141	Smarty, vinyl/ plastic, c-1962	12″	50	73	165
	ALEX-142	Bunny, vinyl/ plastic, c-1962	18″	35	95	150
	ALEX-143	Bunny Baby, vinyl/ plastic, c-1962	17″	95	100	125
	ALEX-144	Katie, vinyl, (F.A.O. Schwartz), c-1962	12″	850	1295	1650
		Tommie, vinyl, (F.A.O. Schwartz), c-1962	12″	850	1295	1650
541	ALEX-145	Unidentified Baby, vinyl	14″		NPA	
	ALEX-146	Pamela, hp, c-1963	12″	275	350	425
	ALEX-147	Unidentified Baby, vinyl	17″		NPA	
	ALEX-148	Janie, vinyl, c-1964	12″	85	125	165
	ALEX-149	Little Shaver, vinyl, c-1964	12″	28	57	90
	ALEX-149-1	Little Orphan Annie, vinyl	14″	185	243	295
	ALEX-150	Little Orphan Annie, vinyl	14″	185	243	295
	ALEX-151	McGuffey Ana, vinyl, c-1965	14″	150	193	235
543	ALEX-152	Baby Ellen, vinyl/ plastic, c-1965	14″	25	57	80
	ALEX-153	Coco, vinyl/plastic, c-1966	20″	950	1000	1650
	ALEX-154	Melanie, vinyl/ plastic, 1966	21″	950	1000	1650
	ALEX-155	Polly, vinyl, c-1966	18″	60	94	150

MTCD Page	Key	Nomenclature	Size	Low	Avg.	High
	ALEX-156	Littlest Kitten, vinyl, c-1966	7½"	55	95	115
544	ALEX-157	Alice in Wonderland, vinyl/plastic, c-1966	14"	50	71	90
		Tweedle Dum, Tweedle Dee, (Old Cottage) compo/ felt	10"		NPA	
	ALEX-158	Nancy Drew, vinyl, c-1967	12"	95	185	245
	ALEX-159	Blue Boy, vinyl, c-1973	11½"	25	40	75
	ALEX-160	Maggie, vinyl, c-1973	17"	85	145	225
545	ALEX-161	Sweet Tears, vinyl, c-1974	9"	20	43	65
			14"	26	47	65
	ALEX-162	Baby Precious, vinyl/ cloth, c-1974	21"	35	84	165
	ALEX-163	Baby Lynn, vinyl/ cloth, c-1974	20"	35	62	90
	ALEX-164	The International Dolls, plastic, 1974	8"	25	51	65

NOTE: The market on these dolls is highly volatile, with specific nationalites edging towards the four-figure bracket. The prices shown, therefore, represent the norm rather than the exception.

MTCD Page	Key	Nomenclature	Size	Low	Avg.	High
548	ALEX-165	Storybook Series, plastic	8"	23	29	90

NOTE: This series is somewhat more stable than the International Series, although there are a few dolls nearing the three-figure mark.

MTCD Page	Key	Nomenclature	Size	Low	Avg.	High
	ALEX-166	Janie, vinyl/cloth, c-1973	14"	45	65	85
			20"	65	85	115

ALLIED DOLL CO.

	Key	Nomenclature	Size	Low	Avg.	High
	ALL-1	Girl, (Allied) compo/ cloth, c-1919			NPA	

ALLIED DOLL & TOY CO.

	Key	Nomenclature	Size	Low	Avg.	High
	ALL-2	Wendy, (Allied) hv, c-1967	14"		15	

LOUIS AMBERG AND SON

MTCD Page	Key	Nomenclature	Size	Low	Avg.	High
549	AMB-1	Papa-Mama Doll, bisque head/B.J. body, c-1903			NPA	
	AMB-2	Bobby Blake, compo/cloth, c-1911			NPA	

		Dolly Drake, compo/ cloth, c-1911			NPA
	AMB-3	Sassy Sue, compo/ cloth, c-1911			NPA
	AMB-4	Swat Mulligan, compo/cloth, c-1911-1914			NPA
550	AMB-5	Little Sister, compo/ cloth, c-1911	14″		NPA
	AMB-6	Character Boy, compo/cloth, c-1912	19″		NPA
	AMB-7	Sis Hopkins, compo/ cloth, c-1911	14″		NPA
551	AMB-8	The Wonder Baby, compo/cloth, c-1913			NPA
	AMB-9a-c	Tiny Tots, compo/ cloth, c-1913	13″		NPA
	AMB-10	Louis Amberg, Portrait, 1913			
552	AMB-11	Little Sweetheart, compo/cloth	16″		NPA
	AMB-12	Truest-to-life Babies, compo/cloth	9″		NPA
	AMB-13	Miss Broadway, compo/cloth	13″		NPA
	AMB-14a,b	Hail Columbia and Yankee Doodle, compo/cloth c-1912	15″		NPA
553	AMB-15a,b	Soldier Boy and Jack Tar, compo/ cloth, c-1914			NPA
	AMB-16a,b	Tango Tots, compo/ cloth, c-1914			NPA
	AMB-17	Jim Dandy, compo/ cloth, c-1914	18″		NPA
	AMB-18	Pouty Pets, compo/ cloth, c-1915	12-16″		NPA
554	AMB-19	Koaster Kid, compo/ cloth, c-1915			NPA
	AMB-20	Koaster Kid, compo/ cloth, c-1915			NPA
555	AMB-21	Sweethearts, compo/ cloth, c-1915			NPA
	AMB-22	Pollyana the Glad Doll, compo/ cloth, c-1917			NPA
	AMB-23	Victory Doll, compo/ B.J. body	15″		NPA
	AMB-23a	Victory			*Catalog Illus.*

MTCD Page	Key	Nomenclature	Size	Low	Avg.	High
	AMB-24	The "Amkid" Doll, bisque/kid, c-1918	19-28"	*Catalog Illus.*		
557	AMB-25	The Educational Doll, compo/cloth, c-1916		NPA		
	AMB-26	Head only, compo, c-1918	8"		45	
	AMB-27	Victory Character Baby, compo, c-1918		NPA		
	AMB-28	Mibs, compo/cloth, c-1921	16"	300	350	425
	AMB-29	New Born Babe, bisque/compo/cloth	26"	600	895	1250
	AMB-29-1	Vanta Baby, compo, c-1927	11"	125	150	225
	AMB-30	Newborn Babe, compo/cloth, 1920s	12"	65	125	145
558	AMB-31	Amberg's Walking Doll, c-1919		ADV.		
	AMB-32	Sunny Orange Blossom, compo/cloth, c-1924	13¾"	NPA		
559	AMB-33	Mibs-type Girl, compo, c-1928		200	250	325
	AMB-34	Body Twist Boy and Girl, compo, c-1928	8"	95	138	165
560	AMB-35	Louis Amberg		*Portrait*		

AMERICAN BISQUE DOLL CO., INC.

	AMER-21	American Bisque Beauty, c-1920		*Catalog Illus.*		

AMERICAN CHARACTER DOLL CO.

(AMERICAN DOLL & TOY MFG. CO.)

MTCD Page	Key	Nomenclature	Size	Low	Avg.	High
561	AMER-22	Fluffy Ruffles, compo/cloth, c-1907			135	
	AMER-23	Fluffy Ruffles, compo/cloth, c-1907			135	
562	AMER-24a-c	Fluffy Ruffles, compo/cloth, c-1908			135	
563	AMER-25	Toddler, compo/cloth, c-1917		*Catalog Illus.*		
	AMER-26	Clown, compo/cloth, c-1918	25"	95	110	175

MTCD					Price	
Page	Key	Nomenclature	Size	Low	Avg.	High
	AMER-27	Child, compo c-1918	23½"	65	135	165
	AMER-28	Baby Petite, compo/ cloth, c-1925	16"	75	95	135
			18"	95	115	148
565	AMER-29	Baby, compo/cloth, c-1925	16"	65	89	95
	AMER-30	Honey Child, compo/ cloth, c-1926	16"	65	95	135
	AMER-31	Sally, compo/cloth, c-1927	16"	50	70	115
	AMER-32	Baby, compo/cloth, c-1930	22"	55	87	100
	AMER-33	Baby Sue, hp/latex/ cloth c-1948-1950	19"	35	49	65
	AMER-34	Baby Sue, hp/ plastic, c-1948-50	14"	35	46	60
567	AMER-35	Baby Sue, vinyl/ cloth, c-1952	17"	30	85	125
	AMER-36	Chuckles, vinyl/ cloth, c-1952	21"	65	95	135
	AMER-37	Chuckles, vinyl/ cloth, c-1952	18"	50	85	125
	AMER-38	Sweet Sue Walker, hp, c-1955	24"	60	95	145
	AMER-39	Sweet Sue, hp, c-1954	15"	35	42	65
	AMER-40	Sweet Sue Walker, hp, c-1954	20"	50	65	85
569	AMER-41	Sweet Sue Walker, hp, c-1954	21"	50	65	85

NOTE: *Prices slightly higher for the 1954 Annie Oakley version in several sizes, dressed as a cowgirl and sometimes called "Dale Evans."*

	AMER-42	Toni, vinyl, c-1955	20"	28	64	150
	AMER-43	Chuckles, vinyl, c-1958	18"	50	75	115
	AMER-44	Sweet Sue Walker, plastic/vinyl, c-1955	23"	60	95	145
571	AMER-45	Toni, hp, c-1958	10"	20	25	32
	AMER-46	Baby Toodles, vinyl, c-1958	14"	15	38	65
	AMER-47	Infant Toodles, vinyl, c-1958	16"	15	38	65
	AMER-48	Infant Toodles, vinyl, c-1958	16"	15	38	65
	AMER-49	Toodle-Loo, "Magic Foam," c-1961	18"	28	50	135
	AMER-50	The New Tiny Tears, vinyl, c-1962	20"		45	
572	AMER-51	Chuckles, vinyl, c-1961	23"	45	62	85

	AMER-52	Chuckles, vinyl, c-1961	23″	45	62	85
	AMER-53	Chuckles, vinyl, c-1961	23″	*Catalog Illus.*		
573	AMER-54	Butterball, vinyl, c-1961	19½″	35	50	95
	AMER-55	Butterball, vinyl/ cloth, voice	22″	35	65	125
574-5	AMER-56-60	The Whimsies; 1-pc. stuffed vinyl bodies, molded heads, assorted characterizations:	21″	18	44	60
		Polly the Lolly				
		Miss Take				
		Zack the Sack				
		Simon (graduate)				
		Dixie the Pixie				
		Fanny (angel)				
		Hedda Get Bedda				
		Strong Man				
		Wheeler the Dealer				
		Tillie the Talker				
		Bessie the Bashful Bride				
		Reggie				
		Susie the Snoozie				
		Zero				
		Lena the Cleaner				
		Monk or Friar				
		Girl Devil				
	AMER-61	Tiny Whimsies, vinyl, c-1961	6″	40	43	48
		Pixie				
		Granny				
		Jump'N				
		Swinger				
		Minnie Mod				
		Go-Go				
577	AMER-62	Popi, snap-apart doll, hp, c-1962	10″		35	
	AMER-63	Tressy Pre-Teen, vinyl, c-1963	14″		18	
	AMER-64	Baby Sue, vinyl, c-1963	17″		45	
	AMER-65	Talking Marie, sv/ hp, c-1963	18″		45	
	AMER-66	Cricket, Tressy's Little Sister, vinyl, c-1965	9″	10	12	18

MTCD Page	Key	Nomenclature	Size	Low	Avg.	High
	AMER-67	Freckles, vinyl/hp, c-1968	13"		25	
	AMER-67-1	Glamourous Pos/n Tressy, vinyl, C-1966	11½"	6	12	22

AMERICAN GLUELESS DOLL CO.

578	AMER-68	Character Baby, c-1918	12-18"		*Catalog Illus.*	

AMERICAN OCARINA & TOY CO.

	AMER-69	American Beauty, c-1919	16-19"		*Catalog Illus.*	

AMERICAN BEAUTY

579	AMER-70	American Beauty, compo, c-1919	16"		295	

AMERICAN PRODUCED STUFFED TOY CO.

	AMER-71	Kutie Kids, compo	14½"		45	

AMERICAN TOY & NOVELTY CO.

580	AMER-72a,b	Two girl dolls of 1918, compo/cloth			*Catalog Illus.*	
	AMER-73	Baby, (Am. Toys) compo/cloth, c-1917			*Catalog Illus.*	

APEX

581	APEX-1	Negro Girl (APEX) stuffed vinyl	22"		35	

ARCADE TOY MFG. CO.

	ARC-1a,b	Boy and Girl (Arcade Toy) compo/cloth, c-1913			*Catalog Illus.*	

ARCY TOY MFG. CO.

	ARC-2	Composition girl doll head, c-1915			*Catalog Illus.*	
	ARC-2a,b	Daddy Long Legs Girl and Boy, 1915			*Catalog Illus.*	

ARMAND MARSEILLE

582	AM-21	Our Pet, bisque/ compo, #992	10"	275	369	425
	AM-22	Bisque Head Girl, A.18M.	42"	1200	1500	2350
	AM-23	Just Me, #310, bisque head toddler	7½"	250	528	1050

MTCD Page	Key	Nomenclature	Size	Low	Price Avg.	High
	AM-24	Bisque Head Girl #300	14½″	225	250	285
583	AM-25	Negro Head #410	2½″	45	75	95
	AM-26	Boy, Toddler body, #352	13½″	325	375	425
584	AM-27	Toddler, #996	15″	150	259	400
	AM-28	Miss Millionaire, #370	23″	165	234	325
	AM-29	Flirty-eyed girl, #990	27″	500	565	650
585	AM-30	Dream Baby, #341	8″	198	240	275
	AM-31	Kid Body Girl, #201013	16½″		NPA	
	AM-32	Kid Body Lady, #3200	19″	165	260	350
586	AM-33	Flirty-eyed Girl, #966	17″	165	196	265
	AM-34	Toddler, #327	22″	450	530	650

ARRANBEE (R & B) DOLL CO.

MTCD Page	Key	Nomenclature	Size	Low	Price Avg.	High
	R&B-13	Bottletot, compo, c-1926	13″	75	95	125
587	R&B-14	Kewty, compo, c-1925-30	14″	45	81	135
	R&B-15	Dutch Boy, compo, c-1930	9″	25	96	115
588	R&B-16a	Nancy, compo	17″	75	125	180
	R&B-16b	Shirley Temple, compo	18″	85	313	550
589	R&B-17	Nancy	19″	75	125	190
	R&B-18	Nancy	19″	75	125	190
	R&B-19	Nancy	19″	75	125	190
	R&B-20	Nancy	17″	75	125	180
	R&B-21	Nancy	17″	75	125	180
	R&B-22a	Nancy as Southern Belle, compo	12″	55	71	125
	22b	Nancy as Southern Belle, compo	17″	75	127	192
590	R&B-23	Drink'n Babe, compo, c-1940, with case & wardrobe	14″		95	
	R&B-23-1	Nancy Lee, hp, c-1947	14″	65	91	135
591	R&B-24	Baby Nancy Lee, syn. rubber/cloth, c-1947	22″	30	32	36
	R&B-25	Little Angel, hp/ cloth/sv, 1947	21″	75	105	135
593	R&B-26	Angel Skin, sv/magic skin, c-1947-1954	13″	25	45	65
	R&B-27	Nanette, hp, c-1953	21″	75	95	165

Page	Key	Nomenclature	Size	Low	Avg.	High
	R&B-28	Nancy Lee, vinyl, c-1952	15″	55	90	135
	R&B-29	Nancy Lee, stuffed vinyl, c-1952	15″	55	90	135
	R&B-30	Little Angel, hp/sv	16″	18	35	65
	R&B-31	Baby Bunting, vinylite plastic/ magic skin, c-1954	15″	25	45	65
595	R&B-32	Taffy, hp walker, c-1954	23″	55	105	145
	R&B-33	Nanette, hp walker, c-1954	21″	75	115	165
	R&B-34	Sweet Pea, vinyl, c-1954		25	45	65
	R&B-35	Little Dear, stuffed vinyl, c-1956	8″	25	30	35
	R&B-36	Littlest Angel, vinyl	11″	8	34	65
	R&B-36-1	Littlest Angel	11″	8	34	65
	R&B-37	Angel, vinyl, c-1956	17″		35	
			21″		45	
597	R&B-38	My Angel Walking Doll, vinyl, c-1956	36″	65	137	185
	R&B-39	Angel Face, various sizes		18	56	95
	R&B-40	Angel Baby, various sizes		18	56	95
	R&B-41	Sweet Angel, sv, c-1956	12″	25	27	35
	R&B-42	My Angel, with curly wig	17″	18	38	65
			26″	25	46	80
	R&B-43	My Angel, vinyl toddler body	17″	18	38	65
			26″	25	46	80
	R&B-44	Littlest Angel, hp, c-1954	11″	8	34	65

ARROW RUBBER

Page	Key	Nomenclature	Size	Low	Avg.	High
598	ARR-1	Crying Baby, (Arrow) vinyl	16″		16	

ART DOLL & TOY CO. INC.

Page	Key	Nomenclature	Size	Low	Avg.	High
	ART-1	Nevvabrake Baby, compo/cloth			*Catalog Illus.*	

AVERILL MFG. CO.

Page	Key	Nomenclature	Size	Low	Avg.	High
	AVRL-8a	Character Dolls, 1915-1916				
599	8b	Dutch Girl			100	
	8c	Cowgirl			100	
	8d	Ranger			100	

MTCD Page	Key	Nomenclature	Size	Low	Avg.	High
	8e	Dutch Boy			100	
	8f	Ranger			100	
	8g	Indian			100	
	8h	Cowboy			100	
	8i	Dutch Boy			100	
600	AVRL-9a	Indians, compo/ cloth, c-1916	16″		100	
	9b		19″		100	
	9c		14″		100	
	AVRL-10a	Papoose, compo/ cloth, c-1916	7″		100	
	10b		11″		100	
	AVRL-11	"Life-like" Baby, compo/cloth			*Catalog Illus.*	
	AVRL-12	Dutch Character Girl, compo/cloth			100	
601	AVRL-13	Sunny Girl, compo/ cloth	16″	100	125	165
	AVRL-14	Baby Booful, compo, c-1920			100	
	AVRL-15	Bye-lo Type, compo/ cloth, c-1925	17″		135	
	AVRL-16	Bye-lo Baby, bisq/ cloth/cell, c-1925	14″	380	492	695
603	AVRL-17	Sunny Babe, compo/ cloth, c-1925	21″	95	135	155
	AVRL-18	Sunny Babe, compo/ cloth, c-1925	18″	85	115	135
	AVRL-19	Clown, compo/cloth, c-1920	14″		165	
	AVRL-20	Bonnie Babe, cell/ cloth, c-1926	16½″	275	325	565
	AVRL-21	Bonnie Babe, bisq/ compo, c-1926		775	843	950
	AVRL-22	Baby Hendren, compo/cloth, c-1930	19″	35	65	90
	AVRL-23	Baby Georgene, compo/cloth, c-1930	23″	35	85	90
	AVRL-24-27	Rag Dolls, yarn hr, mask faces, c-1930-40				
	24	Peasant Boy	13″	25	43	85
	25	Miss Muffet	10″	25	43	85
	26	Girl Scout	13″	25	43	85
	27	Peasant Girl	13″	25	43	85
605	AVRL-28	Baby Georgene, compo/cloth, c-1935	23″	35	85	90

MTCD Page	Key	Nomenclature	Size	Low	Price Avg.	High
	AVRL-29	Walking-Talking Girl, compo/cloth, c-1937	20"	35	65	95
	AVRL-30	Baby, sticky plastic/ cloth, c-1945	26"		35	
	AVRL-31	Georgene "Kirget", oil cloth/cloth, yarn hr, c-1964	18"		45	

B

MTCD Page	Key	Nomenclature	Size	Low	Price Avg.	High
	BAB-1	Babs the Walking Doll	28"		*Catalog Illus.*	
606	BAK-1	Killiblues, compo/ plush, c-1909			165	
	BAW-1	Bawo & Dotter Doll, bisq/compo			*Catalog Illus.*	
	BAHR-1	Bahr & Proschild Baby, compo	15"	225	285	435

BED DOLLS

MTCD Page	Key	Nomenclature	Size	Low	Price Avg.	High
607	BED-1	Flapper-in-a-Swing, compo, c-1920	14"		145	
	BED-2	Baby Bed Doll, compo/cloth, c-1920	20"		135	
	BED-3	Bed Doll Mask Face, ptd, pressed cloth, c-1920	6"		20	
608	BED-4	Lady, mask face, c-1920	28"	25	45	65
	BED-5	Miss Paris, stockinette/compo, c-1920	22"		75	
	BED-6a	Boudoir Doll, compo/cloth	27"		45	
	6b	V for Victory Doll, compo/cloth	30"		65	
	BED-7	Lady Bed Doll, compo/cloth	27"		65	
609	BED-8	Cigarette Smoker, compo/cloth, c-1920	29"	55	243	450
	BED-9	Cigarette Smoker, compo/cloth	27"	55	243	450
	BED-10	A Late Bed Doll, plastic/cloth	25"	35	42	65
611	BELL-1	Belle, vinyl/magic skin, c-1950	18"	35	65	72
	BELL-2	Belle Baby, vinyl, c-1950	19"	35	65	72

| | BEST-1 | The Bester Doll, six sizes | | | *Catalog Illus.* | |
| | BIJ-1a,b | Jitney and Billy with Handcars, (Bijou) | | | *Catalog Illus.* | |

BISQUE DOLLS

	BISQ-30	Negro Child, bisq head	11"	275	315	425
	BISQ-31	German Bisque Girl	18"	225	250	330
612	BISQ-32	German Bisque Toddler	10"	150	165	215
	BISQ-33a,b	All-bisque German Characters			NPA	
	BISQ-34	World War I Characters, Nippon, c-1917 (See BISQ-35)				
613-619	BISQ-35	**IMPORTED BISQUES:**				

FRENCH

Size	Nomenclature	Price
4"	4-jts, CM, G1sE, MP s/s	365
5"	5-jts, CM, G1sE, MP s/s, Wgd	325
7"	5-jts, CM, G1sE, MP s/s, Wgd	325
8"	5-jts, CM, S1pE, MP s/s, Wgd	350

GERMAN

Size	Nomenclature	Price
1"	Sno Babies	125
1¼"	Sno Babies	150
1½"	Sno Babies	180
1½"	1-pc. Pbsq	120
1½"	4-jts, PtdHr, Doll House	135
1½"	4-jts, Wgd, Doll House	135
1¾"	4-jts, MP hr/e/s/s	150
2"	Sno Babies	195
2"	Huggers, Bride & Groom	75
2"	Kewpie Buttonhole	225
2"	Kewpie Scholar	300
2"	4-jts, PBsq, Girls, MP hr/e/s/s	100
2¼"	2-jts, Pbsq, MP hr/e/s/HB	150
2¼"	1-pc, Std Bare Baby	150
2¼"	Kewpie Hugger	300
2¼"	1-pc, Old Man, MP hr/fea/clo	125
2¼"	1-pc, Old Lady, MP hr/fea/clo	125
2¼"	1-pc, Man, MP hr/fea/clo	100
2¼"	1-pc, Lady, Golfer, MP hr/fea/clo	100
2½"	Sno Babies	215
2½"	2-jts, Pbsq, MP hr/e/loop for bow, feet turned	150
2½"	1-pc, Std Baby, MP hr/fea/clo, with lg. bonnet	150
2¾"	1-pc, Std bare baby, MP hr/fea/e	150
3"	1-pc, Child, Std, MP hr/fea/clo, with flower	150
3"	1-pc, Child, Std, MP hr/fea/clo, with sandwich	150
3"	1-pc, MP hr/fea/clo, SGE, OM, 2 teeth	150

3″	Thumb sucker	65
3″	2-jts, MP s/s, PTD/e, Wgd, OL	250
3″	1-pc, Std Girl, MP hr/fea/clo	200
3″	2-jts, MP hr/e	125
3″	4-jts, Baby, MP hr/e	125
3″	Minnie, marked "Disney"	45
3″	Nodder	45
3″	4-jts, Flapper, Pbsq, M hr, Ptd fea/clo	40
3″	Pbsq Character	35
3¼″	Nodder, Boy, with turban & bloomer pants	150
3¼″	2-jts, fat tummy, MP e, Wgd,	150
3¼″	4-jts, Toddler, Pbsq, MP hr/e	150
3¼″	4-jts, Pbsq, MP hr/e/s, in uniforms, as nurse, police, etc.	125
3½″	Mickey Mouse	45
3½″	Minnie Mouse, holding book	38
3½″	Kewpie Huggers	395
3½″	Nodder, Soldier with pointed helmet	175
3½″	2-jts, Ptd e, open head with or. wig	65
3½″	2-jts, CM, Ptd e	50
3½″	2-jts, Sbsq, MP e/s/s, Wgd	175
3½″	2-jts, Baby, MP hr/e, BL, dressed	45
3½″	4-jts, Pale Pbsq, Ptd fea/blue shoes & sock tops	150
3½″	4-jts, MP hr/s/s, Ptd/e, Wgd	250
3½″	4-jts, Gls e, MP s/s, Wgd	250
3½″	Doll House	200
3¾″	2-jts, Pbsq Chubby, SGE	100
4″	1-pc, Character Boy, fat tummy, MO blue swimsuit	60
4″	Kewpie, Marked O'Neill	300
4″	1-pc, Bbsq, Frozen Charlotte	55
4″	2-jts, MP hr/ht/e/s, CL	150
4″	2-jts, MP hr/e/hat band, CL	150
4″	2-jts, MO clo/s/s, CM	75
4″	4-jts, Man, Doll House	50
4″	2-jts, Pbsq, Ptd e, MO hr/s/s	50
4″	2-jts, Pbsq, Ptd e, Wgd, dressed	50
4″	2-jts, MP s/s, MO blonde curls	65
4″	2-jts, MP s/s, MO hr, dressed, CM	75
4″	4-jts, Baby, Ptd fea, brush stroke hair	85
4″	Bye Lo, marked	500
4¼″	Kewpie	245
4¼″	2-jts, MO clo/blonde Dutch-Boy hr	65
4¼″	4-jts, Gls e, CM, Ptd black Mary Jane shoes	150
4½″	1-pc, Soldier with gun	75
4½″	1-pc, Bath Baby, Pbsq, MO hr	40
4½″	2-jts, very fat tummy, OL, MP hr/e	185
4½″	2-jts, Gls e, BL, Character face, undressed	250
4½″	4-jts, MP hr/e, Baby, BL	185
4½″	4-jts, Pbsq, MP hr/e/s/s	185
4½″	4-jts, MP s/s/e, Wgd	215
4½″	4-jts, MP hr/e/s/s	185
4½″	4-jts, MP s/s, Gls e, CM Wgd	275

4½″	4-jts, Gls e, Wgd	80
4½″	5-jts, Gls e, CM, MO s/s	600
4½″	4-jts	195
4½″	5-jts, Brown bisque, Gls e, Wgd, OM with MO teeth	485
4½″	5-jts, CM, Gls e, bare feet	700
4¾″	4-jts, MP s/s, Gls e, Wgd, CM	215
4¾″	4-jts, MP s/s, Gls e, Wgd, OCM	300
5″	1-pc, MP pants/bottle in hand	95
5″	1-pc, marked Heubach, Std Baby, GLE, MP hr/fea/clo	580
5″	1-pc, Betty Boop, Frozen Charlotte	45
5″	2-jts, Boy, MP hr/clo/fea, SGE, fat tummy	270
5″	2-jts, Pbsq, fat tummy, MP hr/e/hb	240
5″	2-jts, MO clo/s/s/, CM	100
5″	2-jts, Ptd e, blue boots, Wgd	115
5″	2-jts, Betty Boop	45
5″	2-jts, Baby Bud	150
5″	2-jts, Kewpie, marked R.O'Neill	110
5″	4-jts, MP s/s, Gls e, Wgd, CM	270
5″	4-jts, MP s/s, Gls e, Wgd, CM	270
5″	4-jts, BL Baby, Gls e, Character face, undressed	350
5″	2-jts, Ptd e, MO hr, MP s/s, CM, dressed	80
5″	2-jts, Ptd e, MP s/s, Wgd, dressed, CM	80
5″	4-jts, MO hr/s/s	50
5″	4-jts, MP hr/s/s/e	200
5″	4-jts, Sbsq, MP hr/e, Girl	125
5″	4-jts, BL Toddler, MP hr/e/blue ribbon	125
5″	4-jts, MP hr/e/s/s, CM	250
5″	4-jts, Pbsq, BL Baby, MO hr	100
5″	4-jts, MP brown e, BL Baby, dressed	80
5″	5-jts, Bye-Lo, marked	600
5″	Boy, MO Sailor suit	85
5″	4-jts, 1920's Girl, marked Germany, PtdBsq, MO hr	25
5⅛″	Pbsq Baby Bud, short shirt, exposed tongue	75
5¼″	4-jts, Cupid's Sister, MP hr/e	240
5¼″	4-jts, MP hr/e/boots/s, CM	270
5¼″	Kewpie, marked	300
5½″	2-jts, Chubby boy, label "Babs Germany"	80
5½″	Baby Bud, PtdBsq, Ptd fea, short shirt	75
5½″	4-jts, MP s/s, lg. Wg	65
5½″	4-jts, Ptd hr/s/s, Wgd	65
5½″	4-jts, MP hr/s/s	300
5½″	4-jts, MP e/s/s, Wgd	300
5½″	4-jts, Gls/e, MP s/s, OM, Wgd	360
5½″	4-jts, ptd, Wgd	65
5½″	5-jts, Gls e, CM, Wgd, bare feet	750
5½″	5-jts, Gls e, MO s/s, CM, Wgd	650
5½″	4-jts, Ptd s/s, Wgd	65
5½″	2-jts, WBsq, Frozen Charlotte, blonde, lustre boots	95
5½″	Chalk Baby	20
5½″	Kestner 180	195
5½″	Cupid-type, MP hr/e/strap with knife, MO movable hat, OL	240

5¾"	4-jts, MP s/s/e, Wgd	175
6"	1-pc, Frozen Charlotte, fat, heavy	45
6"	2-jts, PBsq, Betty Boop, marked Germany	75
6"	2-jts, MO clo/s/s, CM	125
6"	4-jts, PtdBsq, MP hr/e/s, dressed	245
6"	4-jts, MP hr/e/s/s, CM	300
6"	4-jts, MP/e/s/s, Wgd	245
6"	4-jts, Gls/e, MP s/s, OM, Wgd	365
6"	4-jts, Boy, MP hr/fea/clo, Russian suit	245
6"	4-jts, PBsq, Gls/e, Ptd heeled shoes, blue band socks, CM	250
6"	4-jts, PBsq, Flapper, MP hr/fea/clo	225
6"	4-jts, BL Baby, Gls e, character face, undressed	450
6¼"	4-jts, ptd s/s, Wgd	125
6½"	4-jts, PBsq, MP e/s/s, Wgd	212
6½"	Boy, ptd e	60
6½"	5-jts, ptd e, CM	100
6½"	2-jts, Louis Wolfe "Chubby"	425
6½"	4-jts, Kestner Boy, MO hr	175
6½"	4-jts, ptd s/s, Wgd	125
6½"	2-jts, Kewpie, marked R. O'Neill	275
6½"	4-jts, MP e/s/s, 4-button shoes, Wgd	240
7"	2-jts, Baby Bud	200
7"	2-jts, MO clo/s/s, CM	150
7"	4-jts, PBsq, Flapper, MP hr/fea/clo	250
7"	4-jts, Heubach Child, pageboy hair style	550
7"	4-jts, Heubach-type Girl, MO hr	185
7"	4-jts, Heubach Girl, MO hairbows	750
7"	4-jts, Girl, PtdBsq, MP hr/e/s/s, OM, smile with teeth	150
7"	4-jts, PtdBsq, Girl, MP hr/e/s/s	185
7"	4-jts, Kestner, Gls SlpE, OM, MO teeth, MP s/s, Wgd	485
7"	4-jts, MO s/s, Gls e, CM	185
7½"	4-jts, Gls e, OM with teeth, Ptd Mary Jane shoes/s	225
7½"	4-jts, Child, MP hr/e/s/s	365
7½"	4-jts, MP hr with center part/e/s/s, CM	335
8"	4-jts, Ptd s/s, with ribbon bow	135
8"	4-jts, Ptd s/s, with ptd bow	135
8"	Louis Wolfe Baby	225
8"	4-jts, Kestner, Gls SlpE, MP s/s, OM with 4 teeth, Wgd	485
8"	2-jts, Boy, MP hr/fea/clo, stocking cap, knee pants, OM	365
8"	2-jts, SGE, 20's hr	65
8"	4-jts, Ptd s/s, some with ribbons & bows	135
9"	5-jts, Gls e, MP s/s, CM, Wgd	485

JAPANESE

1½"	1-pc, Children	18
1½"	1-pc, Frozen Charlotte Characters	10
2"	1-pc, Std, in white china tub, gilded rim	25
2"	1-pc, Std, (without tub)	15
2¼"	1-pc, Adults	22
2½"	1-pc, Std	18
2½"	1-pc, SBsq Girl	25

2½″	4-jts, BL Baby, MP hr/e, dressed	40
3″	1-pc, Characters	6
3″	2-jts, solid with bonnet head	18
3″	2-jts, SBsq, MP hr/e	72
3″	4-jts, BBsq, with three topknots	18
3½″	1-pc, SBsq, Dutch Girl	40
3½″	1-pc, OL Girl, dressed	50
3½″	2-pc, Happifats, Nippon	100
3½″	1-pc, Three Little Pigs (each)	20
3½″	1-pc, Boy, Poll Parrot Advertisement Character	18
3½″	2-jts, "Jollikid", Nippon, Kewpie hands, MO clo	90
3½″	Doll House, 1920's	20
3½″	4-jts, SBsq, BL Baby, MP hr/e	40
3½″	4-jts, BBsq, Ptd e, with three topknots	40
3¾″	2-jts, Baby Bud, marked Nippon, dressed	120
3¾″	1-pc, Puss N Boots	45
4″	1-pc, Soldiers, Boxed Set of Three	45
4″	1-pc, Cowboy, Poll Parrot Advertisement Character	15
4″	1-pc, Girl with doll, Poll Parrot Advertisement Character	30
4″	1-pc, Character	12
4″	1-pc, Child	20
4″	1-pc, Betty Boop	12
4″	1-pc, Baby Bud, marked Nippon, MO clo/shoes	50
4″	1-pc, Baby Bud, MO suit	50
4″	4-jts, SBsq, MO hr/clo, Wgd	65
4″	Nodder, Girl, red cape, green hat, holding package	35
4″	Nodder, Girl, snow suit, holding teddy bear	40
4″	Queue San	65
4″	2-jts, Hawaiian, grass skirt	50
4″	2-jts, Grandma, gray hr, MO eye glasses	70
4″	4-jts, Boy & Girl, MP hr/e/s, original costumes, PAIR	85
4″	4-jts, BL baby	20
4″	4-jts, BBsq, three topknots	23
4″	2-jts, MO hr ribbon	35
4¼″	Dwarfs, marked Disney	30
4½″	Louis Wolfe "Chubby," Nippon	275
4½″	Baby Bud, marked Nippon	65
4½″	4-jts, BBsq, three topknots, Ptd e	50
4½″	4-jts, Wgd	55
4½″	4-jts, MP s/s, Wgd	55
4½″	4-jts, Ptd e/s/s, Wgd	55
4½″	4-jts, Ptd e/s/s, MO hr	55
4¾″	2-jts, Girl, Nippon, Blue hr band	45
4¾″	Baby Darling, Morimura Bros, Nippon	67
4¾″	Girl, blonde, with Kewpie type body, tiny arms	40
5″	Frozen Charlotte	11
5″	2-jts, MP s/s/shirt/hat, no pants	28
5″	Betty Boop	12
5″	2-jts, MP hr/e/s/s/clo, marked Nippon	35
5″	2-jts, MP hr/e/s/s, nude, marked Nippon	30
5″	4-jts, MP hr/e/s/glasses	75
5″	4-jts, MP hr/e, Ptd bare feet, O/CM, Nippon	75
5″	2-jts, "Wide-Awake", MP s/s, SGE, Nippon	95

5″	Child	20
5″	Kewpie, MP hr/e/s/s, OW bare	60
5¼″	2-jts, velveteen coat	12
5¼″	2-jts, SGE, marcel hr, velvet costume	12
5½″	2-jts, blonde Girl, with blue hair band	18
5½″	1-pc, Little Girl with doll	20
5¾″	2-jts, Ptd hr/hr band, OL	15
5¾″	2-jts, Boy, OL	15
5¾″	2-jts, Ptd/bobbed hr, OL	15
5¾″	2-jts, Ptd/bobbed hr, CL	15
5¾″	4-jts, Ptd s/s, marked Nippon	20
6″	1-pc, MP clo/glasses	35
6″	2-jts, "Wide-Awake", fat tummy, MP s/s, SGE, Nippon	120
6″	4-jts, BBsq, three topknots	60
6″	4-jts, Ptd s/s, some with ribbons/bows	10
6″	4-jts, OL, some with Ptd bows	10
6″	4-jts, BL Baby	60
6¼″	2-jts, MP s/s, Gls e, CM, Wgd	50
6½″	2-jts, Betty Boop, SGE	18
6½″	2-jts, BBsq, Gls e, Hawaiian, Wgd	65
6½″	2-jts, Ptd clo	55
7″	1-pc, Girl, Ptd costume	25
7″	1-pc, Boy, Ptd costume	25
7″	1-pc, MP hr/e, SGE	10
7″	2-jts, Enamel finish, Ptd s/s,	15
7″	2-jts, Enamel finish, Ptd s/s, OL	15
7″	2-jts, Child, MO hr	25
7″	2-jts, SBsq, MP hr/e, SGE, Betty Boop style, CL	72
7½″	1-pc, Betty Boop type, flirty e, Marcel hr	15
7¾″	2-jts, Orphan Annie	50
8″	4-jts, MP hr/e, BL Baby	95
8½″	2-jts, Betty Boop, Gls e, MO clo	38
8½″	4-jts, SBsq Girl, MP hr/e/s/s	84
9″	1-pc, Boy, MO clo, eyes looking up	30

BLOCK DOLL MFG.

620	BLO-1	Answer Doll, hp, (Block)	10″	15	26	35

BORGFELDT, GEO. & CO.

621	BORG-1	Multi-headed imported, bisq, c-1910	NPA
	BORG-2	Tiny Tots Googly, compo/cloth, 1911	650
	BORG-3	Little Bright Eyes Googly, compo/ cloth, 1911	650

MTCD Page	Key	Nomenclature	Size	Low	Avg.	High
	BORG-4	Natural Baby, Kestner, bisq/ compo, 1911		325	375	495
	BORG-5	Fingy-Legs The Tiny Tot, compo/cloth, 1912			125	
	BORG-6	Jolly Kids Googly, compo/cloth				
	6a	Babe			650	
	6b	Harry			650	
	6c	Carrie			650	
	6d	Willie			650	
	6e	Lilly			650	
	BORG-7	September Morn, bisq, 1913			NPA	

BRUCKNER DOLL

MTCD Page	Key	Nomenclature	Size	Low	Avg.	High
622	BRU-1	Bruckner, compo/ cloth	20″	325	400	480

BYE-LO BABY

MTCD Page	Key	Nomenclature	Size	Low	Avg.	High
	BLB-9	Bye-lo Baby, sticky vinyl/cloth	15″		NPA	
	BLB-10	"Indian" Bye-lo, compo/cloth	11″		NPA	

C

CAMEO EXCLUSIVE PRODUCTS

MTCD Page	Key	Nomenclature	Size	Low	Avg.	High
	CAM-33	Baby Blossom, compo/cloth	20″	175	221	265
	CAM-34	Little Annie Rooney, compo, c-1926	16″	375	541	650
	CAM-35	Scootles, compo, C-1930	14½″	200	318	425
	CAM-36	Betty Boop, seg- mented wood/ compo, c-1930	12″	200	375	540
623	CAM-37	Joy, segmented wood/compo	10″	175	208	250
624	CAM-38	Pete the Pup, compo/wood	8″		NPA	
625	CAM-41	Kewpie, compo, c-1940	13″	100	152	275
	CAM-42	Cuddley Kewpies, vinyl/plush	7″	35	42	65
			9½″	65	84	102
	CAM-43	Miss Peep, sv/magic skin, 1950s	17½″	25	36	55
	CAM-44	Sleep-Eyed Baby Mine, patented joints, c-1961	18″	75	100	150

MTCD Page	Key	Nomenclature	Size	Low	Avg.	High
	CAM-45	Colored Miss Peep, soft-stuffed vinyl, patented joints, c-1969	15"	35	44	65
	CAM-46	Scootles, vinyl	14"	75	165	240

CANADIAN DOLLS

MTCD Page	Key	Nomenclature	Size	Low	Avg.	High
626	CAN-1	Negro Child, vinyl, c-1971	13"		45	
	CAN-2	Mounty, vinyl, c-1972	12"		20	
	CAN-3	Young Sasquatch, vinyl	8"		20	

CASELLOID LIMITED

MTCD Page	Key	Nomenclature	Size	Low	Avg.	High
627	CASC-1-3	"True-Life" Dolls, Casseloid,				
	-1	Babyface, c-1952	13"		*Catalog Illus.*	
			17"		*Catalog Illus.*	
	-2	Plastex Baby Doll, c-1940			*Catalog Illus.*	
	-3	Polly Pigtails, plastic/cloth, Puppet, c-1952			*Catalog Illus.*	

CELLULOID DOLLS

MTCD Page	Key	Nomenclature	Size	Low	Avg.	High
629	CEL-17	Boy's head only, (Marks Brothers)	5"		NPA	
			6"		NPA	
	CEL-18	Parsons-Jackson Toddler Girl, c-1913		135	163	190
	CEL-19	American-Made Girl, (Marks Brothers)	25"	225	266	325
	CEL-20	Parsons-Jackson Baby	10"	100	177	275
	CEL-21a	Parsons-Jackson Toddler, SL		125	187	275
	21b	Baby, Parsons-Jackson			Adv.	
	CEL-22a	Minerva/Germany Baby (helmet mark)	13"	75	90	110
	22b	France/GNE Baby	7"	35	59	78
	22c	Irwin Baby	14"	25	33	45
630	CEL-23	Minerva Boy (helmet mark)	13"	50	76	95
	CEL-24	Minerva Girl (helmet mark)	9½"	50	92	125
	CEL-25	Minerva Boy (helmet mark)	11"	85	93	100

MTCD Page	Key	Nomenclature	Size	Low	Price Avg.	High
	CEL-26	Minerva Girl (helmet mark)	14"	95	106	125
631	CEL-27	Schutz-Marke Head, (turtle mark) c-1918	4"		NPA	
	CEL-28	Turtle Mark Girl	15½"	100	125	150
	CEL-29	Turtle Mark Girl	14½"	85	100	125
	CEL-30	Turtle Mark Girl	15½"	95	106	125
	CEL-31	Schutz-Marke Baby	9½"	30	48	65
	CEL-32	Turtle Mark Baby	9½"	30	43	55
	CEL-33	Kestner #200 Boy, (Turtle mark)	10"	75	136	225
632	CEL-34	Mme Hendren Boy (Turtle mark)	15"	100	156	225
	CEL-35	Schutz-Marke Boy, (Turtle mark)	21"	175	258	325
	CEL-36	Boy (Japan)	14"	175	205	245
	CEL-37	SNF Boy (French)	22"	175	190	275
633	CEL-38	Baby, (Occupied Japan-Clover mark)	12"	35	50	65
	CEL-39	Boy, (Occupied Japan)	6½"	22	40	65
	CEL-40	German Girl, c-1970	12"	19	36	55
	CEL-41	Sarold Baby (England)			65	
634	CEL-42	Dutch Lady (Holland) (stork mark)	26"	175	213	375
	CEL-43	Stork Mark Girl	21½"	175	213	225
	CEL-44	K & W Girl, (Germany)	14"	175	250	325
635	CEL-45	Unmarked German Boy	10"	50	57	65
	CEL-46	K & W Baby, Turtle mark	11½"	175	256	325
	CEL-47	Schutz-marke Baby	13"	200	268	335
	CEL-48	French Toddler (windmill mark)	17"	100	215	325
636	CEL-49	One-piece Woman, c-1928	5¾"	30	35	40
	CEL-50	Mask-face Eskimo, cloth body/head, c-1920		65	70	75
	CEL-51	"The All Voice Doll" c-1912	9"	75	100	125
	CEL-52	Negro Baby (German)	11"	75	85	95
637	CEL-53	Miscellaneous Celluloid Dolls: #64-0989 Dressed				

MTCD Page	Key	Nomenclature	Size	Low	Price Avg.	High
		Betty Boop Types	8¼″		30	
		#64-1066 Doll with musical chimes	8-10½″		35	
		#F7161 1-pc, nude, Ptd shoes	3″		10	
		#F7162 1-pc, nude, Ptd shoes	6½″		15	
		#F7171-4 Baby, 4 Jts, Ptd Hr	5-11¼″		30	
		#F7168-9 Baby, 4 Jts, MoHr Wgs	6¼-8½		35	
		#1F5088-9 Baby on satin pillow	3½″		20	
		#2F9466 Baby, 4 Jts, Ptd Hr	8″		30	
		#2F9396 Betty Boop, 2 Jts, MoHr Wg	6″		30	
		#2F9637 Child, 2 Jts, Ptd Hr	7″		20	
		#2F9514 "Picaninnies," 2 Jts, Ptd Hr	2½″		15	
		#64-0810 1-pc molded characters, (12 styles)	5″		15	
		#64-0962 1-pc Children MO clo, (12 styles)	6¾″		20	
		#640968 1-pc Children, MO clo, (24 styles)	7-8½″		20	
		#640983 1-pc Children, MO clo, (24 styles)	7½-8″		25	
		#640974 1-pc Characters, MO clo, (12 styles)	7″		20	
		#640995 1-pc Animal Head Dolls, MO clo, (4 styles)	7″		35	
638	CEL-54	Miscellaneous Celluloid Dolls				
		#640806 Baby, 4 Jts, MP Hr	5¼″		25	
		#64-0816 Betty Boop, 2 Jts, PtdHr, nude	6″		30	
		#64-0992 Negro Baby Doll, Bell Hop	7″		20	
		#2F9386 2 Jts, Character	3½″		15	

MTCD Page	Key	Nomenclature	Size	Low	Price Avg.	High
		#1F9665 1-pc Children, Characters	5″		15	
		#64-0812 Negro Child, 2 Jts, MO clo	4½″		15	
		#64-0819 Baby, 4 Jts, MP hr	6″		20	
		#640980 Santa Claus, 1-pc, MP clo	7″		45	
		#2F9522 Child, 2 Jts, MP hr	6″		20	
		#64-0982 1-pc Children, (12 styles)	7″		15	
		#64-0811 1-pc Children Characters (12 styles)	5″		15	
		#64-0986 Orphan Annie, 2 Jts, MO clo/hr	7¾″		45	
		#64-0972 Baby, 4 Jts, MP hr	8½″		25	
		#2F9761 Children, 2 Jts, Rolling Eyes	4½″		45	
		#64-0990 Dressed Children, 2 Jts	8″		30	
		#64-0978 Betty Boop, 2 Jts	9¼″	-	45	
639	CEL-55	Miscellaneous Celluloid Dolls				
		#F-9220 Betty Boop type in feathers (6 styles)	4½″		25	
		#2F9804 Bathing Girl, with parasol	8″		35	
		#2F9371 School Boys, Girls, Babies (12 styles)	8½″		20	
		#2F9410 Doll, Nursing Set, glass bottle	2½″		20	
		#2F9411 Doll, Nursing Set, glass bottle	3″		25	
		#2F9527 Betty Boop, 2 Jts, nude	6″		30	
		#2F9537 Baseball Players, 1-pc	6″		25	

MTCD Page	Key	Nomenclature	Size	Low	Price Avg.	High
		#2F9539 Assorted Children, 2 Jts, Ptd clo	6″		20	
		#2F9414 Doll in Cradle	2″		20	
		#64-0821 Uncle Sam, 1-pc, MP	6½″		35	
		#2F9412 Doll in Suit Case (bath set)	2½″		25	
		#2F9399 Baby, 4 Jts, Rocking chair	3″		25	
		#2F9800 Doll, 2 Jts, Metal bed	3″		35	
		#2F9370 Assorted Characters & Children, 2 Jts	5½″		20	
640	CEL-56	Miscellaneous Celluloid Dolls				
		#64-0999 Babies, 4 Jts, Rockers	3½″-4½″		15	
		#2F9432 1-pc Betty Boop with violin	5″		30	
		#2F9428 4-Jts, Bare Babies	4″		20	
		#2F9532 2-Jts Betty Boop, Ptd swimsuit	5½″		25	
		#2F9430 2-Jts, Girl with Hr Band	3½″		15	
		#2F9413 Doll in Cradle	1¼″		20	
		#2F9604 2-Jts, Kewpie type, bare	5½″		20	
		#2F9540 Children, 2 Jts, MP clo	6½″		20	
		#2F9392 "Newly Born" 4 Jts, Babies	5″		25	
		#2F9636 2-Jts, Betty Boop, dressed	5¾″		30	
		#2F9385 2-Jts, Kewpie type, dressed	4″		25	
		#2F9792 2-Jts, Kewpie type, chenille outfit	3½″		20	
		#2F9633 Carnival-type in fur outfit, 2 Jts	4⅛″		25	
		#2F9388 2-Jts, Marcel Wg	4″		20	

Page	Key	Nomenclature	Size	Low	Avg.	High
		#2F9541 Santa Claus, Ptd costume	5″		40	
		#2F9793 Pickaninny, 2 Jts, chenille	3½″		15	
		#2F9790 Picaninny in cardboard melon	3½″		20	
		#2F9399 4-Jts, Baby in Rocker	3″		20	
		#2F9393 2-Jts, Betty Boop, nude	5¾″		30	
		#2F9394 2-Jts, Child, nude, hairband	6″		30	
		#2F9531 Assorted Children, MP costumes	4″		20	
641	CEL-57	Miscellaneous Celluloid Dolls				
		#2F9422 Assorted Bathing Suit Children, 2 Jts	5″		20	
		#F9495 Betty Boop, Flirty Eyes, Ptd hr, 2 Jts	6″		30	
		#F9394 Assorted Children, Ptd Bathing Suits, 2 Jts	6½″		25	
		#F9528 Assorted 1-pc Children Ptd clo	6-6½″		20	
		#2F9373 Musical Chime Clown & Girl	8″		35	
		#2F9374 Musical Chime Clown & Girl	9½″		40	
		#F9430 2-Jts, Girl with Hr Band	3½″		15	
		#F9678 Ptd Hr 2-Jtd Girls, Ptd Swimsuits	6¼″		25	
		#F9751 Colored-bead Pull Toys	5¼″		10	
		#1F9662 2-Jts nude, with Marcel Hr	5½″		20	
		#2F9372 Dude, Bell-hop, Clown, etc. Rattle Dolls	9″		25	
		#2F9413 Doll in Cradle	1½″		15	
		#2F9414 Doll in Cradle	2″		20	

		#F9382 "Playmates," Ptd costumes, (6 styles)	5¼"		15	
		#F9383 "Playmates," Ptd costumes, (6 styles)	7¼"		20	
		#F9714 4-Jts, Baby in Paper Peanut Shell	3¼"		35	
		#F9393 2-Jts, Ptd Marcel Hr, nude	5¾"		25	
		#2F9368 Aviator, Sports, Etc. Characters, 2 Jts	6-6½"		20	

CENTURY DOLL CO.

643	CENT-1	Girl, compo/cloth, c-1919	23"	65	91	115
	CENT-2	Girl, compo/cloth	23"	65	91	115
	CENT-3	Chuckles, compo/cloth	12¼"	42	96	165
	CENT-4	Chuckles, compo/cloth	14"	45	100	165
	CENT-5	Bye-lo-type Baby, compo/cloth	13"	225	258	300
	CENT-6	Century/Kestner Baby, bisq/compo	18"	600	676	785
	CENT-7	Chuckles, compo/cloth	21"	65	114	165
	CENT-8	Miss Century "The Doll of the Century," c-1916			*Catalog Illus.*	

CHINA DOLLS

644	CHI-11	Lady, 1870's, Curly Top, cloth body	14"	800	933	1100
	CHI-12	Boy, 5" head	27"	150	300	450
	CHI-13	Boy, 4" head	18"	125	268	425
645	CHI-14	Blonde Boy, head only	5"		NPA	
	CHI-15	Lady, deep shoulder head, only	8"		NPA	
	CHI-16	Lady, pink lustre head only	5¾"		NPA	
	CHI-17	Scotch Boy, pink lustre head/kid body	9½"	225	276	335
	CHI-18	Lady, unmarked		375	418	475
	CHI-19	Colored Head only	2"		NPA	
	CHI-20	Head only, 1¹¹⁄₁₆", 2½" circ.			NPA	

MTCD Page	Key	Nomenclature	Size	Low	Price Avg.	High
	CHI-21	German Half-doll, lady	3¾"	150	230	265
	CHI-22	Mme. Pompadour Dresser Box		75	83	125
646	CHI-23	Door of Hope Doll, wood/cloth, c-1917-1925	11"	200	243	325
	CHI-24	Acupuncture Doll (Sobin Chemicals)	22"		NPA	
	COL-1	Chubby Kid, compo (Columbia Doll)	12"	20	33	65

COMICS, DOLLS FROM THE

MTCD Page	Key	Nomenclature	Size	Low	Price Avg.	High
	COM-A1a	Robin, plastic, (Ideal) c-1967	9"		3	
	A1b	Super Boy, plastic, (Ideal) c-1967	9"		3	
	A1c	Aqua Lad, plastic, (Ideal) c-1967	9"		3	
	COM-A2	Archie, litho cloth	18½"	12	15	18
647	COM-B3	Bat Girl, plastic, 1967	11½"		5	
		Super Girl, plastic, 1967	11½"		5	
		Wonder Woman, plastic, 1967	11½"		5	
		Aqua Woman, plastic, 1967	11½"		5	
	COM-B4a	Batman, vinyl/ plush, 1966	16"		6	
	B4b	Robin, vinyl/plush, 1966	14"		6	
	B4c	Bat Mouse, vinyl/ plush, 1966	14"		6	
	COM-B5	Batman, vinyl/cloth, glove puppet, 1966	5"		2	
648	COM-B6	Batman Troll, vinyl 1967	6"	5	8	10
	COM-B7	Beanie, vinyl/cloth, 1960	16½"	5	15	23
	COM-B8	Betty Boop, 1-pc bisq	3½"	15	24	30
		Bimbo, 1-pc bisq	3½"	15	24	30
		Bingo, 1-pc bisq	3½"	15	24	30
	COM-B9	Betty Boop, cloth (Colorforms)	22"	20	52	78
	COM-B10	Betty Boop, seg- mented wood/ compo	12"	200	375	540
649	COM-B11	Bimbo Orchestra Character, 1-pc bisq (Japan, Borgfeld)	3¾"	15	24	30

MTCD Page	Key	Nomenclature	Size	Low	Price Avg.	High
	COM-B12	Bimbo, segmented wood/compo, 1932	6½"	35	56	75
			9"	65	69	85
	COM-B13	Mechanical Bonnie Braids, key-wind, metal body, c-1952	12"		45	
650	COM-B14	Bonnie Braids Toddler, sv/hp walker, 1951	13"	20	33	54
	COM-B15	Bugs Bunny, felt/ plush	10"		25	
	COM-C2	Captain Action, hp, (Ideal) c-1967	12"		20	
651	COM-C3	The Gene Carr Kids, compo/cloth, 1915				
	C3a	Snowball	14"	85	212	325
	C3b	Mike	14"	85	212	325
	C3c	Blink	14"	85	212	325
	C3d	Jane	14"	85	212	325
	C3e	Skinney	14"	85	212	325
	COM-C3-1	Jane, a Gene Carr Kid	14"	85	212	325
		Mike, a Gene Carr Kid	14"	85	212	325
	COM-C4	Casper the Friendly Ghost, vinyl/plush, c-1960	9"	5	11	18
	COM-C5	Charley Horse, vinyl glove puppet, 1960	10½"	5	15	18
652	COM-D4	Denny Dimwit, compo/wood, c-1948	11"	85	90	125
	COM-D5	Dondi, vinyl/cloth, c-1950			NPA	
	COM-F4	Felix the Cat, segmented wood, c-1928	3½"	65	95	175
	COM-F5	Felix the Cat, compo, chenille tail	13"		450	
	COM-F6	Baby Pebbles Flintstone, vinyl/ cloth, c-1960	15"	15	26	35
653	COM-F7	Baby Puss, vinyl, c-1950	10"	5	11	16
	COM-F8	Barney Rubble, vinyl, c-1960	10"	12	15	18
	COM-F9	The Flintstones and the Rubbles, vinyl				
		Fred	10"	12	15	18
		Wilma	12"	12	15	18

MTCD Page	Key	Nomenclature	Size	Low	Avg.	High
		Barney	10″	12	15	18
		Betty	12″	12	15	18
	COM-F10	Barney Rubble, litho cloth, c-1960	16½″	5	12	15
	COM-F11	Wilma Flintstone, litho cloth, c-1960	20″	5	12	15
	COM-F12	Fred Flintstone Hand Puppet, vinyl/ cloth, c-1962	3″		3	
654	COM-F13	Fluffy Ruffles, bisq/ BJ body, Germany, (Geo. Borgfeldt) c-1908			NPA	
	COM-H1	Henry, rubber, c-1934	8½″		45	
	COM-H2	Heckel (or Jeckel) Hand Puppet, vinyl/cloth, c-1960	5″		6	
	COM-J1a	Joy, compo/cloth, c-1912			NPA	
	J1b	Gloom, compo/cloth, c-1912			NPA	
655	COM-K1	Abe Kabibble, compo/cloth (Bleier Bros)	16″		NPA	
			18″		NPA	
	COM-K2	Krazy Kat, "The Gloom Chaser," felt, (Averill) c-1916	20″		NPA	
	COM-L9	The Dogpatch Family, vinyl (Baby Barry)				
	L9a	Li'l Abner	14″	50	71	135
	L9b	Daisy Mae	14″	50	71	135
	L9c	Mammy Yokum	14″	50	71	135
	L9d	Pappy Yokum	14″	50	71	135
	COM-L10	Little Audrey and Friends, vinyl/ plush, c-1961	9″		25 ea	
		Cinderella				
		Donald Duck				
		Dumbo				
		Merryweather				
		Jiminy Cricket				
		Popeye				
		Mickey Mouse				
		Pluto				
		Goofy				
		Olive Oyl				
		Pinocchio				
		Katnip				

MTCD Page	Key	Nomenclature	Size	Low	Avg.	High
		Spooky Ghost Casper the Friendly Ghost				
	COM-L11	Little Audrey, vinyl	13½″	10	25	32
		Little Audrey, vinyl, jointed, 1960	13″		35	
656	COM-L12	Little Orphan Annie, bisq, c-1933	7½″		50	
	COM-L13	Little Orphan Annie, Sandy, Lillums, and Harold Teen, bisq, boxed set			125	
	COM-L14	Little Orphan Annie, pm or compo, C-1930	12″	35	85	125
		Sandy, pm or compo, c-1930			NPA	
	COM-L15	Little Orphan Annie, litho cloth	17″	15	35	40
	COM-L16	Little Orphan Annie, plastic (Remco) c-1967	15½″	15	30	55
658	COM-L17	The Lone Ranger, compo/cloth, (Dollcraft Novelty)	20½″	250	350	425
	COM-L18	Tonto, compo/cloth, (Dollcraft Novelty)	20½″	250	320	425
	COM-L19	The Lone Ranger, (Hubley/Gabriel) 1973	9½″		10	
	COM-L20	Tonto, (Hubley/ Gabriel) 1973	9½″		6	
	COM-L21	Butch, (Hubley/ Gabriel) 1973	9½″		8	
659	COM-M2	Moon Mullins, nodder, Germany	3¼″		65	
	COM-M3	Jeff, cell, Germany, 1922	3¼″		35	
	COM-N2	Nancy, vinyl/magic skin, c-1955			75	
		Sluggo, vinyl/magic skin, c-1955			75	
660	COM-N3	Nancy, cloth, (Georgene Novelties) c-1960	15″	5	10	18
	COM-N4	Nancy, litho cloth (Stacey Lee Orig) c-1972	20″	16	19	25
	COM-N5a-e	The Nemo Series, bisq, two sizes, c-1914 Dr. Pill,				

661	COM-N6	Princess, Imp, Nemo, Flip Character Boy (Alfred E. Newman), compo/ cloth		50	NPA 65	135
	COM-02	Oswald Rabbit, key-wind walker, cloth/velour	16″		15	
	COM-03	Oswald Rabbit, key-wind walker, plush/cloth, c-1932	17″		20	
	COM-03-1	Oswald Rabbit, plush/cloth, c-1932	15″		15	
	COM-04	Our Gang, hollow bisq figures to paint, (Hal Roach) Boxed SET of nine figures			150	
662	COM-P7	Little Champ, vinyl	14″	30	36	45
	COM-P8	Humphrey, (Ideal) cell/magic skin	16″	40	65	124
	COM-P9	Popeye, rubber, c-1936	13″		35	
	COM-P10	Popeye, compo/ wood, c-1936	15″		85	
	COM-P11	Popeye, litho cloth	15″		25	
663	COM-P11-1	Popeye and Friends, segmented wood	5″		45 ea	
	COM-P12	Popeye, foam, c-1968	12½″	27	38	55
	COM-P13	Popeye, vinyl/cloth, c-1963	21″	18	32	45
	COM-P14	Popeye, vinyl/plush/ felt, GUND, c-1963	9″		18	
	COM-P15	Talking Popeye Hand Puppet, vinyl/cloth (Mattel) c-1966-68	12″	12	16	20
664	COM-P16	Jeep, segmented wood, c-1935	13″		65	
	COM-P17	Olive Oyl, segmented wood, c-1930	5¼″		45	
	COM-P18	Psyllium (Pus-Silly) hard rubber, (Sun Rubber) c-1937	10″		65	
	COM-P19	Psyllium and Popocatepetl, c-1937-38	10″		*Catalog Illus.*	
	COM-P20a	Puzzy, compo, c-1948	15″		135	
		Sizzy, compo, c-1948	15″		135	

MTCD Page	Key	Nomenclature	Size	Low	Price Avg.	High
665	COM-P20c	Puzzy, compo, c-1948	15″		135	
	COM-R1	Rachel, bisq	3½″	45	146	215
	COM-S3	Skippy, bisq, c-1928	5″		65	
	COM-S4	Skeezix, litho oil cloth	14½″	45	135	145
666	COM-S5	Smitty, bisq, Germany, c-1930	3¾″		65	
	COM-S6a	Smitty, cloth, c-1935	14″		45	
			21″		65	
		Li'l Brother Herby, cloth, c-1935	12″		45	
			19″		65	
667	COM-S7	Napoleon alias Snookums, compo/plush, (Samstag-Hilder), c-1910	12″		NPA	
	COM-S8	The Newlywed Kid, Napoleon alias Snookums, c-1909	12″		NPA	
	COM-S9	Newlywed Baby, compo/cloth (Aetna) c-1909			NPA	
	COM-S10	Snoopy Astronaut, vinyl, c-1969	9″		6	
	COM-S11	World's Greatest Super Heroes, vinyl, (Mego) c-1972				
	S11a	Batman	8″		6	
	S11b	Robin	8″		6	
	S11c	Aquaman	8″		6	
	S11d	Superman	8″		6	
669	COM-S12	Superman, head only, vinyl C-1965 (Ideal)	4″		NPA	
	COM-S13	Superman, vinyl/ plush, c-1966	16″		7	
	COM-S14	Sweet Pea, vinyl/ cloth, (Gund)	11½″		45	
	COM-S15	Sweetie Pie, 1-pc vinyl, 1950-60s (Stern Toy)	9½″		18	
	COM-T7	Tom, vinyl/cloth, (Mattel) c-1962	20″		8	
	COM-T8	Trixie, vinyl	8″	6	7	10
	COM-U1	Uncle Wiggly, vinyl/ cloth, c-1953	12½″		NPA	
	COM-W1	Wimpy, rubber, squeeker	8¼″		35	

MTCD Page	Key	Nomenclature	Size	Low	Avg.	High
	COM-W2	Wimpy, compo, rocker-type walker, c-1930	3½″		35	
671	COM-W3	Wimpy, mask face/ cloth, unmarked	17″		35	
	COM-W4	Wimpy, compo, c-1936	19″		20	
	COM-W5	Wonder Woman, head only, vinyl, c-1966, (Ideal)	4″		8	
	COM-W6	Woody Woodpecker, litho cloth, unmarked	13½″		6	
	COM-W7	Woody Woodpecker Hand Puppet, vinyl/cloth (Mattel)	16″		3	
	COM-Y1	Mammy Yokum, vinyl/cloth, Baby Barry, c-1957	21″	50	71	135
	COM-Y2	Mysterious Yokum, soft vinyl/magic skin, c-1953	11″		25	
	COM-Y3	Yosemite Sam, plastic, c-1968, (Dakin)	7¼″	5	11	18
	COM-Y3a	Yosemite Sam, c-1974, (Dakin)		*Catalog Illus.*		

COMPOSITION

MTCD Page	Key	Nomenclature	Size	Low	Avg.	High
672	COMP-1	"Imported Dressed Dolls," compo/ cloth 1928-32		*Catalog Illus.*		
	COMP-2	Baby (Composition Novelty) compo 1916		*Catalog Illus.*		

CORRY, GRACE

MTCD Page	Key	Nomenclature	Size	Low	Avg.	High
	COR-1	Grace Corry Child, compo/cloth	13½″	95	135	185
	COR-2	Grace Corry Boy, compo/cloth	15″	100	145	225

CRECHE DOLLS

MTCD Page	Key	Nomenclature	Size	Low	Avg.	High
	CRE-1	Christ Child, Creche Doll, vinyl, (Ideal) Unmkd	9″	65	135	195
	CRE-1a	The Most Wonderful Story, boxed set, (Ideal) c-1958		NPA		

MTCD Page	Key	Nomenclature	Size	Low	Price Avg.	High
673	CRE-2	John the Baptist, Creche Doll, carved wood/PM, (Italian)	18″		NPA	
	CRE-3	1919 line of one hundred doll styles, (Cresent Toy)			*Catalog Illus.*	

D

MTCD Page	Key	Nomenclature	Size	Low	Avg.	High
	DAI-1	Dainty Doll Baby, compo (Dainty Doll) c-1917			*Catalog Illus.*	
674	DAK-1	Dream Doll, cloth/wire armature, (Dakin)	8″		6	
	DECO-1	Can't Break 'Em Boy, compo/cloth, c-1910-1920	15″		165	

DEE AND CEE, CANADA

MTCD Page	Key	Nomenclature	Size	Low	Avg.	High
	DC-1	Baby, soft vinyl/ stuffed vinyl, c-1950	24″	30	36	45
	DC-2	Mountie, vinyl/hp, c-1950	15″	25	37	50
675	DC-3	Negro Baby, soft vinyl/rigid plastic	20″		40	
	DC-4	Tyrolean Boy, soft plastic c-1955	12″	15	20	35
	DC-5	Small-waisted Girl, vinyl, c-1960	12″	15	25	32
	DC-6	Eskimos, soft vinyl/ plastic (Koweeka) c-1960	14″		45	
			16″		85	

DELUXE READING CORP. (TOPPER CORP)

MTCD Page	Key	Nomenclature	Size	Low	Avg.	High
677	DEL-1	Sleep-eyed Baby, compo, (De Luxe Doll and Toy) c-1919			*Catalog Illus.*	
	DEL-2	Tickles, hp, c-1963	20″	10	23	45
	DEL-3	Baby Brite, vinyl/hp, c-1963	13½″	10	27	45
	DEL-4	Baby Boo, vinyl/hp, c-1965	21″	12	26	50
	DEL-5	Baby Boo, vinyl/hp, c-1965	21″	12	26	50

MTCD Page	Key	Nomenclature	Size	Low	Price Avg.	High
	DEL-6	Little Miss Fussy, soft vinyl/hp, c-1967	18″	10	25	45
	DEL-7	Baby Catch-a-Ball, soft vinyl/hp c-1968	19″	20	28	45
679	DEL-8	Baby Peek 'N Play, soft vinyl/hp, 1968	18″	19	27	40
	DEL-9	Baby Party, vinyl/ hp, 1968	10″	10	24	35
			18″	10	26	45
	DEL-10	Baby Crawler, soft vinyl/hp, 1969	7″	4	13	17
			10″	5	15	18
	DEL-11	Baby Fussy, vinyl/ hp, 1969	10″	5	13	20
	DEL-12	Busy Baby Walker, vinyl/plastic, 1969	10″	6	10	18
	DEL-13	Luv 'N' Care, vinyl/ hp, 1969	18″	15	27	35
	DEL-14	Baby Ride-A-Bike, vinyl/hp, 1969	10″	8	12	25
	DEL-15	Smarty Pants, vinyl/ plastic, 1971	18″	5	7	12
681	DEL-16	Dawn and Friends, vinyl, c-1970	6½″	2	5	10
		Dawn Angie Glori Dale Ron Van Dinah Gary Kip Maureen Melanie Jessica Denise Longlocks				
683	DEL-16-1	The Tom Boy, vinyl, 1965	6½″		7	
	DEL-17a-c	Tear Drops: Belinda, Cybil, Ali, (never marketed)	6″		NPA	
	DEL-18	Gabbie, vinyl/plastic, 1972		10	17	25

DENMARK

	DEN-1a,b	Sexed Twins, vinyl, (Denmark)	11″		50 pr	

DISNEY, WALT

	DIS-15	Mickey Mouse, cloth (Knickerbocker), c-1930	13″	135	160	185

MTCD Page	Key	Nomenclature	Size	Low	Avg.	High
685	DIS-16	Mickey Mouse, compo/wood, c-1930, (Knickerbocker)	9″	55	75	125
	DIS-17a	Mickey Mouse, ptd bisq, w/accordian	5″		40	
	17b	Mickey Mouse, ptd bisq, w/mandolin	5″		40	
	17c	Minnie Mouse, ptd bisq	6″		45	
	17d	Mickey Mouse, ptd bisq	6″		45	
	DIS-18a	Minnie Mouse, segmented wood	3⅞″		45	
		Mickey Mouse, segmented wood	3⅞″		45	
		Minnie Mouse, segmented wood	5⅛″		40	
		Mickey Mouse, segmented wood	5⅛″		40	
	DIS-19	Minnie Mouse, rubber (Sun Rubber)	10½″	12	22	45
	DIS-20a	Mickey Mouse, ptd bisq, c-1928, with ball bat	4⅛″	20	38	45
	20b	Minnie Mouse, ptd bisq, c-1928, with ball glove	4⅛″	20	38	45
	DIS-20-1a	Mickey Mouse, ptd bisq, c-1928	3½″	20	38	45
	20-1b	Mickey Mouse, ptd bisq, c-1928	3½″	20	38	45
	20-1c	Mickey Mouse, ptd bisq, c-1928	3½″	20	38	45
	DIS-21	Mickey Mouse, compo, c-1936	12″	55	75	125
	DIS-22-24	Three Little Pigs, ptd bisq, c-1928	3¼″		45 ea	
	DIS-25	Mickey Mouse, compo, c-1936	12″	55	75	125
	DIS-26	One of the Three Little Pigs, compo, unmarked	9″		165	
	DIS-27	Big Bad Wolf, Ptd bisq (Japan)	3½″		45	
687	DIS-29	Panchito, velvet/felt (Character Novelty Co)	15″		24	
	DIS-30	Dumbo, plush, with music box, (Gund)			26	

MTCD Page	Key	Nomenclature	Size	Low	Price Avg.	High
	DIS-31	Pinocchio, compo/ wood, unmarked	16½″		185	
	DIS-32	Pinocchio Hand Puppet, vinyl/ litho, (Gund)	5″		4	
	DIS-33	Jiminy Cricket Hand Puppet, vinyl/ litho, (Gund)	5½″		4	
	DIS-34	Jiminy Cricket, compo/cloth (head size), (Knicker-bocker)	3¼″		35	
	DIS-35	Donald Duck, compo/wood, (Alexander)	9½″		45	
	DIS-36	Girl, (Rose Red?) compo, (Knicker-bocker) 1937-39	15″		65	
689	DIS-37	Stepmother Marionette, compo/cloth, (Alexander)	12″		65	
	DIS-38	Grumpy, 1-pc, rubber	8″		20	
	DIS-39a	Sneezy, compo	9″	35	65	95
	39b	Sleepy, compo	9″	35	65	95
	39c	Grumpy, compo (Knickerbocker)	9½″		85	
	DIS-40	Happy, compo (Alexander)	9″	60	86	125
	DIS-41	Marionette, Walt Disney, Tony Sarg/Alexander: Seven Dwarfs Snow White Woodsman Prince Charming Stepmother Maid		60	86	125
	DIS-42	Snow White, early flexible vinyl	21″	40	70	165
	DIS-42a	Seven Dwarfs, vinyl	8″-8½″		30 ea	
	DIS-42a	Dopey, from above set	8″		30	
	DIS-43	Snow White, early flexible vinyl	21″	40	70	165
690	DIS-44	Dwarf from Set, vinyl	7″-8½″		25 ea	
	DIS-45	Snow White and the Seven Dwarfs Charms, plastic, (Japan)	¾-1¼″		5 ea	

MTCD Page	Key	Nomenclature	Size	Low	Price Avg.	High
	DIS-46	Mouseketeer Marionette, compo/wood, c-1950	14″		35	
	DIS-47	Lady (Dog from Lady and the Tramp), Hand puppet, vinyl/cloth	3½″		5	
691	DIS-48	Tinkerbell, vinyl	12″		18	
	DIS-49	Peter Pan, vinyl/ cloth/felt, (Ideal)	17″		25	
	DIS-50	Cinderella, topsy- turvey, mask face/ cloth, c-1951	18″		35	
693	DIS-51	Mary Poppins, vinyl/plastic, c-1960	36″	45	60	125
	DIS-52	KO (Small World), vinyl/hp	13″	10	25	30
	DIS-53	Cinderella, (w/extra head) vinyl, 1965	12″		35	
	DIS-54	Small World Dolls (Various Char- acters), vinyl/ plastic	8″	10	25	30
	DIS-55	Ferdinand the Bull, silk/velveteen 1939 (H.G. Stone, London)			NPA	
		Matador, compo/ cloth			NPA	

DISPLAY DOLLS

MTCD Page	Key	Nomenclature	Size	Low	Price Avg.	High
	DISP-1	Mechanical Victory Soldier, compo/ cloth, eight-day clock movement 1918	30″		NPA	
694	DISP-2	Dancers and Musician, PM, (Austria, unmarked)				
	2a	Old Man	12″		NPA	
	2b	Girl	17″		NPA	
	2c	Man	18″		NPA	
	DISP-3	Hans Christian Andersen, PM, (Denmark) c-1930	25½″		NPA	
	DISP-3-1	Mechanical Man, compo c-1940	16″		NPA	

	DISP-4	Trapese Artist, 1-pc compo	13½"		NPA	
697	DISP-5	Farmer, PM, (Germany) c-1883	25"		NPA	
	DISP-6	Mechanical Man, PM, c-1910	31"		NPA	
	DISP-7	Cop-on-the-Beat, PM (German)	22"		NPA	
	DISP-8	Margit Nilsen Manikins, lasti-coid, c-1940	22"		65	
	DISP-9	Fashion Figure, compo, c-1950	31"		65	
	DISP-10a	World War II Bride, rubber/compo	16½"		70	
	10b	World War II Groom, rubber/ compo	17½"		70	
698	DISP-11	Baby, compo, unmarked	22"		NPA	
	DISP-12	Fisk Tire Boy, compo, unmarked, c-1906	21"		NPA	

DOLLHOUSE DOLLS

| 699 | DOL-1 | Grandmother, cell, (helmet mark), (Germany) | 4¾" | | 50 | |

DOLL INDUSTRIES, LTD.

| | DOL-2 | Dollindoll "Walkie Talkie", hp (England) 1952 | 16"-27" | | Catalog Illus. | |

DOLL SHOP, THE

| | DOL-3 | Dolly Dainty, bisq/ compo, c-1910, (The Doll Shop) | 14"-26" | | Catalog Illus. | |

DRAYTON, GRACE G.

| 700 | DRA-1 | Googly, compo | 6½"-6¾" | 135 | 270 | 350 |
| | DRA-2 | Girl, compo/cloth | 13½" | 135 | 185 | 235 |

DREAM WORLD DOLLS

| | DRE-1 | Nun, compo | 11" | 10 | 14 | 18 |

DUCHESS DOLL CORP.

| | DUCH-1 | Cowboy, hp | 7" | | 4 | |

E

EEGEE (GOLDBERGER DOLL MFG. CO. INC.)

Page	Key	Nomenclature	Size	Avg.
701	EG-18a-c	Three dolls from the 1918 line		*Catalog Illus.*
	EG-19	Patsy-type, compo/ cloth, hairbow loop 1920s	15″	45
	EG-20	Girl, compo, hair bow loop 1920s	13″	45
702	EG-21	Baby, compo/cloth	18″	45
	EG-22	Layette Baby, hp/ latex, c-1948, boxed set	14″	45
	EG-23	Bride, compo, c-1948	15″	34
			17″	45
			19″	55
	EG-24	Toddler Boy, hp, c-1948		35
	EG-25	Baby Doll, soft rubber, c-1948	11″	15
		hp/rubber	11″	15
	EG-26a-b	Baby Christine, hp/ rubber/cloth with or without wigs, c-1948	15″	25
			18″	35
			21½″	45
	EG-27	Baby, hp, c-1948	11″	15
			13″	18
			14″	20
			17″	25
	EG-28	Baby Christine, hp/ latex, c-1948	14″	25
			17″	35
			20″	45
704	EG-29	Head only, vinyl, c-1950	5″	NPA
	EG-30	Boy, vinyl/1-pc magic skin body, c-1950	14½″	25
705	EG-31	Baby Yawn, vinyl	12″	25
	EG-32	Roller-Skater, soft vinyl/hp, c-1950	11″	20
	EG-33	Baby, vinyl/latex, c-1951	9½″	10
			13″	12
			16″	14
	EG-34	Baby, hp/latex, c-1951	25″	25
			28″	30

Page	Key	Nomenclature	Size	Low	Avg.	High
	EG-35	Boy, hp/latex, c-1951	25"		25	
			28"		30	
	EG-36	Baby, hp/latex, c-1951	13"		12	
			16"		14	
	EG-37	Girl, hp, c-1951	16"		15	
	EG-38	Boy, soft vinyl/cloth, c-1956	20"		45	
707	EG-39	Baby, hp/latex, c-1951	14½"		20	
			16"		25	
			20"		30	
			25"		35	
			28"		40	
	EG-40	Karena Ballerina, hp/vinyl, c-1958	21"		25	
	EG-41a-c	Little Debutantes, vinyl, c-1958	18"		15	
			19"		20	
			20"		25	
	EG-41-1	Miss Prim, vinyl/ plastic, c-1958	13"		15	
			18"		25	
			28"		35	
	EG-42	Baby Carol, vinyl, c-1958	11"		10	
			14"		15	
			16"		20	
			18"		25	
			20"		30	
	EG-43	My Fair Lady, vinyl, c-1958	20"		35	
	EG-44	Annette, vinyl, c-1961	36"	35	56	85
709	EG-45	Andy, vinyl, c-1963	12"		7	
	EG-46	Annette, vinyl, c-1963	11½"		7	
	EG-47	Gemettes, vinyl, c-1963	15½"		18	
		Miss Emerald				
		Miss Ruby				
		Miss Diamond				
		Miss Amethyst				
		Miss Sapphire				
		Miss Topaz				
	EG-48	Baby Darling, vinyl, c-1963	12"		10	
			16"		12	
			18"		14	
			20"		16	

MTCD Page	Key	Nomenclature	Size	Low	Avg.	High
	EG-49	Charmer Bride Doll, vinyl, c-1963	20"		18	
			25"		25	
	EG-50	Patticake, vinyl/cloth, c-1963	14"		25	
			20"		32	
	EG-51	Tandy Talks, vinyl, c-1963	22"		30	
	EG-52	Princess Boudoir Doll, vinyl, c-1963	14"		18	
	EG-53	Baby Flora, vinyl, c-1963	18"		25	
711	EG-54	Susan Stroller, c-1963			18	
	EG-55	Bubble Bath Baby, c-1963, with bathinette			15	
	EG-56	Kiss-Me Doll, c-1963			8	
	EG-57	Susan Stroller Walking Doll, with stroller and baby, c-1963			12	
	EG-58	Sniffles, c-1963			6	
	EG-59	Sleepy Susan, c-1963, with crib			8	
	EG-60	Kandi, c-1963			6	
	EG-61	Baby Tandy Talks, vinyl, c-1963	20"		25	
	EG-62	Stoneage Baby, vinyl, 1963	12"	4	7	10
712	EG-63	Sniffles, vinyl, c-1963			8	
	EG-64	I'm Hungry, vinyl, c-1963			6	
	EG-65	Cuddly Baby, vinyl			7	
	EG-66	New Born Bundle of Joy, vinyl/cloth	14"		8	
			16"		10	
			20"		14	
		Musical New Born Bundle of Joy	14"		10	
			16"		16	
			20"		18	
713	EG-67	Baby Tandy Talks, vinyl/cotton, c-1963	14"		12	
			20"		18	
	EG-68a-b	Puppetrina, vinyl/cloth, 1963	22"	18	30	40
	EG-68c	Puppetrina, vinyl/cloth, 1963	22"	18	30	40

MTCD Page	Key	Nomenclature	Size	Low	Avg.	High
714	EG-69	Baby Puppetrina, vinyl/cloth	16"		25	
	EG-70	Charmer, vinyl, c-1963	21"		20	
	EG-71	Mary Kate, vinyl, c-1960	10½"		6	
	EG-72	Baby, vinyl, c-1964	17½"		18	
	EG-73	Posi Playmate, vinyl/ soft foam, c-1965			12	
	EG-74	Baby, (Baby Susan or Baby Carol) vinyl c-1966			12	
716	EG-75	Susan, c-1966			15	
	EG-76	Sandi, c-1966			10	
	EG-77	Me and Me Too, Charlot Byj-type girl & dog			6	
	EG-78	Shelly and Her Plush Puppy Fido			8	
	EG-79	Posy Doll, vinyl/ foam, c-1967	13"		6	
	EG-80	Thumkins, vinyl, c-1967, assorted styles	5"		4 ea	
	EG-81	"Hello Dolly", vinyl/ plastic, c-1967	11"		5	
717	EG-82	Kandi, musical, vinyl/cloth, c-1967			18	
	EG-83	Handee Poppet, vinyl head, c-1974				
		Gypsy	24"	12	15	18
		Red Riding Hood	24"	12	15	18
		Alice in Wonderland	24"	12	15	18
		Cinderella	24"	12	15	18
		Bozo the Clown	24"	12	15	18
	EG-84	Bozo Ventriloquist Handee Poppet vinyl head, c-1974	24"	12	15	18
718	EG-85	Baby Luv, vinyl/ cloth	14"	28	32	45
	EG-86	Original artist's model			NPA	

EFFANBEE DOLL CORP.

719	F&B-55a-b	Hugo Baum & Bernard E. Fleischaker			*Portrait*	
	F&B-56	Foxy Teddy Bear, compo/cloth, c-1912			225 ea	

MTCD Page	Key	Nomenclature	Size	Low	Avg.	High
	F&B-57	Candy Kids, compo, c-1915			225 ea	
720	F&B-58	Colored Grumpy, compo/cloth	11½"	100	133	185
	F&B-59	Baby Huggins, compo, c-1913	9"		65	
	F&B-60	Johnny Tu-Face, compo/cloth, c-1912		50	105	165
721	F&B-61	Baby Dainty, compo/cloth, c-1913	15"	25	75	95
	F&B-62	The Tango Kiddies, compo/cloth, 1914			95	
	F&B-63	"My face will be your fortune", 1916			Adv.	
	F&B-64	Little Sweetheart, compo, c-1917-1919	12"		95	
			14"		125	
	F&B-65	Baby, compo, 1916			125	
722	F&B-66	Dolly Dumpling Girl, compo/kid/BJ limbs c-1914-1918	20½"		285	
	F&B-67	Dolly Dumpling Baby, compo, c-1918-1920	16"		265	
	F&B-68	Bathing Bud, compo, 1918			65	
	F&B-69	A Dolly Dumpling Group, 1918			*Catalog Illus.*	
724	F&B-70	Dolly Dumpling Doll, compo/cloth, c-1918				
		#F7756 "Little Girl"	14½"		85	
		#F7757 "Romper Babies"	14½"		85	
		#F7758 "Baby"	14½"		85	
		#F7914 "Baby Dainty"	15"		95	
		#F7915 "Baby Dainty"	18½"		115	
		#F7916 "Baby Dainty"	21½"		135	
		#F7917 "Baby Dainty"	24"		165	
		#F7539 "French Baby" Dressed Doll	15½"		125	
		#F7905 "Our Baby"	14"		95	
		#F7906 "Our Baby"	20½"		115	
		#F7907 "Our Baby"	20"		125	

Page	Key	Nomenclature	Size	Low	Avg.	High
725		#F7538 "Cunning Baby"	15½"		95	
		#F7575 "Cunning Baby"	17"		105	
		#F7758 "Cunning Baby"	17"		105	
		#F7563 "Baby Catherine"	13"		85	
		#F7564 "Baby Catherine"	14½"		95	
		#F7565 "Baby Catherine"	18"		115	
		#F7566 "Baby Catherine"	21"		125	
		#F7539 "French Baby"	15½"		125	
		#F7756 "Little Girl"	14½"		95	
		#F7757 "Romper Babies"	14½"		95	
		#F7576 "Baby Catherine"	20"		125	
		#F7577 "Baby Catherine"	24"		135	
726	F&B-71	Riding Hood Bud, compo c-1919			75	
	F&B-72	Wolf, ptd brown compo, unmarked	9½"	135	175	225
	F&B-73	Baby, compo/cloth, c-1918	16½"		NPA	
727	F&B-74	Girl, (No description in Adv.) c-1920			*Catalog Illus.*	
	F&B-75	Bubbles, compo/ cloth, c-1924	13"	90	95	125
	F&B-76	Bye-lo type, compo/ cell/cloth, c-1925	12"	65	100	135
728	F&B-77	Early Patsy, compo/ cloth, early 1920s	16"		100	
	F&B-78	Early Patsy, compo/ cloth, 1920s	14"		100	
	F&B-79	Girl, compo, 1920-1930s	9¼"		85	
	F&B-80	Whistler Boy, compo/cloth, c-1925	15"		185	
	F&B-81	Heartbeat Lovums, compo/cloth, wind-up heart, c-1920	17"	75	96	135
729	F&B-82	Girl, compo, unmarked, c-1928	11¾"		65	
	F&B-83	Patsy Babyette, compo/cloth	12"	45	68	95

MTCD Page	Key	Nomenclature	Size	Low	Price Avg.	High
	F&B-84	Patsy Lou, compo (NRA), c-1929	22″	45	140	225
730	F&B-85	Patsy Lou, compo, c-1927	22″	45	133	225
	F&B-86	Tousle Head, compo/cloth, c-1928	25″	95	120	150
	F&B-87	Talking Tousle Head (Lovums), compo/cloth	28″	95	120	150
731	F&B-88	Patsy-type, compo, Unmkd	18½″		65	
	F&B-89	Colored Patsyette, brown compo, c-1932	9″	50	95	165
	F&B-90a	Patsy, compo, c-1932	14″	70	99	135
	90b	Patricia, compo, c-1932	15″	70	98	140
732	F&B-91	Mary Ann compo/cloth c-1930	20″	75	102	135
	F&B-92	Patsy-type Boy, compo, c-1930	11″		45	
	F&B-93	Patsy Junior and Friends, c-1930, compo				
	93a	Patsy type, ummarked	11″	25	53	90
	93b	Effanbee Patsy Junior	11″	45	90	135
	93c	Patsy-type, marked Arranbee	12″	55	71	115
	93d	Patsy-type (SALLY/A PETITE DOLL, Amer. Char.)	12″	35	65	95
	93e	Patsy-type, unmarked	12″	25	53	90
733	F&B-94	Colleen Moore Fairy Princess (Wee Patsy), compo, c-1930	5½″	35	81	150
	F&B-95	Babyette, compo/cloth, c-1930-1950	12½″	45	53	80
	F&B-96	Patsy Baby, compo/magic skin, c-1940	12″	40	67	115
	F&B-97	Suzette, compo, c-1930	11″	45	60	75
	F&B-98	Tousle Head, compo, c-1930 (Mickey, Sweetie-Pie & Tommy Tucker)	23″	95	120	150

MTCD Page	Key	Nomenclature	Size	Low	Price Avg.	High
735	F&B-99	Sugar Baby, compo/ cloth, c-1936		40	50	85
	F&B-100	Patsy Tinyette, compo, c-1933	8″	50	63	85
	F&B-101	Little Lady, compo, 1939-1949	22″	75	109	175
	F&B-102	Colored Anne Shirley, compo, c-1935	21″	75	100	135
	F&B-103	Anne Shirley, compo	15″	38	55	85
	F&B-104	Girl, Little Lady body, compo	21″	45	99	175
	F&B-105	Dewees Cochran Girl, compo, c-1936	15″	295	465	750
736	F&B-106	American Children (Dewees Cochran), compo	21″	295	465	750
	F&B-107	American Children (Dewees Cochran), compo, c-1936	17″	265	426	725
	F&B-108	American Children (Dewees Cochran), comp, c-1937	21″	295	465	750
	F&B-109	Ice Queen, compo, c-1938	15″	425	525	850
737	F&B-110	Lucifer, wood, c-1937, marionette	14″	45	110	175
	F&B-111	Emily Ann, compo/ wood, marionette	14″	30	65	90
	F&B-112	Virginia Austin			Portrait	
	F&B-113	Clippo the Clown, compo, c-1937	14″	15	45	95
738	F&B-114	Pop Eye, synthetic rubber/cloth, c-1935			35	
		Olive Oyl, synthetic rubber/cloth			35	
	F&B-115	Musical Patsy (Happy Birthday), c-1940, compo/ cloth	17″		NPA	
	F&B-116	Little Lady, compo, c-1942	18″	75	109	175
	F&B-117	Babyette, compo, c-1945	11½″	45	61	85
739	F&B-118	Little Lady, compo/ cloth	20″	100	175	225
	F&B-119	Candy Kids, compo, c-1946 (Price is for each doll)	12″	50	71	115

MTCD Page	Key	Nomenclature	Size	Low	Price Avg.	High
	F&B-120	Twins, sticky plastic/ cloth, c-1948	13"		85 pr	
740	F&B-121	Patsy, compo, 1946 re-issue, unmarked	14"	30	80	160
	F&B-122	Lil Darlin' Baby, early vinyl/cloth, c-1948	20"		65	
741	F&B-123	Baby, compo/cloth (Mickey, Tommy Tucker) c-1943	21"	35	91	150
	F&B-124	Honey Walker, hp walker, c-1952	18½"	35	58	150
	F&B-125	Cuddle-up, soft plastic/coated fabric, c-1953	27"	50	65	95
	F&B-126	Rootie Kazootie, stuffed vinyl, coated fabric, c-1954	12" 19"		35 55	
	F&B-127	Fluffy (Katie), vinyl, c-1955	8"	12	27	45
743	F&B-128	Candy Ann, stuffed vinyl, c-1955	20"	65	95	165
	F&B-129	Candy Ann, stuffed vinyl, c-1955	20"	65	95	165
	F&B-130a-b	Mother and Child, vinyl/hp, c-1957-59, unmarked, (Child, 7½")	20"	75	95	165
	F&B-131	Patsy-type, vinyl/hp, c-1950, unmarked	15½"	22	39	50
	F&B-132	Twinkie, vinyl, c-1959	15"	13	33	45
	F&B-133	Twinkie, vinyl	16"	13	33	45
744	F&B-134	Baby, vinyl/cloth, c-1962	9"		15	
	F&B-135	Mary Jane, plastic	30"	75	83	125
	F&B-136	My Fair Baby, vinyl, c-1960	22"		35	
745	F&B-137	Honey (Suzie Sunshine in 1964), vinyl, c-1961	18"	35	65	95
	F&B-138	Belle Telle, vinyl/hp, c-1962, talking	18"		35	
	F&B-139	Thumkin, vinyl/ cloth, c-1965	18"		35	
	F&B-140	Miss Chips, vinyl, c-1965	18"	20	22	28
	F&B-141a-b	Half Pint, vinyl, c-1966	11"	15	21	35

MTCD Page	Key	Nomenclature	Size	Low	Price Avg.	High
746	F&B-142	Colored Half Pint, vinyl, c-1966	11"	20	25	35
	F&B-143	Bettina (Precious Baby), vinyl/cloth, c-1967	21"	18	35	60
	F&B-144	Baby Butterball, vinyl, c-1969	12"	8	12	16
	F&B-145	Sweetie Pie, vinyl/ cloth, c-1969	18"	6	10	21
747	F&B-146	Angel Baby (Baby Face, 1969), vinyl, c-1968	14"		40	
	F&B-147	Suzie Sunshine, vinyl, c-1969	18"	8	23	45
	F&B-148	Sugar Plum, vinyl/ cloth, c-1974	20"		25	
	EIS-1	Einco "Baby Dolly", three sizes, 1940 (Eisenmann & Co. London)		25	35	45

ELECTRA (ELEKTRA) NOVELTY CO.

MTCD Page	Key	Nomenclature	Size	Low	Price Avg.	High
749	ELEK-1	Chubby, compo/ cloth, c-1916	33½"	65	85	125
	ELEK-2	Chubby compo/ cloth, c-1916	23"	65	85	125
	ELEK-3	Chubby, compo/ cloth, c-1916	24"	65	85	125
	ELEK-4	Jolly Jumper Boy, compo/cloth, c-1912			85	
	ELEK-5	Mother Hubbard's Dog, compo/cloth c-1911	20"		135	
	ELEK-6a-b	Amy and Laurie, compo/cloth, c-1912			95 ea	
	ELEK-7a-d	Four dolls from the 1915 Elektra line			95 ea	

EMKAY DOLL MFG. CO.

MTCD Page	Key	Nomenclature	Size	Low	Price Avg.	High
750	EMK-1	Baby Marion, pm, c-1917 (Emkay Doll Mfg)			165	

ENGLISH DOLLS

MTCD Page	Key	Nomenclature	Size	Low	Price Avg.	High
751	ENG-1a-c	Three English dolls of 1940			45 ea	
	EST-1	Estrella, compo/ cloth,	19½"		135	
	EUG-1	Lorrie Lee, vinyl (Lorrie Doll) c-1969	8¾"		12	

F

FAIR AMUSEMENT CO.

	FAIR-1	The Eugenic Baby, compo, (Fair Amusement), c-1914			65	
	FAIR-2	Babee, A Eugenic Doll, compo, (Fair Amusement Co) c-1914			65	

FAMOUS DOLL STUDIO

	FAM-1	Ball-jointed Girl, compo, (Famous Doll Studio)	20″		185	
	FAM-2	Sani-Doll, compo/cloth, (Famous Doll Studio), c-1917			65	

FEDERAL DOLL MFG. CO.

	FED-1	Liberty Belle, compo, (Federal Doll) c-1918			95	
752	FED-2	Roze, compo/cloth, (Federal Doll)			65	

FIBEROID

	FIB-1	Laughing Girl, compo/cloth, (Fiberoid), c-1930	28″			45

FISHER-PRICE

	FISH-1	The Fisher-Price Doll Family, vinyl/cloth, c-1973	13″		35 ea	

Jenny   Audrey
Mary   Elizabeth
Baby Ann
Natalie

FLEXO TOYS

755	FLEX-1	Flexo Boy, compo/lead/cloth	11″		45	

FRANKONIA PRODUCTS, INC.

	FRAN-1	Funny Honey, vinyl (Frankonia) c-1965	5″		6	

MTCD Page	Key	Nomenclature	Size	Low	Avg.	High
		FRENCH DOLLS				
	FR-6	Bisque Head Negro Man, French	18″		NPA	
	FR-7	A. Marque Girl, bisq	21″		NPA	
	FR-8	Long-faced Jumeau Girl, bisq	30″		NPA	
	FR-9	Emille Jumeau Lady, bisq	16″		NPA	
	FR-10	French Lady, cell/ bisq	13″		NPA	
	FR-11	Unis France Lady, bisque head	24½″		345	
757	FR-12	Gaultier Bisque Head Girl, BJ body	17″		1750	
	FR-13	Bebe Jumeau, BJ body, bisque head	23″		4200	
	FR-14	Phenix Babe, BJ Body	22″		2650	
	FR-15	Bebe Jumeau, bisq	19″		3200	
	FR-16	Paul Girard Lady, BJ Body	22″		NPA	
	FR-17	Tete Jumeau Girl, BJ Body	18″		NPA	
	FR-18	Unis France Girl, BJ Body	9″	85	277	350
	FR-19	Bisque Head Girl, pm Body	28″		NPA	
759	FR-20	Bisque Head Girl, pm Body	27″		NPA	
	FR-21	Girl, French compo			NPA	
	FR-22	Bent Leg Baby Boy, plastic, c-1973	19½″		65	
	FR-23	Little Brother, Polyflex c-1967, (Clodrey)	20″	55	75	95
	FR-24	Little Sister, Polyflex, c-1967, (Clodrey)	20″	55	75	95
		FULPER ART POTTERY, THE				
	FUL-1	Baby, Bisque head, BJ Body	21″	85	284	500
761	FUL-2	Child, bisque head, BJ body	37″		4250	
	FUL-3	Girl, bisq head, BJ body	21″	265	456	595
	FUL-4a-b	Two Fulper Girls			NPA	
	FUL-5	Toddler, bisque head, BJ body, c-1918	17″	250	353	565

G

GABRIEL, SAM'L SONS & CO

	Key	Nomenclature	Size	Low	Avg.	High
	GAB-1a-b	Mother Goose Dolls (Sam'l Gabriel Sons), 1917			65 ea	
	GAB-2a-d	Mother Goose Dolls (Sam'l Gabriel Sons), 1917			65 ea	

GEM TOY CO.

	Key	Nomenclature	Size	Low	Avg.	High
763	GEM-1a-b	Two dolls of the 1915 line (Gem Toy)			65 ea	
	GEM-2a-b	Two dolls of the 1917 line (Gem Toy)			65 ea	
	GEM-3a-b	"O-U Kids", compo (Gem Toy) 1918			45 ea	

GERMAN-MADE DOLLS

	Key	Nomenclature	Size	Low	Avg.	High
	GER-1	Alice, bisq/kid	12"		165	
	GER-2	Baby Boy, PBsq, brush stroke hair unmarked	4"		125	
	GER-3	GBR. K. Bisque-head Girl, PM body	7"	80	95	125
	GER-4	Bisque-head Girl, BJ Body	40"		NPA	
764	GER-5	Guttmann & Schiffie Girl, bisque head, BJ body	22"		185	
	GER-6	Phyllis, bisq/compo/ muslin, c-1923 (Germany)			325	
	GER-7	All-bisque Doll in Swing, (Germany)	7¾"		195	
	GER-8	Gladdie, red clay head/cloth, c-1929-30	18½"	800	900	1150
765	GER-9	C. M. Bergman Bisque Girl, BJ body, c-1916	25"	250	353	535
	GER-10	P-H./Herzi Toddler, bisq/compo	9"	150	160	195
	GER-11	My Sweet Baby, bisq, compo, BL	10"		195	
766	GER-12	Edmund Steiner Girl, bisq/BJ body	14"	250	325	400
767	GER-13	Otto Reinecke BL Baby, bisq/compo	12"	225	262	335

MTCD Page	Key	Nomenclature	Size	Low	Price Avg.	High
	GER-14	Girl, bisque-head, c-1910, unmkd	38"		NPA	
	GER-15	Bisque head on stick, gls eyes			NPA	
	GER-16	All-bisque Baby, CM (Germany)	6"		135	
	GER-17	B.P. Oriental Child, bisq/compo	17"	425	650	795
	GER-17-1	Kestner #150 Character Baby, bisque-head	15"	300	419	545
	GER-18	G.B./AM #248 Girl, bisq/compo	15"	445	622	800
	GER-19	Bahr & Proschild #585 Character Baby, bisq/compo	14"	300	423	545
769	GER-20a-b	Ski-boy, plastic (Germany)	6¼"	15	23	35
		Swiss Girl, plastic (Germany)	6¼"	15	23	35
	GER-21	German Girl, compo	12"		65	
	GER-22	Toddler, compo	17½"		85	
	GER-23	Girl and General Store, compo/ wood	8"		95 set	
	GER-24	Character Boy, compo/cloth	13"		65	
	GER-25	Girl, compo #502, glass eyes	16"		115	
771	GER-26	Nun, glass eyes, compo			NPA	
	GER-27	German Toddler, compo, glass eyes	18"		165	
	GER-28	Geni, compo/wood	7½"		NPA	
	GER-29	German Baby, compo/cloth	17"		NPA	
	GER-30	Baby, compo (Germany)	11½"		55	
	GER-31	Our Pet, compo	13"		150	
	GER-32	Heidi-type Girl, compo, glass eyes	19"		NPA	
772	GER-33	Girl, compo	8½"		45	
	GER-34a	Old German Man	13"		NPA	
	34b	Old German Woman	10¼"		NPA	
	GER-35	Dutchman, pm/ plush	20"		145	
	GER-36	Chimney Sweep, PM/velvet	20"		145	
	GER-37	Sailor, pm/cloth/ felt	18"		145	

MTCD Page	Key	Nomenclature	Size	Price Low	Avg.	High
774	GER-38	Schildkrot Baby, vinyl, (turtlemark)	16"		25	
	GER-39	Toddler Girl, vinyl	16"		35	
	GER-40	Girl, hp, c-1963	27"		45	
	GER-41	Lilli, Barbie-type doll, c-1954, (Western Germany)	11½"	250	400	550
	GER-42	Little Girl, 1-pc vinyl, (West Germany)	7½"		15	
775	GER-43	A collection of modern German-made dolls available in Canada.			NPA	
	GER-44	Girl, vinyl (Western Germany)	6½"		15	
	GER-45	Sweetheart Dancing Peasant Girl, vinyl/hp	7"		18	
	GER-46a	Cloverleaf mark Boy, plastic 1954	4"		13	
		Cloverleaf mark Girl, plastic 1954	4"		13	

GIEBELER-FALK DOLL CORP

776	GIE-1	Gie-Fa Dolls, five sizes			*Catalog Illus.*	

GOEBEL—See HUMMEL

GOLD DOLL

	GOLD-1	"Indian" Boy, compo/cloth c-1930 (Gold Doll)	11"		65	

GOTZ-PUPPE

777	GOTZ-1	Gotz-Puppe Girl, soft plastic			25	

GROMAN INC.

	GRO-1	Girl, vinyl, (Groman Inc) c-1962	13½"		10	

GUND MFG. CO.

	GUND-1a	Tootsie Boy "Large", compo/cloth, 1912			65	
	1b	Tootsie Girl "Large", compo/cloth			65	

MTCD Page	Key	Nomenclature	Size	Low	Avg.	High
779	GUND-2a-b	The Flippety-Flop Kids "Character dolls," compo/cloth, c-1913			65	
	GUND-3	Creeping Baby, compo/cloth, c-1915			65	
	GUND-4a	Charlie Chaplin, compo/cloth, 1917			95	
	4b	Baby Doll, compo/cloth, c-1917			45	
	GUND-5	Nettie Knit ("doing her bit") 1918	12″		35	
	GUND-6	Rocking Baby, compo/cloth, c-1919			45	
	GUND-7	Mini-Martians, (Deet and Patti):				
		Professor Pook	4½″		3	
		Marti	4½″		3	
		Mini	4½″		3	
		Bonnie	4½″		3	
		Meri	4½″		3	
		Teenie	4½″		3	

H

	H-6	H & B German bisque-head baby	14″	275	325	395

H&Z DOLL & TOY CO

780	H-8	Dainty Marie, compo, c-1919	9″		35	
	H-9	Zaiden, compo			165	

HAHN & AMBERG

781	H-10a	Lucky Bill, plush/compo, 1909	10″		95	
			12″		115	
	10b	Baby Blue, felt/cell, 1909	10″		95	
			14″		125	
	10c	Sassy Doll, silk/velvet/compo 1909			145	
	H-11	Lucky Bill, compo/plush, c-1909	8½″		95	
			10″		115	
			11″		125	

HAMBURGER AND CO.

	HAM-1a-c	Three dolls from 1903 import line			NPA	

MTCD Page	Key	Nomenclature	Size	Price Low	Avg.	High
		HANDWERCK DOLLS				
783	HWK-5	Bisque-head Girl, #7, BJ body	33"	495	647	835
	HWK-6	Bisque-head Girl, #99, BJ body	27"	300	547	815
	HWK-7	Bisque-head Girl #283	27"	325	487	665
	HWK-8	Bisque-head Girl #189	30"	445	615	825
	HWK-9	Viola, bisque head, c-1903	21"	265	408	545
	HAPPIFATS					
	HAP-1a,b	Happifats, bisq, c-1913	3½"		125 ea	
	HAP-2ab	Happifats, compo/ cloth, (K&K Toy) 1917			135 ea	
	HAP-3	Happifats Dishes, German-made			NPA	
	HASBRO					
784	HAS-5	Buddy Charlie, c-1965 (Louis Marx)	12"		15	
	HAS-6	Peteena, poodle head, plastic 1966	9½"	22	25	30
	HAS-7	That Kid, soft vinyl/ rigid vinyl, c-1967	21"	25	45	65
785	HAS-8	Aimee, vinyl, c-1972	16"	15	18	35
	HAS-9	Candy Babies, soft vinyl/cloth, 1972-1973:				
	9a	Dots	9"	7	9	12
	9b	Peppermint Pattie	9"	7	9	12
	9c	Baby Ruth	9"	7	9	12
	9d	Choo Choo Charlie	9"	7	9	12
	HAS-10	Bewiskered G.I. Joes, vinyl, c-1974		8	13	25
786	HAS-11	Leggy, vinyl, c-1973				
		Leggy Kate (#4630) Red Head	10"	5	7	12
		Leggy Nan (#4625) Brunette	10"	5	7	12
		Leggy Sue (#4635) Black with Afro	10"	5	7	12
		Leggy Jill (#4620) Blonde	10"	5	7	12
787	HAS-12	Flutterbyes, 1-pc vinyl, c-1974	1½"		3 ea	

	HAS-13	Sweet Dreams, Rag Doll, c-1974	17"		6	
	HAS-14	Sweet Cookie, soft vinyl/plastic, 1972	18"	12	18	22
	HAS-15	The World of Love, vinyl, c-1971 Love Peace Flower Soul Music	9"	4	6	10
	HAS-16	The World of Love, Adam, vinyl	9"	4	7	12

HAVANA NOVELTY CO.

	HAV-1	The Teddy Doll, bisq/plush, c-1907 (Havana Novelty)			165	

HESS, THEODORE & CO.

789	HESS-1a-b	Two dolls from the 1919 line (Theodore Hess & Co.) compo	14"		65	

HEUBACH DOLLS

	HEU-10	Sun Mark Baby, compo	10"	700	750	795
	HEU-11	Girl, bisq/compo	17"	385	491	595
	HEU-12	Heubach-Koppelsdorf #342 Boy, bisq/pm	7½"	175	190	200
	HEU-13	Boy, Heubach-Koppelsdorf #302	22"	325	560	725
	HEU-14	Molded-hair Girl, bisq/compo	18"		NPA	
	HEU-15	Puss-in-Boots, bisq/PM, c-1920	6¼"		NPA	
	HEU-16	Molded-hair Girl, bisq/compo	18"		NPA	
790	HEU-17	Bisque heads, compo, fully jointed				
	17a	Schoneau & Hoffmeister Hawaiian Girl, (HANNA)	9"	175	255	335
	17b	Heubach-Koppelsdorf African Baby	8½"	165	312	385
	17c	Heubach-Koppelsdorf Mexican Boy	10½"	300	391	475

HIGHGRADE TOY MFG. CO.

	HIGH-1	Girl, compo/cloth, c-1917			65	
	HIGH-2	Girl, compo/cloth, c-1917			65	

HITT, OSCAR

	HITT-1	Snowflake (Oscar Hitt)	3¾"		45	

HONG KONG DOLLS

791	HK-1	Linda, vinyl	14"		10	
	HK-2	Hula Girl, vinyl	9½"		10	
	HK-3	Girl, vinyl	11"		12	

THE E. I. HORSMAN AND AETNA DOLL AND TOY CO.

793	HORS-33	E. I. Horsman, Jr.			*Portrait*	
	HORS-34	E. I. Horsman			*Portrait*	
	HORS-35-37	Scenes in the manu-facture of Horsman dolls., c-1912				
	HORS-38	"New factory of E. I. Horsman and Aetna Doll Co." c-1919				
	HORS-39	Puss-in-Boots, synthetic fur, c-1907			265	
	HORS-40	Campbell Kid, compo/cloth, c-1911	9"	85	135	178
	HORS-41	Can't Break 'Em Girl, compo/cloth (Aetna) c-1909			85	
794	HORS-42	Can't Break 'Em Girl, compo/cloth (Aetna) c-1909			85	
	HORS-43	Billiken, compo/cloth, c-1909		175	200	325
	HORS-44	Samson, compo c-1910			325	
	HORS-45	Sambo, "The Nigger Baby" compo, c-1910	12"		325	
			15"		375	
	HORS-46	Girl compo (Aetna) c-1910			95	
795	HORS-47	Our Baby, compo/velvet, c-1910			85	
	HORS-48	Baby Blue, compo/velvet, c-1910			85	

MTCD Page	Key	Nomenclature	Size	Low	Avg.	High
	HORS-49	Character Baby, compo/velvet, c-1910			95	
	HORS-50a-c	Three models from the 1910 line Dutch Boy, Bellhop, Baby			85 ea	
796	HORS-51	Sister Billiken, c-1909	12″	175	216	275
			15″	200	266	325
	HORS-52	Baby Bumps, compo/velvet, c-1910	12″	95	161	325
	HORS-53	Art Dolls (Thirty Characters), compo/cloth, c-1911			*Catalog Illus.*	
	HORS-54	Campbell Kids and Friends, c-1911			*Catalog Illus.*	
	HORS-55	Character Baby (Art Dolls), compo/cloth, c-1910	11″		165	
797	HORS-56	Laughing Boy, (Art Doll) compo/cloth, E.I.H./1911	17″		195	
798	HORS-57	The Campbell Kid Chorus, c-1911			*News Photo*	
	HORS-58a-b	The Jap Rose Kids, compo/cloth, c-1912			225 ea	
	HORS-59	Fairy, of the Campbell Kid Family, compo/cloth, c-1912			165	
799	HORS-60	Dutch Kids, compo/cloth, c-1912			165 ea	
	HORS-61	Gold Medal Prize Baby (five sizes), c-1911			NPA	
	HORS-62	Sunbonnet Sal, compo/cloth, c-1912			165	
	HORS-63	Suck-a-Thumb, compo/cloth, c-1912			135	
800	HORS-64	Teddy Bull Moose, compo/cloth, c-1912			145	
	HORS-65	Polly Prue, compo/cloth, c-1912			125	

MTCD Page	Key	Nomenclature	Size	Low	Avg.	High
	HORS-66	Nature Babies, 1912				
		Serious Baby				
		Bobby			125	
		Laughing Baby				
		Peterkin			125	
	HORS-67	Schoolboy, compo/				
		cloth, c-1913			95	
801	HORS-68	Boy Scout, compo/				
		cloth, c-1913			95	
	HORS-69	Carnival Baby,				
		compo/cloth,				
		c-1913			95	
	HORS-70	Camp Fire Girl,				
		compo/cloth,				
		c-1911			95	
	HORS-71	Campbell Kid Baby,				
		compo/cloth,				
		c-1913		85	135	178
802	HORS-72	Robbie Reefer,				
		compo/cloth,				
		c-1911			95	
	HORS-73	Baby Premier,				
		compo/cloth,				
		(Aetna) c-1913			95	
	HORS-74	Black Doll, compo/				
		cloth, c-1913			125	
	HORS-75a-b	Our Baby, Two				
		examples of the				
		1913 line			95	
	HORS-76a-c	Three styles of				
		"Bauernkinder,"				
		compo/cloth,				
		c-1914			135	
	HORS-77a-b	Two Campbell Kids,				
		compo/cloth,				
		c-1913			145 ea	
804	HORS-78a-b	Two "American Kids				
		in Toyland,"				
		compo/cloth,				
		c-1913			95 ea	
	HORS-79	One example of the				
		1914 line, compo/				
		cloth			95	
	HORS-80	"The Gee Gee				
		Dolly" (Drayton),				
		two sizes, c-1913			NPA	
805	HORS-81	Baby Butterfly,				
		Oriental Baby,				
		three sizes,				
		compo/cloth,				
		c-1913			265	

Page	Key	Nomenclature	Size	Low	Avg.	High
	HORS-82	Peek-A-Boo, (Drayton), three styles, c-1913			NPA	
806	HORS-83	E.I.H. Boy, compo/ cloth, c-1914-1918	19"		195	
	HORS-84	E.I.H. Boy (Oliver Twist) compo/ cloth, c-1914	16"		165	
807	HORS-85	The Peterkins, compo/cloth, c-1915:				
		Betsy			165	
		Tommy			165	
	HORS-86	Peterkin Boy #1012, compo, c-1918			165	
	HORS-87a-b	Two dolls from 1919 line, compo			165	
808	HORS-88a-c	The Velocipede Kids (The Irish Mail Kids, The Cycle Kids & The Coaster Kids), c-1915, with vehicles			185	
	HORS-89a	Oliver Twist, c-1918			165	
	89b	Peasant Boy, c-1918			145	
	HORS-90	The Adtocolite Doll, two sizes, compo (Aetna), c-1918			NPA	
809	HORS-91	Uncle Sam's Kids, compo/cloth:				
	91a	Miss Sam, c-1917			175	
	91b	Master Sam, c-1917			175	
	HORS-92a-b	Two dolls from the 1919 line			150 ea	
810	HORS-93ab	Little Mary Mix-Up, compo/cloth			165	
	HORS-94	The Horsman Bisque Line, c-1918			NPA	
	HORS-95	Character Baby, compo/cloth	11"		135	
811	HORS-96	E.I.H. Boy, compo/ cloth, c-1923	24"		295	
813	HORS-97	E.I.H. Girl, compo/ cloth, c-1920	18"		95	
	HORS-98	Blue Bird Doll, c-1920			*Catalog Illus.*	
	HORS-99	Heebee (Mate to Shebee), c-1925	10½"	90	135	165
	HORS-100	Gold Medal Baby, compo/cloth	21"	65	120	175

MTCD Page	Key	Nomenclature	Size	Low	Price Avg.	High
	HORS-101	Laughing Dimples, compo/cloth	20″	55	116	185
	HORS-102	Key-Wind Mama Doll, compo/cloth	21″		85	
	HORS-103	Jeanne Horsman, compo/cloth	14″		95	
	HORS-104	Naughty Sue, compo, c-1937	14½″		125	
814	HORS-105	Ma-Ma Papa Doll, compo/cloth	18″		45	
	HORS-106	Toddler Dimples, compo/cloth	20″	35	125	185
	HORS-106-1	Dimples, compo/cloth	19½″	35	125	185
	HORS-107	Baby, hp/cloth/soft sticky plastic c-1948	23″		35	
815	HORS-108	Patsy Look-alikes from Horsman: c-1931-32				
		Babs, compo	12″	25	55	95
		Sue, compo	14″	35	65	100
		Jane, compo	17″	50	103	175
		Sally, compo/cloth	19″	65	95	185
		Nan, compo	20″	75	115	195
		Dainty Dorothy, compo/cloth	20″	75	105	180
816	HORS-108-1	Tynie Baby, compo/cloth, (E.I.H./1924)	21″		95	
	HORS-108-2	Rosebud-type Girl, compo		55	65	125
	HORS-109	Baby Boy, sticky vinyl/cloth	20″		65	
	HORS-110	Baby, vinyl, c-1956, unmarked	18″		20	
	HORS-111	Cindy the Couturier Doll, vinyl/plastic, c-1957	16″	35	50	65
			18″	45	68	75
817	HORS-112	Pretty Poser, vinyl, c-1958	8″		25 in case	
	HORS-113	Ponytail Pam, vinyl, c-1958	17″		85 in case	
819	HORS-114	Tear Belle, vinyl, c-1958	16″		25	
			20″		40	
	HORS-115	Baby Evie, vinyl, c-1958	16″		25	
			20″		NPA	

MTCD Page	Key	Nomenclature	Size	Low	Price Avg.	High
	HORS-116	Little Miss Moppet, vinyl, c-1958	16″		15	
	HORS-117	Pert'n'Pretty, vinyl, c-1958	21″		25	
	HORS-118	Cindy, plastic, c-1958	25″		25	
			36″		NPA	
	HORS-119	Character Baby, early vinyl/cloth	23″		25	
	HORS-120	Girl, 1-pc, vinyl, c-1950	26″	25	48	65
820	HORS-121	Girl, soft vinyl/hp	36″		80	
	HORS-122	Hard Plastic Girl	16″		45	
	HORS-123	Much-loved Baby, 1-pc vinyl	14″		12	
	HORS-124	Baby, soft plastic			6	
	HORS-125	Life-size Infant, soft vinyl/hp c-1961	25″		195	
	HORS-126	Baby, vinyl	11″		5	
	HORS-127	Toddler, vinyl	11″		12	
821	HORS-128	Mademoisella, soft vinyl/hp, (Mademoiselle Dolls)	15½″		65	
822	HORS-128-1	Bootsie, vinyl, 1970	13″		25	
823	HORS-129	Baby Precious, vinyl/cloth, (Irene Szor) c-1963	19″	35	48	65
	HORS-130	Gloria Jean, soft plastic/hp, (Irene Szor) c-1969	16″	35	42	60
	HORS-131a	Hansel, soft vinyl/hp	15″		85	
	131b	Gretel, soft vinyl/hp	15″		85	
824	HORS-132	Nitey-Nite Baby, vinyl/cloth 1963	24″	18	35	50
	HORS-133	Perthy, vinyl, c-1958	13″	12	15	22
			16″	16	19	25
	HORS-134	Girl, vinyl, c-1963	16″	10	14	16
825	HORS-135	Alice, sp/rp, c-1966	28″	45	95	125
	HORS-136	Thirstee-Walker, vinyl, 1962	26″	6	10	18
	HORS-137	Drink and Wet Baby, plastic/vinyl 1964	12″	6	10	15
826	HORS-138	The Pip Squeeks, Singing Group; 1967				
	138a	Cleo, vinyl	12″	7	15	25
	138b	Mark, vinyl	12″	7	15	25
	138c	Anthony, vinyl	12″	7	15	25
	138d	Patty, vinyl	12″	7	15	25
	HORS-139	Bootsie, soft vinyl/hard vinyl, c-1969	12½″		35	

MTCD Page	Key	Nomenclature	Size	Low	Price Avg.	High
	HORS-140	Baby First Tooth, vinyl/cloth 1960s		32	45	65
827	HORS-141	Mary, vinyl, c-1965		7	11	15
		Jerry, vinyl, c-1965		7	11	15
	HORS-142	Re-issue Bye-lo Baby, vinyl/cloth	14"	15	36	65
	HORS-143	Train-a-Baby, vinyl, c-1973	15"		15	
			19"		20	

HOWARD POTTERY CO., ENGLAND

828	HOW-1	Composition Baby, (Howard Pottery), c-1941 (England)			NPA	

HOYER, MARY DOLL CO.

	HOY-1a-b	Mary Hoyer's Brother, hp	14"	65	95	185
	HOY-2	Mary Hoyer Nun, compo, c-1938	14"		225	
	HOY-3	Mary Hoyer, compo	14"	65	85	185

HULSS

829	HULSS-1	German Composi-tion-head Girl	18"	450	500	600

HUMMEL DOLLS (GOEBEL)

830	HUM-1	Mariandl, rubber	11½"	100	156	295
	HUM-2	Baker Boy, rubber	12"	100	156	295
	HUM-3	Rosl, rubber	10¾"	100	156	295
831	HUM-4	Japanese Copy Hummel Boy, vinyl	10¾"		65	
	HUM-5	Ganseliesl, vinyl, c-1973	26cm	20	69	150
	HUM-6	Radi-Bub, vinyl, c-1973	26cm	20	69	150
	HUM-7	Strickliesl, vinyl, c-1973	26cm	20	69	150
	HUM-8	Wanderbub, vinyl, c-1973	26cm	20	69	150
	HUM-9a	Hansl, vinyl, c-1973	20cm	20	69	150
	9b	Gretl, vinyl, c-1973	20cm	20	69	150
	9c	Vroni, vinyl, c-1973	20cm	20	69	150
	9d	Rudi, vinyl, c-1973	20cm	20	69	150
	9e	Seppl, vinyl, c-1973	20cm	20	69	150
	9f	Mariandl, vinyl, c-1973	20cm	20	69	150
	9g	Jackl, vinyl, c-1973	20cm	20	69	150
	9h	Rosl, vinyl, c-1973	20cm	20	69	150
833	HUM-10	Babies, vinyl, c-1973	26cm	20	48	95
	HUM-11	Puppen, designed by Michel Thomas:				

MTCD Page	Key	Nomenclature	Size	Low	Price Avg.	High
	11a	Jacqueline, vinyl, C-1973	36cm		85	
	11b	Gilbert, vinyl, c-1973	36cm		85	
	11c	Jeannette, vinyl, c-1973	36cm		85	
	11d	Pierre, vinyl, c-1973	36cm		85	
	HUM-12	Nina, the Fashion Doll, vinyl, c-1972	38cm	65	78	95
	HUM-12-1	Hein, (Charlot Byj) vinyl, c-1972	26cm		65	
	HUM-13	Sandmannchen (Sandman), vinyl, c-1973	17cm		55	
	HUM-14	Pumuckl, vinyl, c-1973	17cm		50	
	HUM-15	Vagabund, vinyl/ foam, c-1966 (Charlot Byj)	22cm		65	
834	HUM-16	Erbs-Puppen, vinyl, c-1962	26cm		55	
	HUM-17a-e	Lore-Spatzchen, vinyl, c-1972	35cm		85	
	HUM-18	Fratz, vinyl (Charlot Byj) c-1962	23cm	23	38	45
	HUM-19	Jimmy, vinyl (Charlot Byj) c-1966	23cm	23	38	45
835	HUM-20	Trine, vinyl (Charlot Byj) c-1957	26cm	25	42	60
	HUM-21a	Cowboy, vinyl, c-1973	26cm	25	42	60
	21b	Cowgirl, vinyl, c-1973	26cm	25	42	60
	21c	Indianer, vinyl, c-1973	23cm	25	42	60
	21d	Indianerin, vinyl, c-1973	23cm	25	42	60
	HUM-22	Affe Dombi Monkey, vinyl, c-1973	30cm		65	

I

IDEAL TOY CORPORATION

837	IDL-58a	Mr. Hooligan, compo/plush, c-1910			95	
	58b	Mr. Hooligan, compo/plush, c-1910			95	
838	IDL-59	Five items from the 1911 line				
	59a	Baby Mine, compo/ cloth			95	
	59b	Brutus, plush			NPA	

MTCD Page	Key	Nomenclature	Size	Low	Avg.	High
	59c	Dandy Kid, compo/ cloth			95	
	59d	Baby Mine Purse			NPA	
	59e	Ty Cobb, compo/ cloth			125	
	IDL-60	Captain Jinks, compo/cloth, c-1912			95	
	IDL-61a	Naughty Marietta, compo/cloth, c-1912			95	
	61b	Jack Horner, compo/ cloth, c-1912			95	
	IDL-62	"Water Baby", cell/ sponge, c-1912	12"		15	
			14"		20	
839	IDL-63a	Freddie, Country Cousin, compo/ cloth, c-1913			65	
	63b	Flora, Country Cousin, compo/ cloth, c-1913			65	
	IDL-64	Russian Boy, compo/ cloth, c-1912			65	
	IDL-64a	Arctic Boy, compo/ cloth, c-1913			95	
	64b	Baby Marion, compo/cloth, c-1913			65	
	IDL-66	Admiral Dot, compo/cloth, c-1914			75	
840	IDL-67	Character Baby, compo, c-1914			75	
	IDL-68	Four styles from the 1915 line:				
	68a	Broncho Bill, compo/cloth			65	
	68b	Buster, compo/cloth			65	
	68c	Dolly Varden, compo/cloth			65	
	68d	Jenny Wren, compo/ cloth			65	
841	IDL-69	Sanitary Baby, compo/kid, c-1915	16"		85	
			25"		95	
	IDL-70	Baby Talc, compo/ cloth, c-1915			85	
	IDL-71	Columbia Kids Boy, compo/cloth, c-1917			95	

MTCD Page	Key	Nomenclature	Size	Low	Price Avg.	High
	IDL-72	Baby Bi-Face, (Soozie Smiles), compo, c-1916		50	105	165
	IDL-73	Baby, compo, c-1916		50	65	80
842	IDL-74	Columbia Kid, compo, c-1918	12"-24"		95	
	IDL-75	Flossie Flirt, compo/cloth	26"		125	
	IDL-76	Peggy, six sizes, compo/cloth, c-1918	12"-24"		95	
	IDL-77	Baby Mine, compo, c-1919			165	
843	IDL-78	Liberty Boy, compo, c-1918		65	135	175
	IDL-78-1	Liberty Boy, c-1918			165	
	IDL-79	Seven dolls of the 1918 line:				
	79a	#F7715, compo/cloth, 2 styles	13½"		75	
		#F7717, compo/cloth, "Little Girl"	16"		95	
		#F7716 compo/cloth, 2 styles	14½"		85	
		#F7718, compo/cloth	16"		95	
		#F7719, compo/cloth	14½"		85	
	79b	#F7720, compo/cloth	16"		95	
844	IDL-80	Four dolls of the 1918 Ideal line:				
		#7721, compo/cloth	13½"		75	
		#7722, compo/cloth	14½"		85	
		#7723, compo/cloth	16"		95	
	IDL-81	Miss Rosy Cheeks, compo, c-1923			75	
	IDL-82	Smiling Child, compo/cloth, c-1920	22"	25	65	90
	IDL-83	Hush-a-Bye Baby, compo/cloth, c-1925	16½"	35	65	95
	IDL-84	Peter Pan, compo/cloth, c-1928	16½"	35	65	90
845	IDL-85	Snoozie, compo/cloth	16"	85	165	225
	IDL-86	Ticklette, compo/cloth/rubber, c-1931	13"	32	38	65
846	IDL-87a	Curly Tickletoes, compo/cloth/rubber, 1933-1934:				
		61-4610	15"	35	43	75

MTCD Page	Key	Nomenclature	Size	Low	Price Avg.	High
		61-4612	17″	45	57	75
		61-4614	20″	55	69	85
	87b	Ticklette, compo/ rubber/cloth 61-4600, 1933-1934:	13½″	32	38	65
	87c	Flossie Flirt, compo/ cloth				
		71-4630	16″	50	103	175
		61-4634	20″	75	115	195
		61-4632	18″	65	95	185
		61-4636	22″	100	125	195
	87d	Winnie, compo/ rubber, 1933-1934:				
		61-4548	12″	25	55	95
		61-4549	16″	35	69	115
847	IDL-87-1	Unmarked Shirley Temple, compo	18″	85	214	550
	IDL-88	Shirley Temple-type, compo	9″	35	65	90
	IDL-89	Boy in Lee Riders, compo, c-1937	13″	45	65	80
848	IDL-90	Black Snow White, compo, c-1937	13″	35	55	85
	IDL-91	Gabby, compo/wood	10″	85	177	200
	IDL-92	Dimpled CM Girl, compo	16½″	75	185	350
	IDL-93	Girl (Mary Jane or Betty Jane?) 1940s, compo			NPA	
849	IDL-94	Flexy Character, compo, c-1942	12″	85	95	135
	IDL-95	Magic Eyes, compo/ cloth			125	
	IDL-96a	Betty Jane, compo, c-1943	16″	25	55	85
	96b		18″	20	68	115
	96c		20″	35	71	135
850	IDL-97	Honey Baby, compo/ cloth, four sizes, c-1943	16-20″	65	85	135
	IDL-98	Princess Beatrix, six sizes, compo/cloth	16-26″	65	85	135
	IDL-99a-b	Baby Beautiful, compo/cloth, three sizes	16-23″	65	85	135
	IDL-100	Queen of the Ice, compo, c-1943	18″	65	95	145
	IDL-101	Princess Beatrix, compo/cloth	16″	65	85	135
	IDL-102	Teen Star, compo, c-1942	21″	185	267	325

MTCD Page	Key	Nomenclature	Size	Low	Price Avg.	High
853	IDL-103	Plassie, hp/vinyl/ cloth, c-1945	20"	39	50	65
	IDL-104	Snookie, stuffed vinyl/magic skin, c-1950	9½"	15	21	39
	IDL-105	Baby Ruth, vinyl/ waterproof fabric c-1952	16"	35	65	95
	IDL-105-1	Magic Skin Boy, hp head, c-1950	13½"	20	28	42
	IDL-106	Bucilla Thrift Kit Doll, hp, c-1950	11"		10	
	IDL-107	Baby Coos, hp/magic skin	16"	32	35	45
854	IDL-108	Squalling Baby, vinyl/cloth, c-1949	18"	18	35	45
	IDL-109	Baby, vinyl/coated fabric, c-1950	21"		25	
	IDL-110	Saucy Walker, soft vinyl/hp, c-1956	16"	20	29	65
	IDL-111	Molded Hair Boy, vinyl	23"		45	
	IDL-112	Baby Coos, hp/magic skin	13½"	20	28	42
855	IDL-113	Miss Revlon, c-1956	20"	30	52	115
	IDL-114	Patti Prays, vinyl/ cloth, c-1958	20"	15	27	35
857	IDL-115	Patty Playpal, vinyl/ plastic	36"	20	86	135
	IDL-115	Toddler Girl, vinyl/ rv, c-1959	18"	18	27	35
	IDL-116	Saucy Walker, rv/sv	32"	40	65	95
	IDL-117	Saucy Walker, vinyl/ plastic	28"	40	60	95
	IDL-118	Peter Playpal, sv/ plastic, c-1960	38"	85	139	275
	IDL-119	Suzy Playpal, vinyl/ plastic, c-1960	28"	45	62	95
	IDL-120	Suzy Playpal (Penny) plastic/vinyl	32"	45	65	95
859	IDL-121	Shirley Temple as Heidi, vinyl walker, c-1960	15"	40	92	180
			17"	25	89	175
			36"	800	1035	1500
	IDL-122	Daddy's Girl, plastic, c-1960	36"		NPA	
			42"		195	
		Miss Ideal, c-1960- 62, (Terry Twist & Miss Twist)	25"	20	36	65
			30"	40	53	90

MTCD Page	Key	Nomenclature	Size	Low	Price Avg.	High
	IDL-123	Bye Bye Baby, vinyl/ plastic, c-1960	25″		195	
	IDL-124	Mitzi, vinyl, c-1961	11¾″		18	
	IDL-125	Baby Coos, vinyl/ foam, 1961-1963	20″ 24″		45 75	
	IDL-126	Jackie, vinyl, c-1961	15″ 19″ 21″ 25″		15 20 25 30	
861	IDL-127	Bonnie Baby, vinyl, c-1961	12″		15	
	IDL-128	Cream Puff, vinyl, c-1962	19″ 21″ 24″		20 25 30	
	IDL-129	Betsy Wetsy Toddler, vinyl, c-1962	16″ 19″	16 16	22 26	26 40
	IDL-130	Walking Pattite, plastic, c-1961	18″		18	
	IDL-131	Liz, rigid vinyl, c-1962	15½″	17	19	25
	IDL-132	Snoozie, soft vinyl, 1958-1965	14″ 20″		15 20	
	IDL-133	Tearie Dearie, vinyl, 1964-1965	9″	4	12	18
863	IDL-134	Patti, vinyl, c-1965	9″	5	7	10
	IDL-135	Grown-up Tammy, vinyl, c-1965	12″	5	11	18
	IDL-136	Betsy Baby, vinyl, c-1965	13½″		9	
	IDL-137	Betsy Wetsy, soft vinyl/hp, c-1965	20″		15	
	IDL-138	Baby Betsy, vinyl, c-1965	16″		18	
	IDL-139	Katie Kachoo, vinyl, 1967-1970	17″		25	
	IDL-140	Tabatha, soft vinyl, c-1965	11½″		45	
865	IDL-141	Baby Real Live Lucy, vinyl, c-1967	14″	6	10	15
	IDL-142	Tiny Thumbelina, vinyl/cloth, c-1967	14″	4	5	8
	IDL-143	Real Live Lucy, vinyl, c-1965	20″	8	15	20
	IDL-144a-b	Toddler Thumbelina, vinyl, c-1969	9″	6	8	12
	IDL-145	April Showers, vinyl/ hp, c-1969	14″	9	15	22

MTCD Page	Key	Nomenclature	Size	Low	Price Avg.	High
	IDL-146	Playtime Tubsy, vinyl/hp, c-1968	14″		22	
866	IDL-147	The Posie Dolls, vinyl/foam, c-1969:				
	147a	Daisy	18″	9	34	45
	147b	Petal	18″	9	34	45
	147c	Lillie	18″	9	34	45
867	IDL-148	Petal the Posie Doll, vinyl/foam, c-1967	18″	9	34	45
	IDL-149	Lillie the Posie Doll, vinyl/foam, c-1967	18″	9	34	45
	IDL-150	Betty Big Girl, vinyl walker, c-1968	30″	25	61	125
868	IDL-151	Bibsy, vinyl	23″	16	25	30
869	IDL-152	Colored Crissy, sp/rp, c-1968	18½″	40	50	72
	IDL-153	Kerry, Crissy's Friend, sp/plastic c-1969	17½″	12	17	25
	IDL-154	Mia, Velvet's Friend, soft plastic	15″	12	17	25
	IDL-155	Baby Crissy, vinyl/foam-soft skin c-1973	24″	18	26	55
	IDL-156	Brandi, suntan vinyl, c-1971	17½″	15	19	30
	IDL-157	Dina, sp/rp, c-1971	15″	20	26	30
	IDl-158	Cinnamon, sp/rp, c-1971	12″	10	18	30
870	IDL-159	Movin' Groovin' Posin' Cricket, sp/rp, c-1971	16″	20	25	30
	IDL-160	Tearful Tiny Thumbelina, vinyl/cloth, c-1964	14″		23	
	IDL-161	Patti Playful, vinyl/cloth, c-1970	15″	20	48	75
871	IDL-162	Belly Button Baby, sv/hp, c-1970:				
	162a	"Me So Silly", Girl	9″	4	5	10
		"Me So Silly", Boy	9″	4	5	10
	162b	"Me So Glad", Black	9″	4	5	10
		"Me So Glad", White	9″	4	5	10
	162c	"Me So Happy" Girl	9″	4	5	10
		"Me So Happy" Boy	9″	4	5	10
	IDL-163	Lazy Dazy, vinyl/cloth, c-1971	11″	4	7	10
872	IDL-164	Bizzie Lizzie, vinyl/plastic, c-1970	18″	25	26	30

	IDL-165	Play'N Jane, vinyl/plastic, c-1971	17″	6	19	25
	IDL-166	In-A-Minute Thumbelina, plastic/vinyl, c-1971	9″	5	10	18
	IDL-167	Flatsy, flat, wired vinyl, c-1970		4	7	15
873	IDL-168	Cinnamon with Hair-doodler, plastic/vinyl, c-1973	13½″	8	11	18
	IDL-169	Upsy Dazy, plastic/cloth c-1973			10	

IMPERIAL-CROWN TOY, (IMPERIAL CROWN DOLL CO.)

874	IMP-1	Girl, hp/stuffed vinyl, c-1950	16″	16	30	45
	IMP-2	Girl, hp/soft sticky plastic, c-1950	16½″	16	30	45
	IMP-3	Tina Toddler, sp/hp, c-1950	22½″		12	
	IMP-4	Baby, vinyl/hp/cloth	27″		45	
875	IMP-5	Girl, hp/magic skin	14½″	16	30	45

INNOVATION NOVELTY CO.

	INN-1	Soldier, compo/cloth, c-1916			*Catalog Illus.*	

ITALIAN DOLLS

	IT-6	Ratti Girl, vinyl	12″		65	
876	IT-7	Ratti Sexed Boy, vinyl	15″	45	75	90
	IT-8	Ratti Sexed Girl, vinyl	15″	45	75	90
	IT-9	Daniella, vinyl, c-1972	16″		45	
	IT-10	Dark composition girl	15″		135	
	IT-10-1	Cristina, rubber, c-1955	18″		225 *w/wardrobe*	
877	IT-11	Bonomi Boy, (Italo-cremona) vinyl, c-1965	17″		45	
	IT-12	My Baby, sticky plastic, c-1952	20″		100	
878	IT-13	Pinocchio, rubber	10½″		25	
	IT-14	Girl, felt	7″		25	
	IT-15	Bambole Child, vinyl	8½″		20	
	IT-16	Migliorati Child, vinyl	12″	5	10	18

	IT-17	Girl, sp, c-1950			35	
879	IT-18	Bonomi girl, hp, c-1962	12½"		35	
	IT-19	Galafe Minstrel, mask face/cloth	10"		15	
	IT-20	Titti and Son (7" baby) vinyl, (Sebino) c-1972	21"		65	
	IT-21	Furga Girl, vinyl, c-1959	12"	15	23	30
880	IT-22	Marcella (Furga), vinyl	12"		45	
	IT-23	Virga Hobo, hp	7"	8	12	18
	IT-24	Mechanical Tonino, soft vinyl/cloth, c-1950 (Furga)	14"	15	25	35

J

JAPANESE DOLLS

881	JAPA-15	Composition Baby, (Takito, Ogawa) c-1918			*Catalog Illus.*	
	JAPA-16	Baby Lucy, compo (Tajimi Co) c-1917			*Catalog Illus.*	
	JAPA-17	Y-DO-1, Puppet, compo/silk, c-1906 (Cole-Ackerman)			*Catalog Illus.*	
	JAPA-18	Bisque-head Baby, (Nagai & Co) c-1917	12"	125	150	225
			14"	175	225	275
882	JAPA-19	All-bisque Baby	8"		85	
	JAPA-20	Mysterious Dancing Doll, cell	2½"		5 ea	
	JAPA-21	Squeek Toy, rubber-like plastic	10"		5	
	JAPA-22	Dionne-type Toddler, compo	8½"		85	
	JAPA-23	"Grandma" Doll, bisque	4½"		85	
883	JAPA-24a	Water Lily, vinyl (Holiday Fair) 1967	6½"	4	5	9
	24b	Elvira, vinyl (Holiday Fair) 1967	6½"	4	5	9
	JAPA-25a	Sailor, cell/cloth	8"	20	35	45
	25b	Chicago Cub, cell/cloth	8"	20	35	45
	25c	Soldier, cell/cloth	9"	20	35	45
	JAPA-26	Girl, bisque (Japan)	6"	20	26	45
	JAPA-27	Painted-bisque Baby (Occupied Japan)	3½"	20	35	45

MTCD Page	Key	Nomenclature	Size	Low	Avg.	High
	JAPA-28	Bisque Girl	6″	15	23	35
885	JAPA-29	Kewpie Types, soft vinyl	5″		6 ea	
	JAPA-30	Hula Girl, brown vinyl (Forsam)	5″		5	
	JAPA-31a-b	Japanese Charlot Byj Characters, vinyl (price is for each doll)	10″	12	18	21
	JAPA-32	Geisha Girl, rubber	6½″		NPA	
	JAPA-33	Bisque Soldier	3½″	45	48	50
	JAPA-34	Peanut Baby, cell, in paper peanut shell	5″	14	32	45
	JAPA-35	Nippon Baby, bisq/compo	17½″	200	225	275

JOLLY TOY, INC.

MTCD Page	Key	Nomenclature	Size	Low	Avg.	High
	JOL-2	Swiss Boy, sv/rv, c-1962	13″		45	
	JOL-3	Character Girl, sv/rv, c-1960	12″	5	8	15
886	JOL-4	Toddler, vinyl, c-1965	15″		10	
	JOL-5	Girl, vinyl/foam, c-1960			12	
	JOL-6	Jolly, vinyl, c-1960	11″		6	
	JOL-7	Lil Jolly Joker, vinyl, c-1970	8″		15	
	JOL-8	Small Stuff — Topsy, vinyl, c-1960	14½″	3	7	14

JUTTA

MTCD Page	Key	Nomenclature	Size	Low	Avg.	High
	JUTT-1	Jutta, bisq/BJ body, #1349	12″	300	390	550

K

K AND K

MTCD Page	Key	Nomenclature	Size	Low	Avg.	High
887	K&K-2	Flossie Fisher's Own Doll, c-1916	15½″		85	
	K&K-3	Flossie Fisher's Own Doll, 1917-1921	15½″		85	
888	K&K-4a-c	Three dolls from the Playmate line, c-1917		85	95	115
	K&K-5	Happifat, compo/cloth	10″		325	
889	K&K-6	Kewpie, compo/cloth, c-1918	18″		395	

Catalog Illus.

MTCD Page	Key	Nomenclature	Size	Low	Avg.	High
	K&K-7	Dolls from the 1918 line, compo/cloth: #F7520, Girl, three styles	13½"		75	
		#F7521, Girl, two styles	15"		85	
		#F7522, Girl, two styles	15"		85	
		#F7523, Girl	17"		95	
		#F7524, Girl	17"		95	
		#F7525, Girl	18"		95	
		#F7542, Girl	19"		115	
		#F7526, "French Model" Girl	18"		115	
		#F7527, "French Model" Girl	19"		125	
		#F7528, "French Model" Girl	19"		125	
		#F7540, "French Model" Girl	15"		95	
		#F7541, "French Model" Girl	17"		115	
890	K&K-8	Dolls from the 1918 line, compo/cloth; #F7547, Hollikid	12½"		85	
		#F7740, Red Riding Hood	15"		85	
		#F7521, Girl, two styles	15"		85	
		#F7784, Wardrobe Doll, Girl, w/case	11½"		75	
		#F7785, Wardrobe Doll, Girl, w/case	11½"		75	
		#F7786, Wardrobe Doll, Baby, w/case	11½"		75	
		#F7727, "Little Girl," three styles	13½"		75	
		#F7739, "Little Girl," two styles	14½"		85	
		#F7728, "Little Girl," three styles	14½"		85	
		#F7520, "Little Girl," three styles	13½"		75	
891	K-1	Painted Bisque-head Baby, compo/cloth	23"		165	
	K&S-1	K-Star-S Girl, bisque	6"		NPA	
	KAHN-1a	Bwana Tumbo, c-1920, (Kahn & Mossbacker)			*Catalog Illus.*	

MTCD Page	Key	Nomenclature	Size	Low	Price Avg.	High
	1b	The Girl of the Golden West, c-1920, (Kahn & Mossbacker)			*Catalog Illus.*	
KAMMER & RHEINHARDT						
892	KR-7	The Flirt, c-1908	25″	750	850	1250
	KR-8	#121 Toddler, bisq/pm	15″	300	663	935
	KR-9	#100 Our New Baby, brown compo, c-1910	15″	500	600	750
	KR-10	#728 Boy, cell/compo	15″	175	225	275
KAMPES						
893	K&M-1a-b	Kamkins, pressed cloth, c-1928	19″	275	375	425
KANKO						
894	KAN-1	Kanko, Walking Doll, compo/cloth, (Albert Kahn) c-1920-24	18″		NPA	
KAULITZ, MARION						
	KAU-1	Kaulitz Swiss Girl, compo, c-1908	21″		NPA	
COLOR PLATES						
895	COLOR-1-A	Child, Bisque-head, BJ body, (ref: FUL-2)	37″		4250	
	COLOR-1-B	Baby, Bisque-head, BJ Body, (ref: FUL-1)	21″	85	284	500
	COLOR-1-C	Girl, Bisq/BJ compo/wood, (Heinrich Handwerk)	36″	1000	1500	2250
	COLOR-1-D	American Beauty, compo, c-1919, (ref: AMER-70)	16″		295	
	COLOR-1-E	Bisque-head Girl, A.18 M., (ref: AM-22)	42″	1200	1500	2350
	COLOR-2-A	Hilda, #237, bisq/compo, (ref: KEST-14)	14″	1400	1600	1950
	COLOR-2-Ba	Baby Bumps-type, compo/cloth	7″	75	136	195
	COLOR-2-Bb	Baby, Nippon, bisq/pm, (ref: JAPA-11)	11″		90	

MTCD Page	Key	Nomenclature	Size	Low	Avg.	High
	COLOR-2-C	#236 Toddler Girl, bisq/BJ body, (ref: SFBJ-2)	27"	1000	1611	2245
	COLOR-2-D	FS&C #1295 Toddler, (Germany), (ref: SCH-3)	14"		425	
	COLOR-3-A	Our Pet, bisq/compo #992, (ref: AM-21)	10"	275	369	425
	COLOR-3-B	Boy, Heubach-Koppelsdorf #302, (ref: HEU-13)	22"	325	560	725
	COLOR-3-C	Child, #214, bisq/compo/BJ body, (ref: KEST-15)	21"	225	340	450
	COLOR-3-D	OM German Child (ref: BISQ-5)	25"	375	425	475
	COLOR-4-A	Edmund Steiner Girl, bisq/BJ body, (ref: GER-12)	14"	250	325	400
	COLOR-4-B	Door of Hope Doll, wood/cloth, c-1917-1925 (ref: CHI-23)	11"	200	243	325
	COLOR-4-C	E.I.H. Boy (Oliver Twist) compo/cloth, c-1914 (ref: HORS-84)	16"		165	
	COLOR-4-D	E.I.H. Boy, compo/cloth, c-1914-1918 (ref: HORS-83)	19"		195	
	COLOR-5-A	Dream Baby, compo/cloth	15"	275	379	425
	COLOR-5-B	Flapper-in-a-Swing, compo, c-1940, (ref: BED-1)	14"		145	
	COLOR-5-C	K Star R Toddler, bisq/BJ compo, (ref: KR-8)	14"	300	663	935
	COLOR-5-D	Hedgehogs, synthetic prickly hair felt/vinyl, pair, (Prices given are for old models, not the present production): Mecki & Micki, 28cm	11"	85	95	165
	COLOR-6-A	Humpty Dumpty, Ptd linen, unmkd	16"		65	

	COLOR-6-Ba	Man, felt/cloth	15"		225	
	COLOR-6-Bb	Man, felt/cloth	16"		225	
	COLOR-6-C	Bye-lo Baby, bisq/ cloth/cell, c-1925 (ref: AVRL-16)	14"	380	492	695
	COLOR-6-D	Hansel, sv/hp (ref: HORS-131a)	15"		85	
		Gretel, sv/hp (ref: HORS-131b)	15"		85	
	COLOR-7-A	Lone Ranger, compo/cloth, (Dollcraft Novelty) (ref: COM-L17)	20½"	250	350	425
	COLOR-7-B	Tonto, compo/ cloth (Dollcraft Novelty) (ref: COM-L18)	20½"	250	320	425
	COLOR-7-C	See COLOR-7-A				
	COLOR-7D	Mickey Mouse, cloth, c-1930, (Knickerbocker) (ref: DIS-15)	13"	135	160	185
	COLOR-7-E	Doctor Doolittle, vinyl/cloth, (ref: PORT-D10)	22"	20	30	45
	COLOR-8-A	Snow White, mask face/cloth, (Play-toy) 1940s	16"	35	64	145
		Dwarfs, mask face/ cloth (Playtoy) 1940s (price for each)	11"	35	65	95
	COLOR-8-B	Bisque-head Girl, A.18 M., (ref: AM-22)	42"	1200	1500	2350
	COLOR-8-C	Otto Reinschke, BL Baby, bisq/compo (ref: GER-13)	12"	225	262	335
	COLOR-8-D	Shebee (mate to Heebee) c-1925, (ref: HORS-99)	10½"	90	135	165
	COLOR-9Aa	Tynie Baby-type (ref: BISQ-18)	6½"	225	370	450
	COLOR-9-Ab	Herm Steiner, New Born Babe #240, (ref: BISQ-17)	10"	175	223	270
	COLOR-9-Ac	Dream Baby, bisque-head/cloth, (ref: AM-3)	10"	225	250	330

	COLOR-9-B	Brother, compo/ cloth (Horsman), 1937	22"	95	135	165
	COLOR-9-C	BSW Toddler, (Germany), (ref: SCH-2)	15"	185	426	525
	COLOR-9-D	Bisque Shoulder-head Girl #370, (ref: AM-9)	20"	225	238	300
	COLOR-10-A	Bisque-head Girl (Gebruder-Ohlhaver) (ref: REV-1)	17"	300	375	450
	COLOR-10-B	Girl, bisq/BJ body (ref: FUL-3)	21"	265	456	595
896	COLOR-10-C	Loula Long Combs, artist's model-ing compound, compo	24"		750	
	COLOR-10-D	Mitzie Green's Art Needlework Quilt Kit with doll, 1931			65	
	COLOR-11-A	Snoozie, compo/ cloth (ref: IDL-85)	16"	85	165	225
	COLOR-11-B	Boy, 1-pc cell, MP, (Japan)	9"		30	
		Girl, 1-pc cell, MP, (Japan)	9"		30	
	COLOR-11-C	#121 Toddler, bisq/ pm, (ref: KR-8)	15"	300	663	935
	COLOR-11-D	Brother Coos, hp/ cloth/compo, (ref: IDL-28)	30"		95	
	COLOR-12-A	K Star R #728 Toddler, Boy, bisq/BJ compo (ref: KR-10)	14"	175	225	275
	COLOR-12-Ba	Character Boy, compo/cloth (M.T. Co.) c-1910 (ref: MT-1)	14"		135	
	COLOR-12-Bb	Character boy, compo/cloth, c-1910 (ref: UNMKD-69)	15"		95	
	COLOR-12-C	#728 Boy, cell/compo (ref: KR-10)	15"	175	225	275
	COLOR-12-Da	Baby #152 (ref: KEST-8)	13"	300	346	450

MTCD Page	Key	Nomenclature	Size	Price Low	Avg.	High
	COLOR-12-Db	Kestner #150 Character Baby bisque-head, (ref: GER-17-1)	15″	300	419	545
	COLOR-13-A	Chad Valley Girl, velveteen/cloth	17″	250	450	475
	COLOR-13-B	Little Angel, hp/ cloth/sv, 1947 (ref: R&B-25)	21″	75	105	135
	COLOR-13-Ca	Baby, 351.14K bisq/ pm, (ref AM-5)	17″	325	350	450
	COLOR-13-Cb	Baby, 352, bisq/ compo/cloth, (ref: AM-7)	12″	200	225	300
	COLOR-13-D	Bahr & Proschild Baby, compo, (ref: BAHR-1)	15″	225	285	435
	COLOR-14-A	Boy, bisq/pm (ref: HEU-12)	7½″	175	190	200
	COLOR-14-B	OM German Bisque (ref: BISQ-8)	24″	375	450	525
	COLOR-14-C-D	Cristina, rubber, 1955, (ref: IT-10-1)	18″		225 w/wardrobe	
	COLOR-15-A	AM 750 Baby, bisq/ pm	9″	225	279	325
	COLOR-15-B	Coleman Dolly Walker, c-1917, (ref: W-T-1)	29″		325	
	COLOR-15-C	Mae Starr, compo/ cloth, c-1930, (ref: W-T-9)	28″	295	345	425
	COLOR-15-D	Bonnie Babe, cell/ cloth, c-1926, (ref: AVRL-20)	16½″	275	325	565
	COLOR-16-A	Lion Uniform Doll, old heavy plastic (ref: ADV-L6)	13″	35	65	85
		New thin plastic	13″	25	35	65
	COLOR-16-B	Lenci College Girl, felt/cloth, Unmkd	17″	395	500	750
	COLOR-16-C	Carolle, hp (UNICA, Belgium)	19″		85	
	COLOR-16-D	BL French Baby, Unmkd, (ref: PM-2)	10½″	200	250	325
	COLOR-16-E	Chad Valley, Princess Elizabeth mask face/cloth England, (Hygienic Toys)	19″	450	475	595

MTCD Page	Key	Nomenclature	Size	Low	Avg.	High
	COLOR-16-F	Charlie Chaplin, vinyl/cloth, (Bubbles, Inc.) 1972		25	39	55
	COLOR-16-G	Blythe, plastic/ vinyl, c-1973, (ref: KEN-5)	12"	6	9	11
	COLOR-16-H	Girl, compo/cloth, c-1918, (ref: UNMKD-82)	20"		145	
	COLOR-16-I	Girl, 1-pc vinyl, c-1950, (ref: HORS-120)	26"	25	48	65
	COLOR-16-J	Two-faced Baby, vinyl/plastic, (Frankie R. Berg) c-1950, (ref: MULTI-17)	16"		45	
	COLOR-16-K	Debbie (Fleischaker) c-1951, (ref: ALEX-93)	22"	85	135	160
	COLOR-16-L	Baby First Tooth, vinyl/cloth, (ref: HORS-140)		32	45	65
	COLOR-16-M	Baby Luv, vinyl/ cloth, (ref: EG-85)	14"	28	32	45
	COLOR-16-N	Perfect Girl, compo/ cloth, (ref: PER-1)	21"		85	
	COLOR-16-0	Schilling Talking Doll, MP Hr, (ref: W-T-17)	22"	40	60	95
	COLOR-16-P	Cindy, plastic, c-1958, (ref: HORS-118)	25"		25	
	COLOR-16-Q	Monica Elizabeth, hp, (ref: MON-3)	17"	95	219	325

KAYBEE DOLL & TOY CO.

913	KB-1	Four dolls from the 1918 line		*Catalog Illus.*		
	KB-2	Part of the 1918 line		*Catalog Illus.*		
	KB-3	Girl, vinyl, c-1966	19"	NPA		

KAYSAM CORP.

	KS-1	Girl, sv/rv, c-1961	20"		25	
914	KS-2	Character Girl, vinyl	19"		20	

KEHAGIAS, GREECE

	KEH-1	Kehagias Girl, sv/rv, 1966-1970 (Greece)	11"		25	

MTCD Page	Key	Nomenclature	Size	Low	Price Avg.	High
		KENNER PRODUCTS CO.				
	KEN-1	Crumpet, sv/hp, c-1970	18″	9	15	20
915	KEN-2	Mad Cap Molly, plastic, c-1971	12″		6	
	KEN-3	Garden Gal dolls, vinyl, c-1973:				
	3a	Marigolds	6½″		5	
	3b	Bachelor's Buttons	6½″		5	
	3c	Zinnias	6½″		5	
916	KEN-a-b	Jenny Jones and Baby John, vinyl, (Baby John, 2½″) c-1973	9″	10	15	25
	KEN-5	Blythe, plastic/vinyl, c-1973	12″	6	9	11
	KEN-6	Baby Alive, foam-stuffed vinyl, c-1973	16″	12	15	18
917	KEN-7	Baby Yawnie, sv/ cloth, c-1974	14″	10	12	18
	KEN-8	Nancy Nonsense, vinyl/plastic, c-1974	18″	9	12	18
	KEN-9	Dusty, vinyl, c-1974	11½″	5	10	18
918	KEN-10a	Steve Scout, vinyl, c-1974	9″	6	8	10
	10b	Bob Scout, vinyl, c-1974	9″	6	8	10
	KEN-11	Betty Crocker, litho cloth, c-1974	13″	12	15	18
	KEN-12	Gabbigale, vinyl/hp, c-1972	18″	8	15	20
		KERR & HINZ				
919	KERR-1	Baby and High Chair, bisq dolls	3½″	9	15	25
		J. D. KESTNER				
	KEST-9	Girl, bisq/leather	18″	300	375	475
	KEST-10	#154 Girl, bisq/kid	25″	325	451	750
	KEST-11	Lettie Lane's Daisy, #171, bisq/compo/ BJ body	18″	275	376	585
921	KEST-12	Dutch Boy Fisher-man, #174, bisq/ compo/BJ body, c-1918	11½″	250	316	390
	KEST-13	Girl, bisq/kid	29″	350	563	835
	KEST-14	Hilda, #237, bisq/ compo	14″	1400	1900	2450

MTCD Page	Key	Nomenclature	Size	Price Low	Avg.	High
	KEST-15	Child, #214, bisq/ compo/BJ body	21"	225	340	450
	KEST-16	Baby, #260, bisq/ compo	11¼"	225	378	595
	KEST-17	Oriental Baby, #243, bisq/compo	18"	1600	1800	2250

KLEY & HAHN DOLLS

MTCD Page	Key	Nomenclature	Size	Price Low	Avg.	High
	K&H-1	#571 Baby, bisq/pm	37½"		NPA	
	K&H-2	#525 German Bisque- head Baby	9"	400	450	550
922	K&H-3	#320 Character Girl, bisq/compo	16½"	895	1350	2250
	K&H-4	#250 Girl, bisq/BJ compo body	24"	250	366	545

KEWPIES

MTCD Page	Key	Nomenclature	Size	Price Low	Avg.	High
	KEW-4a	Whoopy Clowny, rag, 1931-1932	14"		NPA	
	4b	Cuddly Kewpie, rag, 1931-1932	11½" 14"	55 65	85 95	125 135

L

MTCD Page	Key	Nomenclature	Size	Price Low	Avg.	High
923	LANG-1a-g	"El-Be-Co" Dolls, (Langrock Bros), compo/cloth, c-1917			65 ea	

LASTIC-PLASTIC

MTCD Page	Key	Nomenclature	Size	Price Low	Avg.	High
	LAS-1	The Angel Child (Mommy's Little Angel), vinyl/ cloth, c-1951	17"		NPA	
924	LAS-2	Our Own Little Girl (Our Little Girl) stuffed vinyl, c-1951	22"	65	85	125

LAUREL DOLL CO.

MTCD Page	Key	Nomenclature	Size	Price Low	Avg.	High
	LAU-1	Gabby, vinyl, unmarked (Laurel Doll)	36"		45	

LEATHER DOLLS

MTCD Page	Key	Nomenclature	Size	Price Low	Avg.	High
925	LEA-1	Sonny, a Tuco Leather Doll, (Notter) c-1915	8"		*Catalog Illus.*	
	LEA-2	Baby's Friend (M.S. Davis & Co) c-1907	12"		*Catalog Illus.*	

	LEA-3	Nine items of 1917 line:			Catalog Illus.	
		Cow Boy				
		Soldier Boy				
		Uncle Sam				
		Indian Girl				
		Cow Girl				
		Navy Boy				
		Dutch Girl				
		Indian Chief				
		Clown				
		Nurse				
		Dutch Boy				
	LEN-1	Unusual Lenci Baby, compo/cloth, c-1950	15"		NPA	
	LILLY					
926	LIL-1	Lilly, bisq/kid			NPA	
	LORRIE DOLL CO					
	LOR-1	Lorrie Brown Baby, vinyl/cloth, c-1962	21½"		25	
927	LOR-2	Lorrie Toddler, vinyl, c-1971	15½"		20	

M

MACE, L.H. & CO.						
	MAC-1a-d	Four dolls from the 1911 line, (L.H. Mace & Co.)			Catalog Illus.	
	MACON					
929	MAC-2	Macon Baby, compo/cloth	22½"		35	
MAIDEN AMERICA TOY MFG. CO.						
	MAID-1	Maiden America, The National Doll, compo, c-1915			Catalog Illus.	
	MAID-2a-b	M.A.T. Characters, compo/cloth c-1919			Catalog Illus.	
	MAID-3a-j	Group of M.A.T. Character Dolls compo/cloth, c-1919			Catalog Illus.	
MANHATTAN DOLL CO.						
	MAN-1	The Doll Beautiful, seven sizes, from 12" to 30", c-1919	12-30"	65	135	195

MTCD Page	Key	Nomenclature	Size	Low	Avg.	High
	MAN-2	Walking Doll, wood/ compo, c-1919	28"		135	
	MANNEQUINS					
931	MANN-1	Marianne, compo, c-1943	11¾"		45	
	MANN-2	Fashiondol, compo, c-1943	12½"		45	
	MARSHALL FIELD & CO.					
	MAR-1	Dandy, A doll from the toy display of Marshall Field & Co., c-1908			*Catalog Illus.*	
	MARTI ANNA					
	MAR-2	Marti Anna, compo/ cloth, c-1940	18"		165	
	LOUIS MARX & CO.					
	MARX-3	Captain Tom Maddox, c-1967	11¼"		15	
	MARX-4	Stony "Stonewall" Smith, c-1964	11"		15	
932	MARX-5	Astronaut, vinyl	7½"		15	
	MARX-6	Mike Hazard, Double Agent, vinyl, c-1961	11"		15	
	MARX-7	Fighting Eagle, vinyl, c-1967	11½"		15	
933	MARX-8a	Janie West, vinyl	9"		12	
	8b	Josie West, vinyl	9"		12	
	MARX-9	Jane West, vinyl, c-1967	11"		12	
	MARX-10	Chief Cherokee, vinyl, c-1967	11½"		12	
	MARX-11	Daniel Boone, vinyl, c-1967	11"		12	
	MARX-12	Geronimo, vinyl, c-1967	11½"		12	
	MARX-13	Bill Buck, scout, vinyl, c-1967			12	
		Zeb Zachary, trooper, vinyl, c-1967			12	
		Captain Tom Maddox, vinyl, c-1967			12	
	MARX-14	Miss Seventeen, plastic, c-1961	15"		25	
			18"		35	

Page	Key	Nomenclature	Size	Low	Avg.	High
935	MARX-15	Twinkie, with wardrobe, accessories			25 complete	
	MATCHBOX DIV., LESNEY PROD. CORP.					
936	MAT-1	The Fighting Furies, plastic, c-1974:				
		Captain Peg-Leg	8½″		15	
		Captain Hook	8½″		15	
	MATTEL, INC.					
941	MATT-28	Shrinkin' Violet, rag doll		35	42	45
	MATT-29	Tatters, Rag Doll		15	20	25
	MATT-30	Drowsey, vinyl/cloth		4	12	20
942	MATT-31	Baby Teenie Talk		6	9	15
	MATT-32	Baby Coleen, vinyl/cloth		6	10	20
	MATT-33	Storybook Kiddles:				
		Cinderiddle		6	9	15
		Liddle Biddle Peep		6	9	15
		Liddle Red Riding Hiddle		6	9	15
		Liddle Middle Muffet		6	9	15
	MATT-34	Baby Small Walk		8	10	15
	MATT-35	Patootie, vinyl/cloth		5	8	12
	MATT-36a,b	Pretty Pairs, Angie 'n' Tangie		10	16	25
	36c,d	Nan 'n' Fran		10	16	25
	36e,f	Lori 'n' Rori		10	16	25
943	MATT-37	Tutti		6	9	18
	MATT-38	Baby First Step		10	29	45
	MATT-39	Rock Flowers,				
		Rosemary		8	10	15
		Heather		8	10	15
		Lilac		8	10	15
		Iris		8	10	15
		Doug		8	10	15
	MATT-40	Baby Love Light		6	9	12
	MATT-41	Baby Go Bye-Bye and Her Bumpety Buggy		5	12	25
	MATT-42	Tippy Toes		10	15	22
944	MATT-43	Baby Fun		6	11	20
	MATT-44	Sketchy		9	24	30
	MATT-45	Red Riding Hood, rag		4	9	15
		Wolf		4	9	15
	MATT-46	Lancelot Lion, rag doll		4	9	15
	MATT-47	Tea Party Kiddles		4	7	10

Page	Key	Nomenclature	Size	Low	Avg.	High
945	MATT-48	Off to See The Wizard Hand Puppet		2	7	10
	MATT-49a	Baby Tender Love		5	8	15
	49b	Tearful Baby Tender Love		5	8	15
	MATT-50	New Chatty Cathy		10	18	25
	MATT-51	Tiny Swingy		6	11	15
	MATT-52	New Tiny Chatty Baby		8	15	20
	MATT-53	New Chatty Baby		10	16	25
946	MATT-54	Bed Time Baby, rag		3	7	10
	MATT-55a-d	Fashion Teener		6	9	15
	MATT-56	Bend-able Leg Ken		3	10	15
	MATT-57a	Talking Christie		4	10	18
	57b	Talking Brad		3	11	25
	MATT-58	Peachy and Her Puppets		10	13	18
	MATT-60	Newborn Baby Tender Love		5	10	18
947	MATT-59	Randi Reader		10	12	18
	MATT-61	Baby Beans, The Hold-Me-Tights:				
	61a	Cry Baby Beans		4	7	20
	61b	Booful Beans		4	7	20
	61c	Talking Baby Beans		4	7	20
	61d	Puffen Bean Puppet		4	7	20
	61e	Punky Bean Puppet		4	7	20
	61f	Biffy Beans		4	7	20
	61g	Biffy Beans		4	7	20
948	MATT-62	Splash Happy Sal			15	
		Splash Happy Hal			15	
	MATT-63	Saucy		7	15	25
	MATT-64	Cynthia		12	17	28
	MATT-65	Hi Dottie		6	11	18
	MATT-70	Quick Curl Casey		8	12	18
	MATT-73	Quick Curl Kelly		7	12	18
949	MATT-66	Big Jim		5	9	15
	MATT-67	Big Josh		5	9	15
	MATT-68	Big Jack		5	9	15
	MATT-69	Big Jeff		5	9	15
	MATT-71	Barbie's Friend Francie		4	10	15
	MATT-72	Mod Hair Ken		6	12	18
	MATT-74	The Sunshine Family		8	12	18

McCLURG, A.C. & CO

Page	Key	Nomenclature	Size	Low	Avg.	High
950	McC-1	Character doll from 1911 line			*Catalog Illus.*	

MEAKIN & RIDGWAY INC

Page	Key	Nomenclature	Size	Low	Avg.	High
	MEAK-1	Three dolls from 1919 line, bisq/ cloth			*Catalog Illus.*	

MECHANICAL DOLLS

Page	Key	Nomenclature	Size	Low	Avg.	High
	MECH-1	Man, pm/wood, unmarked	12″		NPA	
		Bear, pm/wood, unmarked	10½″		NPA	
951	MECH-2	French Dancing Dolls from Samstag & Hilder, c-1906			*Catalog Illus.*	
	MECH-3	Tommy Golfer, compo, 1931-1932	13″		65	
	MECH-4	Hawaiian Girl, compo, key-wind, unmarked	14″		35	
	MECH-5	Swimming Doll, cell wind-up, c-1936	5″		25	
	MECH-6	Jr. Life Guard, The Swimming Doll, early plastic, key-wind, c-1967	10″		30	
	MECH-7	Baby Princess, vinyl, key-wind, c-1967	11″		12	
952	MECH-8	Crawling Baby Boy, sp/metal/hp, unmarked	7″		25	
	MECH-9	Crawling Baby, metal/plastic, key-wind (Irwin)	5″		15	

METAL DOLLS

Page	Key	Nomenclature	Size	Low	Avg.	High
	MET-5	American Baby Face Doll, c-1903, (Metal Doll Co.)			*Catalog Illus.*	
	MET-6	The All Steel Doll, (Metal Doll Co.) c-1903			*Catalog Illus.*	
	MET-7	The Metal Doll Co. factory in Pleasantville New Jersey, 1903			*Catalog Illus.*	
953	MET-8a-b	Mama Doll, 1914-1916	17″	75	100	125
	MET-9	Baby, c-1918 (Atlas Doll & Toy)	14-18″	50	87	125
	MET-10	Hug Me Kid, c-1919 (Atlas Doll & Toy)			135	

	MET-11a-b	Treat 'Em Rough Kiddies, c-1919, (Art Metal Works)		45	85	135
954	MET-12	Unmarked Boy, white bisq gauntlet hands	16½″	75	100	125
	MET-13	"Talking" Mama Doll, various sizes, c-1920 (Art Metal Works)		75	125	150
	MET-14	Dimples-type Baby, cloth body	16″	75	100	150
	MET-15	Baby, unmarked	12″	50	75	95
	MET-16	Dream Baby-type doll, cloth body, c-1925	12½″	50	95	150
	MET-17	Girl, compo limbs, (Bell mark)	13″	50	75	95
	MET-18	A group of metal-headed dolls from Sears 1931-32 catalog, cloth bodies, compo limbs:				
		Minerva Girl Doll, mohair wig	15″	55	75	95
			17″	75	95	125
			20″	85	105	135
		"Wear Well" Girl Doll, molded hair	19″	60	85	125
		Cunning Baby Doll (Dimples-type)	14½″	75	95	135
		"Wear Well" Girl, molded hair	15″	55	75	95
		Girl doll with human hair wig	17½″	85	108	145

METTI, THE HOUSE OF

956	METT-1	Mon Cherie, vinyl, c-1973, unmarked			20	
	METT-2	Baby, vinyl, c-1973			15	
	METT-3	Piccaninny, dark brown oily vinyl, unmarked	10½″		25	
	METT-4a	Baby Brother, oily vinyl, sexed	16″		25	
	4b	Baby Sister, oily vinyl, sexed	16″		25	

MTCD Page	Key	Nomenclature	Size	Low	Price Avg.	High
957	MGM-1	Lindy-Sue (F&B Fluffy-type) vinyl, (Molly E)	10½"		15	
	MGM-2	Perky (F&B Fluffy-type) vinyl, (Molly E)	10½"		15	
	MIN-1	Darling Baby (original box) compo, (Minerva Toy Co)	9"		65	
	MIR-1	Little Buck, c-1919 (Miranda & Co.)	10"		NPA	
		Squaw, c-1919 (Miranda & Co.)	12"		NPA	
	MIS-1	Baby-Aire type, compo, unmarked, 1920-1930	22"		65	
	MIS-2-3	Mistress Patty P. Comfort, hot water bottle doll, c-1913			*Catalog Illus.*	
	MIT-1	The Yankee Doll with Moving Eyes, c-1913 (Mitred Box Co.)			*Catalog Illus.*	
	MIT-2a-b	The Yankee Doll, compo (Mitred Box Co.) c-1912	12-13"		*Catalog Illus.*	
958	MIT-3	The Yankee Doll c-1912 (Mitred Box Co.)	15"		*Catalog Illus.*	
	MOD-1	Three dolls from the 1915 line of Modern Toy Co., compo/cloth: College Boy Petite Polly Co-Ed			*Catalog Illus.*	
	MON-1	Monica, plastic/ compo, c-1945	21"	95	219	325
960	MON-2	Monica Lind, compo, c-1940		95	219	325
	MON-3	Monica Elizabeth, hp	17"	95	219	325
	MRP-1	MRP Boy, head only, sv/magic skin	4½"		10	
	MRP-2	Early vinyl Girl, head only	4½"		10	
961	MT-1	Character Boy, compo/cloth, c-1910, (M.T.Co.)	14"		135	

MTCD Page	Key	Nomenclature	Size	Price Low	Avg.	High
		MULTIFACE DOLLS				
962	MULTI-12	Topsy-Turvy, litho cloth, c-1901, (Albert Bruckner/ Horsman)	14½″	125	239	475
	MULTI-13	Topsy-Turvy, unmarked compo	17″	45	60	75
	MULTI-14	Topsy-Turvy, compo	7½″	45	60	75
	MULTI-15	Molded Baby, 1-pc, c-1957, (Bonny Tex Co.)	9″		35	
	MULTI-16	Trilby (Little Sister), c-1951, sv/cloth (Ideal)	18″		165	
963	MULTI-17	Two-faced Baby, vinyl/plastic, (Frankie R. Berg) c-1950	16″		85	
	MULTI-18	Rubber 3-face Baby, c-1960	11″		20	
964	MULTI-19	Two-faced Girl, vinyl, (Hong Kong) c-1960	9″		25	
	MULTI-20	Two-faced Girl, plastic/vinyl, (Hong Kong) c-1960	14″		25	
		MUTUAL DOLL CO. INC.				
965	MUT-1	Bundie Doll, compo c-1919	12″		95	
	MUT-2	Baby Bundie, compo, c-1918-19	12″		95	
			16″		135	
	MUT-3	Joseph L. Kallus			*Portrait*	
	MUT-4	Group of Baby Bundies, c-1919			*Catalog Illus.*	
966	MY-1	My Da-zee, wood (W.C. Horn Bro & Co.) c-1912	6″		135	
	MY-2	My Sweetheart, bisq/ BJ body, (A.W.)	28″	325	375	495

N

		NANCY ANN STORYBOOK DOLLS, INC.				
	NAN-1	From a Muffie folder			*Catalog Illus.*	
	NAN-2	Muffie, plastic	8″	15	28	40
	NAN-3	Nancy Ann, plastic, jtd knees	10½″	12	15	25

MTCD Page	Key	Nomenclature	Size	Low	Price Avg.	High
	NAN-4	Nancy Ann, vinyl/hp	10"	12	15	25
	NAN-5	Boy, hp	7"		20	
	NASCO					
969	NAS-1	Nasco Sleeping Baby, vinyl/cloth	16"		NPA	
	NATIONAL JOINT LIMB DOLL CO.					
	NATL-1	Miss Najo, compo/ pm	12-26"		*Catalog Illus.*	
	NATL-2	Baby, compo/pm	12-19"		*Catalog Illus.*	
	N.D. CO.					
970	NDC-1	Charles Baby, bisq/ compo	22"		65	
			24"		85	
		Toddler, compo/ cloth	14"		45	
	NATURAL DOLL CO. INC.					
	NATL-3	Hard Plastic Walker Bride, c-1960	17"		35	
	NED-1	The Nedco Doll, cloth/pm, c-1919, (New England Doll Co.)			*Catalog Illus.*	
	NEW ERA NOVELTY CO., INC.					
971	NEW-1	Our Baby, compo, c-1915			95	
	NEW-2	Nanco Babies, compo, c-1916			*Catalog Illus.*	
	NEW-3	Yama Yama Doll, compo, five sizes	13½"-30"		*Catalog Illus.*	
	NEW-4	Yama Yama Doll, c-1918			*Catalog Illus.*	
972	NEW-4	Skooter Kid, compo/ cloth, 1915-1918	16×15×5½"		*Catalog Illus.*	
	NEW TOY MFG. CO.					
	NEW-5	Coquette, compo/ cloth, c-1912	10"	65	81	165
	NEW-6a	"Wall Eye Dolls," Jack, compo/cloth	14½"	275	475	650
	6b	"Wall Eye Dolls," Jill, compo/cloth	14½"	275	475	650
	NEW-7a	"The Brick Top Twins," Googly Girl, compo/cloth, c-1912	14½"	275	475	650

MTCD Page	Key	Nomenclature	Size	Low	Price Avg.	High
	7b	"The Brick Top Twins," Googly Boy, compo/cloth, c-1912	14½"	275	475	650
975	NEW-8	Items from 1912 line of New Toy Mfg. Co., compo/cloth, c-1912:	10-12"			
	8a	Coquette		65	81	165
	8b	Sailor Girl		65	81	165
	8c	Sailor Boy		65	81	165
	8d	Country Boy		65	81	165
	8e	Baseball Player		65	81	165
	8f	School Boy		65	81	165
	8g	School Girl		65	81	165
	8h	Jockey		65	81	165
	8i	Clown		65	81	165
	NEW-9	Soldier Dolls, compo/cloth c-1914:	10-16"			
		c-1914:	10-16"			
	9a	German		65	81	165
	9b	English		65	81	165
	9c	French		65	81	165
	9d	French		65	81	165
	9e	English		65	81	165
	9f	Russian		65	81	165
	NEW-10	Baby Bunting, Bear 2-faced Doll			165	
	NEW-11	Three styles from 1915 line:				
	11a	All-composition doll	7½"	65	90	165
	11b	Harlequin Doll, compo	7½"	65	90	165
	11c	Baby, compo	7½"	65	90	165
	NEW-12	Newbisc Baby, eleven sizes, (Nutoi), with or without wigs, c-1918		65	90	165
976	NEW-13	Three dolls from 1918 line, with or without wigs:				
	13a	Baby, compo	14"	65	81	165
	13b	Girl, BJ compo		65	81	165
	13c	Girl, compo/cloth	22"	65	81	165
	NEW-14	Baby Doll from 1919 line			135	
	NEW-15	Toddler, Midolly Dolls from the 1920 line				

Catalog Illus.

MTCD Page	Key	Nomenclature	Size	Low	Price Avg.	High
	NEW-16	Maytime Girl, a Newbisc Doll, (18 sizes) c-1919			NPA	
	NIBUR NOVELTY CO.					
977	NIB-1	Toddler, compo/ cloth, molded hr, 1923-1925	21"		45	
	NONBREAKABLE DOLL & TOY CO.					
	NON-1	Clownee, One of the Jam Kiddos, compo/cloth, c-1915			*Catalog Illus.*	
	NON-2	CAPO Non-Break- able Dolls, some stuffed, some compo, with or without wigs, c-1916	24-36"	65	90	175
	NON-3	Jam Kiddos, compo, c-1915				
	3a	Sailor Boy		65	85	165
	3b	Sweet Lavendar		65	85	165
	3c	Buster Brown		65	85	165
978	NON-4	CAPO Baby, compo, c-1917		65	85	165
	NORTH POLE DOLLS					
979	NP-1	The North Pole Doll, three sizes cell/fur, (Hahn & Amberg) c-1909			145	
	NP-2	Eskimo, compo (Horsman), c-1909	12"		145	
		Lt. Peary, compo (Horsman), c-1909	12"		165	
		Dr. Cook, compo (Horsman), c-1909			165	
	NP-3a	Peary, cell/cloth, (Strobel & Wilken), c-1909			135	
	3b	Cook, cell/cloth, (Strobel & Wilken), c-1909			135	
	NOVELTY DOLLS					
981	NOV-1	Joss, the God of Sunshine, compo, c-1909			35	
	NOV-2	Lotus Flower, (S.K. Novelty) c-1915			25	

MTCD Page	Key	Nomenclature	Size	Low	Price Avg.	High
	NOV-3	Mechanical "Long Voice" dolls, cell (Marks & Knoring) c-1916		15	26	35
	NOV-4	Mechanical "Voice" dolls, cell, (Marks & Knoring) c-1916		15	26	35
	NOV-5	Sailor Boy, Voice doll, compo/cloth, c-1918			35	
	NOV-6a	Dressed Kewpie, compo/cloth	21½"		NPA	
	6b	Kewpie on Pedestal, compo, undressed	12½"		35	
	6c	Kewpie on Pedestal, compo, dressed	12½"		45	
	NOV-7	Voice dolls, c-1918, compo/cloth		15	26	35
	NOV-8	Dainty Marie, compo (Shimmie Minnie)	9"	25	32	35
	NOV-9	Tiss Me, 1-pc plaster compo, (Borgfeldt) c-1919	6½"	20	35	45
982	NOV-10	Winkie, compo (Max Merten) c-1919		20	35	45
	NOV-11	Blynkie, Hair Wig, (Jones-Moran Doll Mfg.) c-1920		20	35	45
	NOV-12	Tumble-Bo, pm/ compo (Hy Mayer) c-1919		25	35	45
	NOV-13a	Kewpie, compo (Hyman and Oppenheim) c-1918		25	45	65
	13b	Splashme, compo (Hyman and Oppenheim), c-1918		25	35	45
983	NOV-14	Splashme, 1-pc compo	6"		35	
	NOV-14a-d	Four models from the 1919-1920 line (Tip Top Toy Co):				
	14a	Miss Summertime		25	35	45
	14b	Georgiette		25	35	45
	14c	Cherry Blossom		25	35	45
	14d	Atlantic City Belle		25	35	45
	NOV-15	Squat-Me, 1-pc compo	5½"		25	

MTCD Page	Key	Nomenclature	Size	Low	Price Avg.	High
	NOV-16	Pretty Polly, compo (Seamless Toy Corp) c-1919	9″		45	
984	NOV-17	Republic Doll & Toy Co. Dolls, compo, with or without wigs:				
	17a	Smiles, (20 styles) c-1919		25	35	45
	17b	Kweenie, c-1919		25	35	45
	17c	Salute (Soldier or Sailor), c-1919		25	35	45
	NOV-18	Miss Summertime, 1-pc compo, unmarked	10½″		35	
	NOV-19	Beach Flirt, compo, bathing cap or wig, (Fair & Carnival Supply), c-1919		25	35	45
	NOV-20	Impie, compo (Ben-Arthur Studios) c-1919		25	35	45
985	NOV-21	A Kutie Kid, compo (Seamless Toy Corp.) c-1919		25	45	65
	NOV-22	Fan-ie Baseball Doll, (Estelle Allison) c-1919	7¼″		55	
	NOV-23	Imported China doll novelties, c-1928:				
		Jtd bisq baby, boxed nursing set	2½″		15	
		Jtd bisq girl, boxed bath set	3″		20	
		Jtd bisq baby, boxed nursing set	3¼″		25	
		Jtd bisq baby, boxed nursing set	3¾″		30	
		Jtd bisq baby, wicker crib	4½″		35	
		Jtd bisq baby, wicker basket	4½″		35	
		Jtd bisq baby, china "wicker" basket	4″		35	
986	NOV-24	My Playmate, compo (Geo. Borgfeldt) c-1930	6½″		15	
	NOV-25	Drayton-types, 1-pc compo, unmarked, c-1920	4½″		45 ea	

MTCD Page	Key	Nomenclature	Size	Low	Price Avg.	High
	NOV-25-1	Pudgie, compo (Tip Top Toy), c-1919	12"		25	
	NOV-26	Doll Lamp, hp, 1940s	11"		25	
987	NOV-27	Assorted novelty items from 1936 Stack Mfg. Co. catalog:				
	27a	Feather-Dressed Celluloid Doll	7"	30	35	40
	27b	Bisque Doll in Carriage	5"		45	
	27c	Dressed Bisque Doll	6"		18	
	27d	Celluloid Feather Doll	6"		15	
	27e	Celluloid Doll, nude	6"		15	
	27f	Boxed set, Doll with moving arms	3"		30	
	27g	Boxed set, Doll with moving arms	3"		30	
	27h	Bisque Doll in Trunk	4½"		25	
	27i	Wood Segmented Characters	5"		45 ea	
	NOV-28	Crawling Baby, 1-pc plaster compo	10"		NPA	
988	NOV-29	Assorted novelty items from 1936 Stack Mfg Co. catalog:				
	29a	Battling Sailor (Popeye), compo	12"		85	
	29b-d	Fiberboard Characters	9½"		10 ea	
	29e	Hamburger King (Wimpy), compo	19"		20	
	29f	Sheba Feather Doll, compo	22"		35	
	29g-h	Bathing Girl Beauties, compo	14"		25	
	29i	Maribou Compo Doll Lamp	22"		45	
	29j	China Half-Doll Clothes Brush	4½"		35	
	29k	Zaza Dolls, rubber	12"		NPA	
	29l	Clown Doll, compo	27"		45	
	29m	Baby Doll Cricket, cell head			15	
	29n	Noisy Shaker Doll Wand	18"		15	
	29o	Jester Doll Wand	21"		15	
	29p	Celluloid Shaker Doll			15	

MTCD Page	Key	Nomenclature	Size	Low	Avg.	High
	29q	Compo-head Chenille Manikin	10"		15	
	29r	Celluloid-head Baby Doll Horn	15"		15	
	29s	Minnie Mouse, wood	3⅞"		40	
	29t	Mickey Mouse, wood	3⅞"		45	
	29u	Minnie Mouse, wood	5⅛"		40	
	29v	Mickey Mouse, wood	5"		45	
	29w	Nick, plastic (Mickey Mouse)	12"	55	75	125
	29x	Fan Dancer (Sally Rand), plaster	12"		35	
	29y	Movie Star, (Mae West), plaster	13"		35	
	29z	Curly Top (Shirley Temple), plaster	14"		45	
990	NOV-30	Clown, compo/cloth, c-1940, unmkd.	15"		25	
	NOV-31	Heart Beat Baby, compo/cloth/vinyl, c-1948	17"		45	
	NOV-32	Baseball Player, compo/cloth, c-1943	26"		45	
	NOV-33	Mexican Man, (Jerry Elsner Co), c-1950	7½"		15	
991	NOV-34	Noddy, 1957, Enid Blyton character:				
	34a	Noddy, Chad Valley Line, rubber	11"		25	
	34b	Big Ears, Chad Valley Line, rubber	12"		25	
	34c	Noddy in Bendy-Land (Bendy Toys)			25	
	34d	Noddy, nodder head (Merrythought Ltd.)	11"		35	
	NOV-35	"Jayne Mansfield" Hot Water Bottle, vinyl (Poynter Products), c-1957	21½"		65	
	NOV-36	Pagliacci Clown, vinyl/cloth, c-1958	29"		25	
992	NOV-37	Walker Girl, compo, (Germany) c-1959			35	
	NOV-38a-b	Trolls, vinyl, c-1965		3	6	10
	NOV-39a-b	Trolls, 1-pc vinyl	8"	5	9	15
	NOV-40a-c	Children, 1-pc molded vinyl	2¼"-3¼"		3 ea	

993	NOV-41	Angel, Rag Doll, felt (Italy), c-1960	10"		10	
	NOV-42	"Pregnant" Rag Doll (Pintel of Paris)			35	

O-P

	PAC-1	Beygrau Baby (Pacific Coast Doll Mfg. Co.) c-1918			65	
	PAL-1	Girl, 1-pc vinyl-plastic (Palan Jay) c-1965	11"		5	
994	P&M-1	Walker Girl, plastic/vinyl (P&M Doll Mfg. Co) c-1963			25	

PAPIER MACHE DOLLS

	PM-2	Bent-leg Baby, (French), unmarked	10½"	200	250	325
	PM-3	SP Toddler Girl, Gls SlpE	20"		100	
	PM-4	R.A. Googly	6½"	85	123	165
	PM-5	Christmas Doll from Paris, cloth body, c-1910, unmarked	14"	200	225	275
	PM-6	G.W. Girl, Gls SlpE	21½"	100	258	350
	PM-7	Unmarked Girl, (J.C. Penney Co), c-1920	24½"	250	308	350
	PM-8	Unmarked Girl, (German), Gls SlpE	12½"	90	100	125
997	PM-9	Bent-limb Baby	9"		45	
	PM-10	Unmarked Girl	12½"	85	90	125
	PM-11	Unmarked Baby, cloth body	8"		35	
	PM-12	Walking Mammy, (Noma Toy Co), c-1947, unmarked	10"	30	45	65
	PM-13	Girl, Gls SlpE	17"		75	

PEDIGREE SOFT TOYS LTD., LONDON

	PED-1	Walker Boy, hp, c-1948	20"		45	
	PED-2a-c	Three Toddler dolls from the 1939 line, compo		25	45	75

MTCD Page	Key	Nomenclature	Size	Low	Price Avg.	High
998	PED-3-6	Toddler and Baby Dolls from the 1939 line		25	45	75
	PED-7a-d	Saucy Walkers, hp, c-1952		35	60	75
1000	PED-8	Pin-Up Doll, hp, c-1952		35	60	75

PEERLESS DOLL CO., NY

1001	PEER-1a-d	Four dolls of the 1917 line, compo/ cloth			65	

PERFECT TOY MANUFACTURING CO.

	PER-1	Perfect Girl, compo/ cloth	21"		85	

PERMOLIN PROD. CO. INC.

1002	PER-2a	Trulie Good, compo, with or without wigs, c-1918	14"		45	
	2b		15"		65	

PERSONALITY DOLLS

	PERS-A2a	Gomez Addams	5¾"		12	
	A2b	Morticia Addams	5"		12	
	A2c	Uncle Fester	4¾"		12	
	PERS-B3	Baby Roslee, Walking Talking Doll, compo/cloth	23"		125	
	PERS-B4	Baby Sandy, compo, c-1930	7"	90	116	200
1003	PERS-B5	The Beatles, compo, c-1954:				
		Paul McCartney	8"	31	38	45
		George Harrison	8"	31	38	45
		Ringo Starr	7"	31	38	45
		John Lennon	8"		75	
	PERS-B6	The Beatles, solid vinyl, Set	4½"	35	40	55
	PERS-B7	Ellie May Clampett, (Beverly Hillbillies), vinyl (Unique), c-1960	12"		15	
	PERS-B8-B10	Bonanza "Full Action Figures" (American Character) c-1965:				
	B8	Hoss Cartwright (Dan Blocker)	8"		75	

MTCD Page	Key	Nomenclature	Size	Low	Price Avg.	High
1004	B9	Little Joe Cartwright (Michael Landon)	8″		50	
	B10	Ben Cartwright (Lorne Greene)	8″		50	
	PERS-B11	James Bond, vinyl, (Ideal)	12½″	10	15	25
	PERS-B12	Oddjob, vinyl (Gilbert), c-1965	10½″		15	
1005	PERS-B13	Daniel Boone, sv/hv, (Remco), c-1964	5″		20	
	PERS-B14	Bozo the Clown, vinyl/plush, (Knickerbocker)			15	
	PERS-B15	Kitty Karry-All from the Brady Bunch, vinyl, (Remco), c-1969	20″		20	
1006	PERS-B16	John Bunny (1883-1915) compo/ cloth (Amberg), c-1914	12″		165	
	PERS-B17	John Bunny, One of the Vitagraph Players, (Amberg), c-1914, compo/ cloth			165	
	PERS-C3	Ben Casey's Perfect Patient, vinyl, c-1963	15″		25	
	PERS-C4	Prince Charles, vinyl/ stuffed head	17¼″	30	45	65
1007	PERS-C5	Bonnie Prince Charlie, vinyl/ magic skin	21″	30	45	65
	PERS-C6a	Charlie Chan, vinyl, Hand puppets (Ideal), c-1973			5	
	C6b	Number One Son, vinyl, Hand puppet (Ideal), c-1973			5	
	PERS-C7	Charlie Chaplin, compo/cloth, c-1918	8½″		65	
	PERS-C8	Charlie Chaplin, compo/cloth c-1918	30″		45	
1008	PERS-C9	Charlie Chaplin, compo/cloth, c-1915			95	
	PERS-C10	Charlie Chaplin Doll and J.L. Amberg			*Portrait*	

Page	Key	Nomenclature	Size	Low	Avg.	High
	PERS-C11	Charlie Chaplin, c-1915			135	
	PERS-C12	Charlie Chaplin as The Tramp, litho cloth, (Kenner), c-1973	14″	20	38	55
	PERS-C13	Winston Churchill, compo (Small World Emporium), c-1960	4″		25	
1009	PERS-C14	Chitty Chitty Bang Bang Characters (Caractacus Pott, Truly Scrumptious, Jemima, and Jeremy), vinyl, (Mattel)	1¼-2¼″		45 set	
	PERS-C15	Clarabelle Clown, bendable vinyl	6″		6	
	PERS-C16	Jackie Coogan, head only, c-1921	5″		25	
	PERS-C17	Jackie Cooper, compo, (Petite)	12″		185	
1010	PERS-C18	General Custer, solid vinyl (Marx), c-1968	11½″		15	
	PERS-D3	Dionne Baby, all felt, c-1940	23″	225	250	425
	PERS-D4	Marie Dionne, mask face stockinette	21″	225	250	425
1011	PERS-D5	Yvonne Dionne Baby, compo/ cloth, c-1935	23″	175	256	395
	PERS-D6	Yvonne Dionne, Toddler, compo/ cloth, 1936	13½″	95	241	345
	PERS-D7	Dionne copy, PtdBsq, (Japan), c-1934	7½″	20	25	35
1012	PERS-D7a	Dionne Quintuplets, compo, c-1936, (Price for each Quint)	17″	115	267	395
	PERS-D8	Dionne Quintuplets, compo copies, c-1936 (Price for set)	6½″	45	56	75
	PERS-D9	Deanna Durbin Walker, wooden midriff, (Ideal)	15″	150	314	485

MTCD Page	Key	Nomenclature	Size	Low	Price Avg.	High
	PERS-E5	Eloise Rag Doll (Amer. Char.)			35	
1013	PERS-E6	General Dwight D. Eisenhower, vinyl	11"		55	
	PERS-F4	Family Affair's Talking Buffy and Mrs. Beasley, (Mattel), c-1970	10¾"	10	25	45
	PERS-F5	Family Affair's Talking Mrs. Beasley, (Mattel), c-1973	15½"		30	
	PERS-F6a	Fat Albert, hand puppet, vinyl, (Ideal) c-1973			5	
	F6b	Weird Harold, hand puppet, vinyl, (Ideal) c-1973			5	
1015	PERS-F7	Sally Field as The Flying Nun, vinyl, (Hasbro), c-1967	4¼"	12	15	18
	PERS-F8	Talking W.C. Fields, litho cloth, c-1972	17"	10	18	25
	PERS-G1	Judy Garland, stuffed Lastic Plastic, (Lastic Plastic Inc), c-1952	28"		NPA	
	PERS-G2	Ginny Tiu, vinyl	14½"	45	65	80
	PERS-G3	Barry Goldwater, hv, (Remco), c-1964	6"	10	20	25
	PERS-G4	Elizabeth Woodville Grey, "A Doll of Destiny," (A&H Doll), c-1953	11"	15	20	25
	PERS-H4	Ski Girl, compo, c-1943	26"		75	
	PERS-H5a-b	H.R. Pufnstuf Puppets, vinyl, (Remco) c-1971 Jimmy Witchie Poo Dr. Blinkley Orson Vulture Seymour Spider Cling Pufnstuf Clang			5 ea	
1016	PERS-J1	Former President Lyndon Baines Johnson, hv, c-1964	6"	10	20	25

MTCD Page	Key	Nomenclature	Size	Low	Avg.	High
	PERS-K1	"Jacqueline Kennedy" (Onassis), vinyl/ plastic (Alexander) c-1961	19"	600	720	900
	PERS-K2	"Jacqueline Kennedy" (Onassis), (Kaysam), c-1961	24"	25	65	85
	PERS-K3	"Jacqueline Kennedy" (Onassis), (also called "Gigi"), c-1961	25"	25	65	85
	PERS-K4	King Kong, vinyl, (Mattel), c-1966	12"		8	
1017	PERS-K5	Robert (Evel) Knievel, vinyl, (Ideal) c-1972	7"	7	9	12
	PERS-L1	Lamb Chop, vinyl, c-1962	14"		35	
	PERS-L2a	Laurel, 1-pc vinyl (Lakeside Toys)	5¾"		15	
	L2b	Hardy, 1-pc vinyl (Lakeside Toys)	4¾"		15	
	PERS-L3	Piper Laurie, hp, (Alexander)	14"	250	300	325
			21"	300	350	395
1018	PERS-L4a	Colored Terri Lee, hp	16"	70	110	165
	L4b	Colored Jerri Lee, hp	16"	70	110	165
	PERS-L5	Terri Lee Drum Major	16"		165	
	PERS-L6	Terri Lee, soft, stuffed, sticky plastic	16"		165	
	PERS-L7	Colored Jerri Lee, compo, c-1948	16"	75	115	185
1019	PERS-L8	Terri Lee, compo, c-1948	16"	75	115	185
	PERS-L9	Terri Lee, rubber compound	16"		165	
	PERS-L10	Tiny Jerri Lee, hp	10"	45	61	85
	PERS-L11	Jerri Lee, hp		70	110	165
1020	PERS-L12	Mary Jane, Terri Lee LAL, hp, Walker, unmkd, c-1953	16"	35	85	145
1021	PERS-L13	Terrl Lee, sv, (price for complete doll)	5"		85	
	PERS-L14	Harold Lloyd, Rag doll, litho cloth	11½"		85	

MTCD Page	Key	Nomenclature	Size	Low	Avg.	High
	PERS-L15	Harold Lloyd, cell, c-1934	3½"		15	
	PERS-M9	The Mamas and the Papás, vinyl, (Hasbro) c-1967:				
	M9a	Michelle Phillps	4"		5	
	M9b	John Phillips	4"		5	
	M9c	Denny Doherty	4"		5	
	M9d	Cass Elliot	4"		10	
	PERS-10	The Man from U.N.C.L.E., solid vinyl, (Gilbert) c-1965:				
	10a	Illya Kuryakin (David McCallum)	12"		25	
	10b	Napoleon Solo (Robert Vaughn)	12"		25	
1022	PERS-M11	Mickey Mantle, compo nodder	7"		35	
	PERS-M12	Charley McCarthy, unmkd, c-1938	13"	45	65	95
	PERS-M13a-b	Miss America, vinyl (Mattel), c-1966	11½"	10	18	25
	PERS-M14a-d	The Monkees Singing Group: Peter Tork, Mickey Dolenz, Davy Jones, Mike Nesmith, (Hasbro), c-1967	4½"		45 set	
1023	PERS-M15a-c	The Munsters, sv/hp, (Remco), c-1965			25 set	
	15a	Herman Munster	6½"		8	
	15b	Lily Munster	4¾"		8	
	15c	Grandpa Munster	4¾"		8	
	PERS-M16	Billy Munster, vinyl, (Ideal), c-1965	8¼"		15	
	PERS-M17	Myrtle, Talking Rag doll, (My Three Sons) (Mattel) c-1969	14"		10	
	PERS-M18	The Triplets, vinyl, (My Three Sons) (Remco) c-1968, (price for each doll)	9"	6	9	15
1024	PERS-N1	"Broadway" Joe Namath, solid vinyl, (Mego), c-1970	12"	12	15	25

MTCD Page	Key	Nomenclature	Size	Low	Price Avg.	High
	PERS-N2	Nash-on-Nasser, vinyl squeek toy, (Rosenel) c-1969	7″		5	
	PERS-N3	Lori Martin as Velvet Brown, (National Velvet) vinyl/hp, (Ideal), c-1961	38″	295	395	525
	PERS-N4a	Richard Nixon, rubber eraser, c-1968	2¾″		3	
	N4b	Spiro Agnew, rubber eraser, c-1968	2¾″		3	
	PERS-P5	Patti Partridge, (The Partridge Family) sv (Ideal) c-1971	16″		8	
1025	PERS-P6	Laurie Partridge of the Partridge Family, vinyl/ plastic	19″	15	35	65
	PERS-P7	Kathy-Jo, (Petticoat Junction) vinyl (Remco) c-1969	9″		8	
	PERS-Q1	Queen Elizabeth and Prince Phillip, hp, (Alexander) Unmkd (Price is for pair)	18″	595	750	900
1026	PERS-R2	Rickey Jr. stuffed vinyl/vinyl, (Amer. Char), c-1955	16″	18	39	75
	PERS-R3	Jackie Robinson, compo, c-1950	13″		150	
	PERS-R4	Sally Rand, Fan Dancer, plaster, c-1936	12″		35	
	PERS-R5	Basketball Player, brown compo	16″		30	
1027	PERS-R6a-b	Dale Evans Rogers, hp, unmkd (Alex)	14½″		NPA	
	PERS-S10	LuAnn Simms, hp walker, 1940-50	16″		40	
1028	PERS-S11	The Snow Baby, Marie Ahnighito Peary, 1913			*News Photo*	
	PERS-S12	The Snow Baby, Marie Ahnighito Peary, 1913			*News Photo*	
	PERS-S13	Snow Baby, bisq/pm (AM-1894 head)	12″		225	

MTCD Page	Key	Nomenclature	Size	Low	Price Avg.	High
1029	PERS-S14	Snow White, compo (Amer. Toy & Mfg.) c-1918			*Catalog Illus.*	
	PERS-S15	Carnival Shirley Temple, 1-pc plaster	12"		45	
	PERS-S16	Shirley Temple, compo	18"	85	210	550
	PERS-S17	Shirley Temple Baby, compo/cloth, (Ideal)	27"	650	850	925
1030	PERS-S18	Shirley Temple Soaps	5"	20	30	35
	PERS-S19	Canadian Shirley Temple (Reliable, 1939)		85	125	145
	PERS-S20	Shirley Temple, v/plastic (Ideal)	36"	600	1035	1500
	PERS-S21	Shirley Temple Comes Back, 1973			*News Photo*	
	PERS-S22	Re-issue Shirley Temple, vinyl, (Ideal), 1972	15"	40	92	180
1031	PERS-S23a	Re-issue Shirley Temple, vinyl, (Ideal), 1972	16¼"	25	36	72
	PERS-S23b	Re-issue Shirley Temple, vinyl, (Ideal), 1972	16½"	25	36	72
1032	PERS-T1	Tinker Bell, litho cloth, (Mattel), c-1968	19"	5	8	10
	PERS-T1-1	Tiny Tim, vinyl	4"	10	15	20
	PERS-T2	Topo Gigio, hand puppet, vinyl/cloth, c-1964	11½"	10	15	20
1033	PERS-T3	Topo Gigio, vinyl/cloth, c-1964	12"	15	20	25
	PERS-T4	Topo Gigio, Rag Doll, (Lamar Toy), c-1960	16½"	15	20	30
	PERS-T5	Twiggy, the English Model, vinyl, (Mattel), c-1966	11"	15	43	65
	PERS-U1	Political Head, compo, unmkd	4"		15	
1034	PERS-W3	Lawrence Welk's Champagne Lady, vinyl/hp, (Effanbee)	19"		85	
	PERS-W4	Mae West, plaster compo	13"		35	

	PERS-W5	Linda Williams (Angela Cartwright), vinyl/ plastic (Tops in Toys) c-1960	30″	35	65	95
	PERS-W6	Angela Cartwright with a 14″ Linda Williams doll			*Catalog Illus.*	
	PERS-W7	Jane Withers, compo (Alexander)	12½″	400	450	525
1035	PERS-W8	Jane Withers, CM, compo, unmkd	14″	125	200	265
	PERS-W9	Flip Wilson/ Geraldine Talking Rag Doll (Shindana), c-1970	16½″	4	8	20

PETRI & BLUHM

1037	PET-1a-b	American Babies, Two dolls from the 1915 line, (Petri & Bluhm)			85	

PLATED MOULDS, INC.

	PLA-1	Girl, sv, c-1961	19″		15	
	PLA-2	Baby, vinyl	13″		15	
	PLA-3	Baby, vinyl, c-1961	20″		18	
	PLA-4	Baby, sv/cloth, c-1961	20″		18	
	PLA-5	Baby, vinyl, c-1961	19½″		18	
	PLA-6	Girl, vinyl, c-1966	18½″		15	

POLISH

1039	POL-1	Polish Child, mask face/cloth	9″		15	

POLITZER TOY MFG.

	POL-2a-b	Two styles of the 1914 line, compo/ cloth, Soldier, sailor, baseball dolls			85	
	POL-3a-c	Three dolls from the 1914 line, compo/ cloth			65	

POOR

	POOR-1	Poor Pitiful Pearl LAL, compo/cloth	15″		55	

PROGRESSIVE TOY CO

	PRO-1	Our Little "Sweetness" Love Pirate, compo, c-1919		25	35	45

PULLAN DOLL CO., CANADA

	PULL-1a	Boy, sv/hp			20	
	1b	Girl, sv/hp			20	
	PULL-2	Cliquot Club Eskimo, compo	14″	30	65	115

PUPPETS AND MARIONETTES

1041	PUPP-8	Batman, plastic, (Hazelle, Inc.), c-1967-68	16″	15	25	35
		Robin, plastic, (Hazelle Inc), c-1967-68	14½″	15	25	35
	PUPP-8-1	Pillow Baby (Hand Puppet) compo/cloth, c-1930		25	35	65
	PUPP-8-2	Pillow Baby (Hand Puppet) compo/cell, c-1925		35	65	85
	PUPP-9	Boy, compo, (Sarg/Alexander), c-1938	11″	65	100	125
	PUPP-10	Dopey, compo/wood (Alexander)	9″		65	
	PUPP-11a	Hansel, wood	13″		65	
	11b	Gretel, wood	13″		65	
	PUPP-12	Character, compo/wood (F&B)	12″		45	
	PUPP-12a	Champy the Lion, vinyl/felt	4″		5	
	12b	Mr. Fox, vinyl/felt	3½″		5	
	PUPP-13	The Munsters, vinyl/cloth, c-1965:				
	13a	Grandpa			5	
	13b	Lily Munster			5	
	13c	Herman Munster			5	
	PUPP-14	Pelham Puppet, c-1952			*Catalog Illus.*	

Q

1042	Q-1a-b	Two dolls from 1918 line, Quaker-Doll Co.			*Catalog Illus.*	

R

RALEIGH DOLLS, THE

Page	Key	Nomenclature	Size	Low	Avg.	High
1043-50	RAL-1	Jessie McCutcheon Raleigh and Dolls, c-1917			*Portrait*	
	RAL-1a	Detail of RAL-1			*Portrait*	
	RAL-2	Jessie McCutcheon Raleigh, 1919			*Portrait*	
	RAL-2a	Detail of RAL-2			*Portrait*	
	RAL-3a	#F7470, Dearie, Wgd	11½″		250	
	3b	#7472, Dearie, Wgd	18½″		425	
	3c	#F7471, Dearie, Wgd	16½″		350	
	RAL-4	#F7478, Kiddie Kar Kiddie, Wgd	18½″		425	
	RAL-5	#F7481, Debutante, Wgd	18½″		425	
	RAL-6	#F7417, Curly MoHr Wgd Toddler	18½″		425	
	RAL-7	#F7431, Painted Hair Baby	18½″		425	
	RAL-8	#F7405, Bobbed-Hair Wgd Baby	18″		425	
	RAL-9	#F7452, Miss Traveler, Toddler, Wgd	18½″		425	
	RAL-10	#F7477, Summer Girl, Toddler, Wgd	13½″		285	
	RAL-11	#7436, Mother's Darling Baby, PtdHr	18″		425	
	RAL-12	#F7547, Bye Bye Baby, PtdHr	18″		425	
	RAL-13	#7410, PtdHr Toddler	13½″		285	
	RAL-14	#F7412, PtdHr Toddler, Barette	11½″		250	
		F7413, PtdHr Toddler, Barette	10½″		235	
		#F7414, PtdHr Toddler, Barette	18½″		425	
	RAL-15	#F7411, PtdHr Toddler, Barette	18½″		425	
	RAL-16	#F7400, PtdHr Baby	10½″		235	
		#7401, PtdHr Baby	12½″		265	
	RAL-17	#F7403, Bobbed MoHr Wg Baby	10½″		235	
		#F7404, Bobbed MoHr Wg Baby	12½″		265	

MTCD Page	Key	Nomenclature	Size	Low	Price Avg.	High
RAL-18a		#F7425, Baby Stuart, PtdHr	11½"		250	
	18b	#F7426, Baby Stuart, PtdHr	13½"		285	
RAL-19a		#F7418, Baby Petite, PtdHr	10½"		235	
	19b	#F7419, Baby Petite, PtdHr	12½"		265	
RAL-20		#F7408, Baby, 3-pc Worsted suit	18½"		425	
RAL-21		#F7430, Bed Time Baby, PtdHr	12½"		265	
RAL-22		#F7420, Baby Petite, PtdHr	18"		425	
RAL-23		#F7408, Evelyn, Toddler	11½"		250	
		#F7409, Evelyn, Toddler	13½"		285	
RAL-24		#F7473, Little Playmate, Wgd	13½"		285	
RAL-25		#F7474, Johnny Jump-Up, Wgd	13½"		285	
RAL-26a		#F7415, Curly MoHr Wg Toddler	11½"		250	
RAL-26b		#F7416, Curly MoHr Wg Toddler	13½"		285	
RAL-27a		#F7406, Baby, 2-pc Knit Suit	11½"		250	
RAL-27b		#F7407, Baby, 2-pc Knit Suit	13½"		285	
RAL-28		#F7463, Honey Bunch, Wgd	11½"		250	
RAL-29		#F7460, Sonnie, PtdHr	13½"		285	
RAL-30a		#F7451, Rosemary, PtdHr	11½"		250	
	30b	#F7452, Rosemary, PtdHr	13½"		285	
RAL-31		#F7455, My Favorite, PtdHr	11½"		250	
RAL-32		#F7454, Marjorie, PtdHr	11½"		250	
RAL-33a		#F7475, Bobbie Burns Lassie	10½"		235	
	33b	#F7476, Bobbie Burns Lassie	18½"		425	
RAL-34		#F7457, Miss Sunshine, PtdHr, Barette	13½"		285	
RAL-35		#F7462, Kinder-garten Girlie, Wgd	11½"		250	

MTCD Page	Key	Nomenclature	Size	Low	Price Avg.	High
	RAL-36	#F7459, Winter Girl, PtdHr	13½″		285	
	RAL-37	#F7466, Curly Locks, Wgd	11½″		250	
		#F7477, Curly Locks, Wgd	13½″		285	
	RAL-38	#F7429, Little Brother, PtdHr, Toddler	13½″		285	
	RAL-39	#F7402, Baby, PtdHr	18″		425	
	RAL-40	#F7427, School Girl, PtdHr	11½″		250	
	RAL-41	#F7456, Dorothy, Toddler, PtdHr	11½″		250	
	RAL-42a	#F7464, Betty Bonnet, Toddler, Wgd	11½″		250	
	42b	#F7465, Betty Bonnet, Toddler, Wgd	13½″		285	
	RAL-43	#F7428, Baby Sister, Toddler, Wgd	11½″		250	
	RAL-44	#F7453, Jane, PtdHr	11½″		250	
	RAL-45	#F7435, Mother's Darling Baby, PtdHr	12½″		265	
	RAL-46	#F7483, Polly, Toddler, Wgd	18½″		425	
	RAL-47	#F7479, Little Princess, Toddler, Wgd	18½″		425	
	RAL-48	#F7480, Vacation Girl, Wgd	18½″		425	
	RAL-49	#F7461, Nancy C, Baby, PtdHr	11½″		250	
		#F7458, Nancy C, Baby, PtdHr	13½″		285	
	RAL-50	The Construction of the Raleigh Doll, c-1918			*Catalog Illus.*	
	RAL-50-1	Peeps, The Fairy Doll, c-1918	12″		*Catalog Illus.*	
	RAL-51	Tiny Tot, c-1919	18″		*Catalog Illus.*	
	R.A.					
1050	RA-1	R.A. Girl, bisq/pm (Germany)	13″	85	171	250
	RAVON					
	RAV-1	Raving Beauty, hp (RAVON)	18½″		25	

RAYCO

	RAY-1	"Barbie of Norway" (RAYCO)	12"		25	

REGAL DOLL MFG. CO. NEW YORK

Page	Key	Nomenclature	Size	Low	Avg.	High
	REG-1a	Boy, compo, c-1919	13½"	25	35	45
	1b	Girl, compo, c-1919	13½"	25	35	45
1051	REG-2	Hug Me, compo/ cloth (Kiddie Pal Dolly), c-1925	25"	55	70	95
	REG-3	Kiddie Pal, Character Baby, compo/cloth	19"	70	95	135
	REG-4	Kiddie Pal Dollies, compo/cloth, c-1928:				
	4a	#1F5324, Sleeping Eyes	17"		55	
	4b	#1F5310, Compo Legs	20"		85	
	4c	#1F5361, Sleeping Eyes	18"		65	
	4d	#1F5367, Kiddy Pal	20"		85	
	REG-5	Kiddie Pal Dollies, compo/cloth, c-1928:				
	5a	#1F5337, MoHr Wg	19"		85	
	5b	#1F5340, Crying Voice	19"		85	
	5c	#1F5122, Sleeping Eyes	26"		95	
	5d	#1F5120, Sleeping Eyes	20"		90	
	REG-6	Kiddie Pal Doll, compo/cloth, c-1928	26"		95	

REGAL TOY CO. LTD., CANADA

Page	Key	Nomenclature	Size	Low	Avg.	High
1053	REG-7	Eskimo Boy, vinyl, c-1963	11½"		65	
	REG-8	Baby Twinkle, vinyl	9"		15	
	REG-9	Eskimo, plastic/vinyl	10"		45	
	REG-10	Indian Girl, vinyl	12"		25	
1054	REG-11a	Sexed Baby Boy, vinyl, c-1967	16"		45	
	11b	Sexed Baby Boy, vinyl, c-1967	12"		25	
	11c	Sexed Baby Girl, vinyl, c-1967	16"		45	
	REG-12	Girl, vinyl, c-1971	18"		15	

MTCD Page	Key	Nomenclature	Size	Low	Avg.	High
	REG-13a	Girl, vinyl, c-1960	15″		5	
	13b	Girl, vinyl, c-1960	17″		10	
	REG-14	Michelle, vinyl, c-1974	14½″		35	
	REISMAN CO					
1055	REI-1	Komikal Musikal Klown, c-1915	18″		85	
	RELIABLE DOLLS					
	REL-1	Indian Girl, compo, c-1920	12½″		45	
	REL-2	Girl, compo	18″		35	
	REL-3	Mounty, compo, c-1920	16″		65	
	REL-4	Toddler, compo, c-1930	14″		32	
1056	REL-5	Dolls from the 1939 line:				
	5a	Wetums			NPA	
	5b	Baby Bunting			NPA	
	5c	Peggy			NPA	
	REL-6	Nurse, compo/cloth, c-1940	18″		45	
	REL-7a	Wetums, compo	12″		20	
	7b	Baby, compo	12″		20	
	REL-8	Wetums Baby, compo, c-1940	21″		35	
1057	REL-9	Toddler, hp, c-1950	10″		15	
	10b	Baby, plastic	20″		15	
	REL-11a	Baby, vinyl	18″		15	
	11b	Baby, vinyl	16″		12	
1058	REL-12a	Baby, vinyl/cloth	21″		15	
	12b	Baby, vinyl	16″		12	
	REL-13	Mitzi, dark vinyl, c-1974	17½″		20	
	REMCO INDUSTRIES INC.					
1059	REM-5	The Frogman, U. S. Navy Commando, hi-impact plastic, c-1961	30″		25	
	REM-6a	Betty in the Beauty Parlor, hp	10½″		15	
	6b	Johnny in the Barber Shop, hp	10½″		15	
	REM-7	Snugglebun, plastic/ vinyl, c-1965	16″	6	13	20
	REM-8	Lil Soldier Joe, vinyl/ plastic, c-1965	5″		10	

MTCD Page	Key	Nomenclature	Size	Low	Price Avg.	High
1060	REM-9a	Cowboy Pete, vinyl, c-1965			10	
	9b	Black Bart, vinyl, c-1965			10	
	9c	Fatso, vinyl, c-1965			10	
	REM-10	Li'l Winking Herby Hippy, vinyl, c-1967	16″	15	25	35
	REM-11	Baby Chatterbox, hp/vinyl, c-1967	14″	10	13	15
	REM-12-a-b	Mr. & Mrs. Mouse & House, vinyl, 1966			15 set	
1061	REM-13	Baby Glad'N'Sad, vinyl/hp, c-1966	15″		15	
	REM-14	Bottle Babies, vinyl, c-1967	3¾″		5 ea	
1062	REM-15	Tippy Tumbles, vinyl, c-1968	16″	8	11	15
	REM-16	Tumbling Tomboy, vinyl/hp, c-1969	17″	8	11	15
1063	REM-17	Jumpsy, vinyl/hp, c-1970		10	14	18
	REM-18	Tiny Tumbles, vinyl/hp, c-1970	8″		10	
	REM-19	Tiny Tumbling Clown, white plastic, c-1970	8″		10	
	REM-20	Katrina, Spongee Plastic Body, c-1967	13″		12	

Remco Brown-Eyed Series:

MTCD Page	Key	Nomenclature	Size	Low	Price Avg.	High
1065		Jumpsy, Brown Eyes		18	19	25
		Baby Whistle, Brown Eyes		16	20	25
		Baby Laugh-A-Lot, Brown Eyes		16	20	25
		Tiny Tumbles, Brown Eyes		16	20	25
		Kewpie, Brown Eyes	8″	15	27	35
		Polly Puff, Brown Eyes			29	
		Tippy Tumbles, Brown Eyes		15	18	25
	REM-21	Brown-Eye Winking Winny, c-1968	15″	15	24	35
	REM-22	Brown-Eye Baby Grow-A-Tooth, c-1968	15″	18	26	35

MTCD Page	Key	Nomenclature	Size	Low	Price Avg.	High
	REM-23a	Brown-Eye Tina, vinyl/hp, c-1969	15″	16	25	35
	23b	Brown-Eye Billy, vinyl/hp, c-1969	16″	17	26	35
	REM-24	Brown-Eye Tumbling Tomboy, c-1969	17″	20	24	30
	REM-25	Brown-Eye Twins, vinyl, c-1969, (Price for each doll)	9″	9	14	18
	REM-26	Brown-Eye Baby Know-It All, c-1969	17″	29	33	45
	REM-27	Brown-Eye Growing Sally, c-1969	6¼″		8	
	REM-28	Brown-Eye Bunny Baby, c-1969	18″	18	27	35
	REM-29	Baby Know-It-All, vinyl/hp	17″		25	
1066	REM-30	Chew-Chew Baby, hp/vinyl, c-1968	14″		15	
	REM-31	Bunny Baby, vinyl/ hp, c-1969	17″		25	
	REM-32	Ragmop, Rag Doll, c-1969	6″		4	
			15″		6	
			25″		10	
1067	REM-33	Baby Walk'N'Run, vinyl/plastic, c-1969	15″		12	
	REM-34	Baby Sister Grow-A-Tooth, vinyl/ plastic, c-1969	14½″		15	
	REM-35	Baby Grow-A-Tooth, hp/vinyl, c-1968	15″	18	21	25
	REM-36a-g	Heidi and Friends, vinyl, c-1967 a–Heidi b–Winking Heidi c–Hildy d–Herby e–Jan f–Pip g–Spunky	4½-5½″	3	5	8
1069	REM-37	Kewpies, vinyl, c-1968	8″		25	
			14″		45	
	REM-38	Baby Whistle, vinyl/ cloth, c-1970	15″	15	18	25
	REM-39	Baby Laugh-A-Lot, vinyl/plush, c-1970	16″	15	18	25

MTCD Page	Key	Nomenclature	Size	Low	Avg.	High
1070	REM-40	Baby Goldilocks, hp/vinyl, c-1970	12"		15	
	REM-41	Finger Dings, vinyl, c-1970:	6"		3 ea	
		Sally Ice Skater				
		Millie Mod				
		Betty Ballerina				
		Adventure Boy				
	REM-42	Finger Ding Flower Kids, vinyl, c-1971:				
	42a	Li'l Buttercup	6"		3	
	42b	Li'l Daisy	6"		3	
	42c	Betty Ballerina	6"		3	
	42d	Li'l Rose	6"		3	
	REM-43	Li'l Polly Puff, vinyl/cloth, c-1970	12"		10	
	REM-44	Hug-A-Bug, plastic, c-1972	3⅞"		3	
1071	REM-45	Dune Buggy Baby, plastic/vinyl, c-1972	12"	6	10	15
	REM-46	Sweet April, vinyl/hp, c-1971	5"	10	15	25
	REM-47	Mimi, vinyl/hp, c-1973, Black	19"	20	30	55
		White	19"	17	27	50
	REMPEL MFG. CO.					
1072	REMP-1	Indian, 1-pc rubber	6½"		18	
	REVALO					
	REV-1	Bisque-head Girl, (Gebruder- Ohlhaver)	17"	300	375	450
	RHEINISCHE GUMMI UND CELLULOID FABRIK					
	RHE-1	Turtlemark Baby, Sexed Girl, vinyl	14"		75	
	RHE-2	Turtlemark Baby, Sexed Girl, vinyl	15"		75	
	RHE-3	Turtlemark Baby, Sexed Boy, vinyl	16"		75	
	RIKKER BROS.					
1073	RIK-1	Made-in-Holland Dolls, bisq/compo, asstd			*Catalog Illus.*	
	RITE-LEE					
	RITE-1	Miss Lynne, soft brown vinyl	19"	35	72	105

MTCD Page	Key	Nomenclature	Size	Low	Avg.	High
	RODDY					
	ROD-1	Saucy Walker Type, hp	16″	30	35	45
1074	ROD-2a-c	Three examples of 1952 line		30	35	45
	ROSEBUD					
	ROSE-1	Rosebud, hp/vinyl	21″	18	26	35
	ROSE-2	Baby, hp, c-1950	6″		8	
	ROSE-3	Boy, hp	10″		12	
	ROTH					
	ROTH-1	Beauty Doll, compo/cloth, c-1915	25″		95	
	ROVEN					
1075	ROV-1	Lucky Lisa, vinyl/ hp, c-1971	22″		45	
	ROYAL DOLL CO.					
	ROY-1	Boy, compo/cloth, c-1918	23½″		65	
	ROY-2	Boy, vinyl, c-1964	12″	12	18	25
1076	ROY-3	Lady, brown vinyl, c-1950	19½″		45	
	ROY-4	Baby, vinyl/plastic, c-1961	14½″		45	
	ROY-5	Emma Sue, brown hp walker, c-1950	18″		85	
1077	ROY-6	Lady, plastic/vinyl, c-1960	24″		65	
	ROY-7	Girl, hp/vinyl, twist waist c-1960	21½″		85	
	ROY-8-9	Lonely Lisa, vinyl/ wired, bendable body/cloth, c-1964	21″	22	46	85
	RUBBER DOLLS					
1078	RUB-7	The Crying Baby, (Baumann Rubber Co), c-1903			*Catalog Illus.*	
	RUB-8a-b	Miss Sunshine and Billy Boy (Faultless Rubber Co), c-1918 Also: Sweetie Nurse Fairy Boy Scout Sailor Boy			15 ea	

MTCD Page	Key	Nomenclature	Size	Price Low	Avg.	High
	RUB-9	Miss Sunshine, rubber/cloth, unmkd, c-1918	13½"		65	
	RUB-10	Novelty Baby, c-1925	5"		35	
1079	RUB-11	Bent-Limb Baby, c-1930	14"	35		
	RUB-12	Bent-Limb Baby	17"	45		
	RUB-13	Baby Darling, 1-pc, c-1931-32	8"	*Catalog Illus.*		
	RUB-13-1	Sonny, c-1940	9½"		25	
1081	RUB-14	Jill, 1-pc (Sun Rubber Co), c-1934	5"		6	
	RUB-15	Catalog cuts from 1930-1935 Butler Bros. catalogs		3	6	10
	RUB-16	Assorted Rubber Dolls and Toys from 1936 Stack Mfg. Co.	13½-16"	5	8	15
	RUB-17	Tom Mix, Cowboy Movie Star, 1936	10"		25	
	RUB-18	Popeye, c-1936	13"		35	
	RUB-19	Hobo, (Rempel), c-1940	7"		18	
	RUB-19-1	Zaza Dolls, inflatable, c-1936	12"		NPA	
1082	RUB-20	Baldy, 1-pc (Seiberling) c-1933	7½"		6	
	RUB-21	Baldy, Ptd swimsuit (Seiberling)	7"		8	
	RUB-22	Steha Girl (Germany)	10"		20	
1083	RUB-23	Baby, Magic Skin, c-1948, unmkd	8½"		15	
	RUB-23-1	Patty Pigtails, plastic/rubber, (Eastern Rubber)	9"		12	
	RUB-24ab	Boy and Girl, Jtd Shoulder, c-1940	10"		35 pr	
	RUB-25	Seated Bathtub Baby, c-1948, unmkd	5"		12	
	RUB-26a-c	Three babies, c-1948, unmkd	5-6"		5 ea	
	RUB-27	Magic Skin Baby, c-1948, unmkd	9½"		25	
	RUB-28	Davy Crockett-type Boy, molded hat/ clo, (Rempel) c-1950	8"		15	
1084	RUB-29	Steha Girl	15½"		50	

MTCD Page	Key	Nomenclature	Size	Low	Avg.	High
	RUB-30	Dree-Me-Dee (Sun Rubber)	10"		20	
	RUB-31	Bonnie Bear (Sun Rubber) c-1950	5½"		20	
		Wiggy Wags, (Sun Rubber) c-1950	5½"		20	
	RUB-32	Happy Kappy, 1-pc (Sun Rubber)	7"		20	
	RUB-33	Rompy, (Sun Rubber)	7"		20	
	RUB-34	Boy, (Sun Rubber)	8½"		20	
1085	RUB-35	Betty Bows, (Sun Rubber) c-1953	11"	13	20	25

RUSHTON

	RUSH-1	Hobo, vinyl/cloth	19½"		35	

S

	SD-1	SD Smiling Baby, vinyl/cloth	13"		25	
	SAL-1	Sally Lou (Sally Lou Dolls), c-1940	19½"		45	

SAMSTAG & HILDER BROS.

1086	SAM-1ab	Two dolls from the 1903 line			*Catalog Illus.*	
	SAM-2	Merry Widow, bisq/ BJ compo, (E.U. Steiner) c-1908			*Catalog Illus.*	
	SAM-3	The Majestic Doll (E.U. Steiner), c-1908			*Catalog Illus.*	
	SAM-4	Peter Pan Acrobats, compo/cloth (Steiner, Germany) c-1908:				
	4a	Captain Hook, Acrobat			NPA	
	4b	Peter Pan, Acrobat			NPA	
	4c	Peter Pan, Acrobat			NPA	
	SAM-5a-c	Hug-Me Kiddies, Four sizes, compo/ felt, c-1912		275	475	650
1088	SAM-6	The One Dollar Doll, (Germany), c-1912			NPA	
	SAM-7ab	Faddy Fads, compo/ cloth, c-1914			NPA	
	SAM-8	Blow 'Em Up Willie (Balloon Kids), three sizes, c-1914			NPA	

MTCD Page	Key	Nomenclature	Size	Price Low	Avg.	High
	SAM-9	Whistling Jim, c-1914	13½″	600	650	750
	SAM-10	The Mama Doll, c-1914	9″	Catalog Illus.		
1089	SAM-11	Babs, bisq, six sizes, (Germany), c-1914	3″-10″	100	150	250
	SAM-12	Fairy Zoo-Dolls, The Two-in-One Dollies, c-1910:				
	12a	Bears, elephants, lions, donkeys, cats, dogs	10″		225	
			12″		245	
			14″		265	
			16″		295	
			18″		325	
	12b	Peacocks, pheasants, owls, roosters, frogs, blackbirds, parrots	10″		225	
			14″		245	

SASHA DOLLS

MTCD Page	Key	Nomenclature	Size	Price Low	Avg.	High
1090	SASH-1a	Sasha, rv, (England)	16″	15	28	35
	1b	Gregor, rv, (England)	16″	15	28	35
	1c	White Baby, (England)	12″	20	25	29
	SASH-2a	Cora, very dark rv, (England)	16″		55	
	2b	Caleb, very dark rv, (England)	16″		55	
	2c	Black Baby, very dark rv, (England)	12″		55	

SAYCO

MTCD Page	Key	Nomenclature	Size	Price Low	Avg.	High
1091	SAY-1	Toughie, vinyl, c-1949	21″		18	
	SAY-2	Baby Toughie, vinyl, c-1949	20″		15	
	SAY-3	Baby Beth, stuffed vinyl, c-1962	18″		18	
	SAY-4	Girl, vinyl/plastic, c-1959	36″	25	43	50

SCHLEICH

MTCD Page	Key	Nomenclature	Size	Price Low	Avg.	High
1092	SCH-1	Bendable figure, solid vinyl, (Germany)			15	

MTCD Page	Key	Nomenclature	Size	Low	Avg.	High
	SCHMIDT					
	SCH-2	BSW Toddler, (Bruno Schmidt, Germany)	15"	185	426	525
	SCH-3	FS&C #1295 Toddler (Germany)	14"		425	
	SCHOEN					
	SCH-4a	Hansel, compo/cloth, (Germany), c-1913			165	
	4b	Gretel, compo/cloth, (Germany), c-1913			165	
	SCH-5	Baby, compo, c-1917			95	
	SCHONEAU & HOFFMEISTER					
1093	SCH-6	#1909 Bisque-head Girl	17"	175	325	375
	SCH-7	Black Hanna, bisq head	6¾"	150	217	325
	SCH-8	Painted Bisque-head Girl	18"	175	325	395
	SCH-9	Painted Bisque-head Girl	24"	325	465	675
	SCH-10	#1909 Bisque-head Girl	24"	325	465	675
	SCHOENHUT, A., CO.					
1095	SCH-12a	Albert Schoenhut and Sons			*Portrait*	
	12b	Albert Schoenhut			*Portrait*	
	SCH-13a	Max, wood, c-1907	7½"		225	
	13b	Moritz, wood, c-1907	7½"		225	
	SCH-14	Rol'y Dolly, Rol'y Poly Toys, c-1908-1909	Lg		225	
			Sm		90	
1096	SCH-15	Carved-Hair Boy			650	
	SCH-16	Walkable Doll, wood, c-1919	11"	395	416	475
			14"		450	
			17"	300	356	475
	SCH-17	Walker, MoHr Wg	11"	300	389	495
	SCH-18	The "Dolly Face" Doll, HH Wg	19"	300	349	425
	SCH-19	Rare Composition, MP Hr	12½"		350	
	SHUCO					
1097	SCH-20	Wind-up Clown, beats drum, (Germany)	4½"		15	

	SEAMLESS TOY					
	SEA-1	Bent-limb Baby, compo, c-1918			85	
	SEA-2	Ball-jointed Girl, (Seamless Toy Corp), c-1919			165	
	SEARS ROEBUCK					
1098	SEA-3	Little Cherub, BJ compo, c-1910	19″		165	
	SELIGMAN & BRAUN					
	SEL-1a-e	Five Character Dolls of the 1911 line: School Girl School Boy Bridget Mike Indian		95	165	225
	S.F.B.J.					
	SFBJ-1	Bent-Limb Baby, #251, compo	13″	450	541	850
1099	SFBJ-2	#236 Toddler Girl, bisq/BJ compo	27″	1000	1611	2245
	SHACKMAN					
	SHA-1	Beatnik, wood/ rubber ball head	7″		8	
	SHINDANA					
	SHI-1a-d	Lil Souls, rag dolls, set of four sizes 6″, 7″, 10″			25 set	
	SHI-2	Baby Zuri, vinyl, c-1972	12″	15	23	25
	SIMON & HALBIG					
1100	S&H-6	#1078 Bisque-head (Germany)	14″	275	383	450
	S&H-7	Bisque-head/BJ- body Girl	25″	400	565	850
	SPANISH DOLLS					
	SPA-1	Toyse Sexed Boy, vinyl	11″		35	
	SPA-2a	Munecas de Alba (Pirula) Boy, vinyl	10″		40	
	2b	Munecas de Alba (Pirula) Girl, vinyl	10″		40	

MTCD Page	Key	Nomenclature	Size	Low	Price Avg.	High

STANDARD DOLL CO.

	Key	Nomenclature	Size	Low	Avg.	High
	STAN-1	Six dolls from the 1917 line:				
	1a	Scotch Highlander			85	
	1b	Uncle Sam			95	
	1c	Miss America			95	
	1d	French Zouave			95	
	1e	Cadet			85	
	1f	Baby			75	

STANDARD SPECIALTY CO.

	Key	Nomenclature	Size	Low	Avg.	High
1102	STAN-3	Flicks Kids, three sizes, compo/cloth, c-1915			85 ea	

STAR TOY & NOVELTY CO.

	Key	Nomenclature	Size	Low	Avg.	High
	STAR-1	Baseball Boy, compo/cloth, c-1914			85	
		Policeman, compo/ cloth, c-1914			85	
		Jockey, compo/ cloth, c-1914			85	
		Infant, compo/cloth, c-1914			75	
	STAR-2	Baby, twelve styles, compo/cloth, c-1916			75	
	STAR-3	Yama Kid, compo/ cloth, c-1915	19"		85	
			25"		95	
			30"		100	

STEIFF TOYS & DOLLS

	Key	Nomenclature	Size	Low	Avg.	High
		General Price Guide — Dolls:				
			To 9"	125	165	225
			10-12"	175	200	325
			13-15"	200	250	395
			15-18"	250	350	525
			19" & Larger	350	450	725
	STE-1	Fraulein Margarete Steiff, 1909			*Portrait*	
	STE-2	Brownie Policeman and the Kentucky Donkey, wool/silk/ plush/felt, c-1905			*Catalog Illus.*	
	STE-3	Five dolls from the 1909 line:				
	3a	Hubertus		200	250	300
	3b	Alida (large)		200	250	300

187

MTCD Page	Key	Nomenclature	Size	Low	Price Avg.	High
	3c	Olaf		200	250	300
	3d	Alida (small)		175	225	275
	3e	Anthony		200	250	300
1104	STE-4	Private Sharkey, U.S. Soldier, felt clothes, c-1909		450	650	795
		Sargent Kelly, U.S. Soldier, felt clothes, c-1909		450	650	795
	STE-5	Billy, felt, c-1909			165	
	STE-6	Group of Character Dolls, c-1910		*Catalog Illus.*		
	STE-7	Steiff Characters, c-1912		*Catalog Illus.*		
	STE-7a	Detail of STE-7, c-1912		*Catalog Illus.*		
1105	STE-8a	Hedgehogs, synthetic prickly hair, felt/ vinyl, pair,				

(Prices given are for old models, not the present production):

MTCD Page	Key	Nomenclature	Size	Low	Price Avg.	High
		Macki and Mucki, 12 cm	4¾″	45	65	95
		Mecki and Micki 17cm	6¾″	65	85	125
		28 cm	11″	85	95	165
		50 cm	19¾″	125	165	225
	STE-9	Gucki the Dwarf, rubber/cloth, animal fur side burns & beard	12″	175	200	325

STEINER DOLLS

MTCD Page	Key	Nomenclature	Size	Low	Price Avg.	High
1106	STE-10	Edmund Ulrich Steiner, 1916		*Portrait*		
	STE-11	Bisque-head Girl (Herm Steiner)	12″	150	167	195
	STE-12	Herm Steiner Girl, bisq/BJ body	20½″	165	257	375
	STE-13	Herm Steiner Bent-limb Baby	12″	225	281	395

STEINFELD BROS.

MTCD Page	Key	Nomenclature	Size	Low	Price Avg.	High
1107	STE-14a-d	Racketty-Packetty Kiddies, compo/ cloth, c-1913	18″	95	165	225

STEINHARDT, A. & BRO.

MTCD Page	Key	Nomenclature	Size	Low	Price Avg.	High
	STE-15	Mr. Twee Deedle, two sizes, felt, c-1911		125	175	235

MTCD Page	Key	Nomenclature	Size	Low	Avg.	High
	STE-16	Neverbreak Character Dolls, compo/cloth, c-1910:				
	16a	Smiling Sue, white, (Mulatto is Honey Boy)		65	95	135
	16b	Teddy, Jr., velvet/ cloth/satin		65	95	135
1108	STE-17	Four Character Dolls of 1911 line, compo/cloth:				
	17a	Dutch-She			85	
	17b	Marceline, The Hippodrome Clown			95	
	17c	Dutch-He			85	
	17d	Pierrot, The Clown Doll			75	

STERLING DOLL INC.

MTCD Page	Key	Nomenclature	Size	Low	Avg.	High
	STE-18	Football Player, compo/cloth	29"		45	

STROBEL & WILKEN CO.

MTCD Page	Key	Nomenclature	Size	Low	Avg.	High
1109	STRO-1	Nationality Dolls from the 1905 line, compo/cloth			*Catalog Illus.*	
	STRO-2a-c	The Smiling Jubilee Babies, c-1909			*Catalog Illus.*	
	STRO-3	Bent-limb Baby, c-1909		95	165	235
	STRO-4ab	Diabolo Boy and Girl, c-1908			*Catalog Illus.*	
1110	STRO-5	Susie's Sister (American Art Dolls line), Ptd Fea, c-1915	17"		NPA	
	STRO-6	Seven dolls from the 1916 "American Art Dolls" line:				
	6a	Faith			165	
	6b	Ulrich			165	
	6c	Liesel			165	
	6d	Jimmy			165	
	6e	Blanche			165	
	6f	Boy Scout			185	
	6g	Buddy			165	
1112	STRO-7	Brighto the Live Wire Kid, bisq, c-1914			225	

SUPER DOLL, INC.

	Key	Nomenclature	Size	Low	Avg.	High
	SUP-1	Girl, vinyl, c-1963	16½″		12	

SUPERIOR DOLL MFG. CO.

| | SUP-2 | Baby, compo | | | NPA | |

SUTTON, A.D. & SONS

| | SUT-1 | Novelty Girl, plastic (Hong Kong) | 11″ | | 12 | |

T

TAMMEN H.H. CO.

	Key	Nomenclature	Size	Low	Avg.	High
1113	TAM-1	Ramona, c-1916			NPA	
	TAM-2	Skookum Group, c-1916, (Price is for each doll)		35	58	85
	TAM-2b	Skookum Family Group, wool/felt/ cotton (Price is for set of three dolls)		45	85	125
		Chief, mask face	16½″			
		Sqaw, mask face	14″			
		Papoose, mask face	3″			

TIMPO TOYS LTD.

| | TIM-1a-d | From the 1941 line | | | *Catalog Illus.* | |
| | TIM-2a-j | Timpo Toys Rag dolls, mask faces, c-1943 | | | 35 ea | |

TIP TOP TOY CO.

	Key	Nomenclature	Size	Low	Avg.	High
1115	TIP-1a	Paul, compo/cloth, c-1912	15½″	275	475	650
	1b	Virginia, compo/ cloth, c-1912	15½″	275	475	650
	TIP-2	Little Boy Blue, BL Baby, c-1913			95	
	TIP-3a	Gertie, compo/cloth, c-1913		60	75	95
	3b	Bertie, compo/cloth, c-1913		60	75	95
	TIP-4	Cy from Siwash, compo/cloth, c-1913		60	75	95
	TIP-5	"Kewpies are now made in America," c-1917	13″		*Catalog Illus.*	
	TIP-6	Composition Shoulder-head Girl, c-1918			NPA	

MTCD Page	Key	Nomenclature	Size	Low	Price Avg.	High
	TOOTSE					
1117	TOO-1	Tootse, compo toddler	14″		*Catalog Illus.*	
	TOO-2	Tootse, compo	14″		95	
	TREGO					
	TRE-1	The Trego Doll, (AM #390), BJ body	21″ 25″	175 275	241 354	325 425
	TRION TOY CO.					
	TRI-1	Cheery, c-1916			165	
	TRI-2	Little Rascal, compo/ cloth, c-1915			135	
	TRI-3	Ma Bell Marianne, compo, c-1919			135	
	TRI-4	"Sanitrion" Bath Dolls, 2 sizes, compo/loofah, c-1918			45 ea	

U

	UNEEDA DOLL CO.					
	UNEE-13	Bent-limb Baby, compo, c-1918	25″	65	83	95
1118	UNEE-14	Sticky vinyl Girl, 1-pc body, molded hair, 1948-1952	21″	18	29	45
	UNEE-15	Sticky vinyl Boy, molded curls, 1948-1952	18″	18	29	45
	UNEE-16	Bent-limb Baby, plastic, c-1955	10½″		15	
1119	UNEE-17	Purty, rv/sv, c-1955	14″	20	26	35
	UNEE-18	Walking Doll, sv, walker-type plastic body, c-1952	23″	12	18	25
	UNEE-19	Molded-hair Girl, c-1959	14″	15	17	20
	UNEE-20	Debbie, vinyl, c-1960	11″	12	18	21
	UNEE-21	Girl, hp/vinyl, c-1960	15″		15	
1120	UNEE-22	Baby Dollikins, sv/hp, c-1960	21″	20	33	55
	UNEE-23	Baby Dollikin, sv/hp, c-1960	21″	20	33	55
	UNEE-24	Dollikin, plastic, c-1960	11″	4	8	15
	UNEE-25	Colored Walker, sv/hp, c-1960	35″		35	

MTCD Page	Key	Nomenclature	Size	Low	Price Avg.	High
1121	UNEE-26	Fairy Princess, PVC, c-1961	32″	14	40	55
	UNEE-27	Saranade Phonograph Doll, vinyl/hp, c-1962	21″	18	36	50
	UNEE-27a	Saranade	21″	18	36	50
1122	UNEE-28	Blabby, vinyl, c-1962	14″	10	16	25
	UNEE-29	Suzette, plastic, c-1962	12″	6	20	35
	UNEE-30a-b	Wishniks, vinyl, c-1960	8″	5	8	10
	UNEE-31	Wishnik, vinyl	7″	5	8	10
1123	UNEE-32	Baby Trix, foam, c-1965	19″	5	14	21
	UNEE-33	Weepsy Wiggles, vinyl/cloth c-1963	19″		45	
1124	UNEE-34	Child, sv/hp, c-1964	17″	10	16	25
	UNEE-35	Troll, vinyl, c-1965	3½″	9	11	15
	UNEE-36	Pee Wee, vinyl, c-1967	4″	4	10	15
	UNEE-37	Hee Wee, vinyl, c-1967	4″	4	10	15
	UNEE-38	PlumPees, vinyl, c-1967		4	11	15
1125	UNEE-39	Bareskin Baby, vinyl/hp, c-1968	12½″	8	15	25
	UNEE-40	Tummy-The Pudgy Pixie, vinyl, c-1973	9″	3	7	12
	UNEE-41ab	Tiny Sophisticates, vinyl/plastic, 1973	6″	3	5	10
1126	UNEE-42	Jennifer Fashion Doll, teen-type, vinyl body, c-1973	18″	5	14	20
	UNEE-43ab	Clover Fashion Doll, teen-type, vinyl/plastic body, c-1973	15″	5	11	18
	UNEE-44	Magic Meg with Hair That Grows, teen type, vinyl/plastic, c-1973	16″	6	13	20
1127	UNEE-45ab	Purty Toddler, three styles, vinyl/plastic, c-1973	11″	6	14	20
	UNEE-46ab	Minuette, vinyl/plastic, c-1973	8″	3	9	15

UNGER DOLL & TOY CO.

	UNG-1	Carnival Character, compo		10	26	35

UNMARKED DOLLS

Page	Key	Nomenclature	Size	Low	Avg.	High
	UNMKD-61	Girl, leather body, Ptd fea, c-1900	25"		495	
1128	UNMKD-62	Colored SL Baby, compo/pm	4¼"		35	
	UNMKD-62-1	Chubby Kid-type Child, compo	24½"	45	65	85
	UNMKD-63	Toddler Boy, compo	11¾"		125	
	UNMKD-64	Character Boy, compo/cloth, c-1910	16"		85	
1129	UNMKD-65	Character Boy, compo/cloth, c-1910	17"	65	80	95
	UNMKD-66	Boy, compo/cloth, c-1910	11"		65	
	UNMKD-67	Character Girl or Boy, compo/cloth, c-1910	13"		85	
	UNMKD-68	Character Boy, compo/cloth, c-1910	14½"		75	
	UNMKD-69	Character Boy, compo/cloth, c-1910	15"		95	
	UNMKD-70	Character Baby, compo/cloth, c-1918	22"		65	
	UNMKD-71	Character Boy, compo, c-1910	13"		125	
1131	UNMKD-72	Coquette-type Girl, compo/cloth, c-1910	9"	65	81	165
	UNMKD-73	Character Molded-hair Girl, compo/ cloth, c-1910	14"		95	
	UNMKD-74	Grumpy Boy, compo/cloth, c-1910	16"		145	
	UNMKD-75	Character Boy, compo/cloth, c-1910	11"		75	
	UNMKD-76	Head only, compo, PtdE, c-1910	7½"		NPA	
	UNMKD-77	Character Boy, compo/cloth, c-1910	21"		95	
	UNMKD-78	Character Laughing Baby, compo/ cloth, c-1918	24"		125	

MTCD Page	Key	Nomenclature	Size	Low	Price Avg.	High
	UNMKD-79	Laughing Girl, compo/cloth, c-1910	13½″		125	
1132	UNMKD-80	Buster Brown-Type Boy, compo/cloth, c-1910	31″		NPA	
	UNMKD-81	Girl, compo/cloth c-1910	18″		145	
	UNMKD-82	Girl, compo/cloth, c-1918	20″		145	
	UNMKD-83	Toddler, compo/cloth, c-1921	10″		95	
1133	UNMKD-84	Girl, compo/cloth, c-1918	17″		95	
	UNMKD-85	Girl, compo/cloth, c-1920	12″		165	
	UNMKD-86	Baby, compo, c-1921	17″		125	
	UNMKD-86a	Baby, compo, c-1921	17″		125	
	UNMKD-87	Girl, compo, c-1920	16½″		85	
	UNMKD-88	Boy, compo/cloth, c-1918	18½″		95	
1134	UNMKD-88-1	Girl, compo/cloth	17″		85	
	UNMKD-89	Mama-type Girl, compo/cloth, c-1920	18″		65	
	UNMKD-90	Girl, compo, c-1920	8″		65	
1135	UNMKD-91	Girl, compo/cloth, c-1920	15″		95	
	UNMKD-92	Girl, compo	10″		65	
	UNMKD-92a	Girl, compo	10″		65	
	UNMKD-93	Patsy-type, compo, c-1929	24″		145	
	UNMKD-94	Patsy-type, compo, c-1925	18″		125	
	UNMKD-95	Character Boy (Dr. Dafoe), compo, c-1938	14″	400	445	495
	UNMKD-96a	Girl, compo, c-1938	11″	35	56	75
	96b	Girl, compo, c-1938	14″	50	65	95
1137	UNMKD-97	Girl, compo/cloth, c-1930	22″	65	87	95
	UNMKD-98	Girl, compo/cloth, c-1930	17″	65	87	95
	UNMKD-99	Girl, compo/cloth, c-1930	15½″	45	74	85
	UNMKD-100	Child, compo/cloth, c-1930	19″	65	87	95
	UNMKD-101	Topsy Baby, compo/cloth, c-1920	16″	45	53	65
	UNMKD-102	Boy, c-1935	14½″	35	46	50
	UNMKD-103	Girl, compo, c-1936	18″	50	105	135
	UNMKD-104	Baby, compo, c-1930	12″	25	39	45

	UNMKD-105	Baby, compo/cloth, c-1929	17½″	45	63	75
	UNMKD-106	Chinese Mandarin, compo/cloth, c-1938	16½″		NPA	
	UNMKD-107	Girl, compo/cloth, c-1930	13″		45	
1138	UNMKD-108ab	Twins, compo/cloth, c-1925	21″	45	92	165
	UNMKD-109	Wide Awake-type, compo, 1910-1920	13″		125	
	UNMKD-110	Molded-hair Girl with braids, c-1920	14″		45	
	UNMKD-111	Girl, compo/cloth	24″	45	78	150
1139	UNMKD-112	Boy Baby, compo/ cloth, c-1925	21″		85	
	UNMKD-113	Girl, compo, c-1938	17″		85	
	UNMKD-114	Character Girl, SGE, watermelon smile	20″		95	
	UNMKD-115	Girl, compo, c-1920	14″		95	
1140	UNMKD-116	Girl, compo, c-1930	13″		65	
	UNMKD-117	Cowboy, compo/ cloth, 1938-1940	13″		45	
1141	UNMKD-118	Dutch Boy, c-1930	10½″		NPA	
	UNMKD-119	Girl, compo, c-1940	27″		65	
	UNMKD-120	Laughing Boy (Lastic Plastic), sticky vinyl/cloth body, c-1949	19″		65	
	UNMKD-121	Girl, sticky vinyl	15½″		65	
	UNMKD-122	Lady, brown Ptd compo, c-1940	14″		85	
	UNMKD-123	Vinyl Adult head, cloth body	42″		NPA	
	UNMKD-124	Dionne-type, compo, c-1938	20″		95	

U.S. TOY & NOVELTY CO.

1142	US-1	Wauketoi, The Walking Farmer Boy, w/cart, c-1919			*Catalog Illus.*	

THE UTLEY CO.

	UT-1ab	The Fabco Dolls, c-1917	14-26″		*Catalog Illus.*	
	UT-2	The Tuco Doll, four styles of wigs, c-1918	14-26″		*Catalog Illus.*	

| | UT-3a-e | The Rollinson Doll; faces are three-dimensional stockinet, c-1916 | | | *Catalog Illus.* | |

V

VALENTINE DOLLS

1144	VAL-1	Valentina Ballerina, sv/hp, c-1950, (14″ including stand)	11″	15	19	25
	VAL-2	Bride, hp, c-1950	14″	15	20	30

VENTRILOQUIST DOLLS

	VEN-1	Kenny Tok, compo/cloth (Reliable Toy Co. Toronto), c-1939			35	
	VEN-2	Willie Talk, compo/cloth (Horsman), c-1939			35	
	VEN-3	Howdy Doody, vinyl/cloth, (Ideal), c-1954	21″		18	
	VEN-4	Ricky Lane, vinyl/cloth, c-1964	24″		35	
	VEN-5	Simon Sez, vinyl/cloth, (Horsman) c-1973	30″		30	
1147	VEN-6	Freckles, vinyl/cloth (Uneeda), c-1973	30″		30	
	VEN-7	Willie Talk, vinyl/cloth (Horsman), c-1973	24″	9	12	15
	VEN-8	Emmett Kelly, Willie the Clown, vinyl/cloth (Juro), c-1974	30″		45	
	VEN-9	Hayley O'Hara, vinyl/cloth (Juro), c-1974		8	10	15
	VEN-10	Mortimer Snerd, Friend of Edgar Bergen, vinyl/cloth (Juro), c-1974			30	
	VEN-10-1	Blabby, vinyl/cloth, c-1973	24″		10	
	VEN-11	Ventriloquist Dummy, vinyl/cloth (Juro), c-1974			10	

MTCD Page	Key	Nomenclature	Size	Low	Avg.	High
	VEN-12	Honey Munch, vinyl/ cloth (EEGEE), c-1974	21"		45	
	VOGUE DOLLS, INC.					
1148	VOG-8a-d	Pre-Ginny Compositions	8"	35	90	150
	VOG-9	Girl, compo	8"	35	90	150
	VOG-10ab	Make-up Dolls, compo, c-1943	12"		35 ea	
	VOG-11	Jennie, compo, c-1947	18"		75	
1149	VOG-13	Ginnette, vinyl	8"	20	25	40
	VOG-14	Ginny, hp	8"	30	48	90
1150	VOG-15	Ginny Baby	8"	5	11	18
			12"	6	8	15
			16"	12	18	30
			20"		NPA	
	VOG-16	Lil Imp	11"		18	
		Wee Imp	8"		10	
	VOG-17a	Jan		15	22	45
	17b	Jill		15	22	45
	VOG-18	Jeff		15	24	45
	VOG-19	Ponytail Teen, a "knock-off" of Brickette, vinyl, c-1960	20"	25	37	55
	VOG-20	Musical Baby Dear, c-1962	12"		NPA	
			18"		NPA	
1151	VOG-21a	Bobby Dear "One" and Baby Dear "One" (old face), c-1962	25"		265 pr	
		Baby Dear "One" (alone), old face	25"	30	81	150
1152	VOG-22ab	Miss Ginny, plastic, c-1972	16"	6	15	18
	VOG-23	Lil Imp, c-1964	10½"	18	38	75
1153	VOG-24	My Angel, vinyl/ plastic	14½"		NPA	
	VOG-24a	My Angel, vinyl/ plastic, c-1965	14½"		45	
	VOG-25	Love Me Linda, vinyl, c-1965	15"	19	31	45
	VOG-25a	"Pretty as a Picture" (Love Me Linda), 1967-1968		19	31	45
	VOG-26	Baby Dear "One" (new face) vinyl/ cloth, c-1971	25"	5	8	15

Page	Key	Nomenclature	Size	Low	Avg.	High
1154	VOG-27	Star Bright, vinyl/ hp, c-1966	19"		25	
	VOG-28	Baby Star Bright, vinyl/cloth, c-1966	18½"		20	

W

	WAL-1	The Juggling Clown, (Walbert Mfg.), c-1916			*Catalog Illus.*	

WALKING-TALKING DOLLS

Page	Key	Nomenclature	Size	Low	Avg.	High
	W-T-11	Mechanical Girl (Waltershausen Doll Mfg.), c-1905			*Catalog Illus.*	
	W-T-12	Jenny Lind, The Talking Singing Doll (Jenny Lind Doll Co), c-1916			*Catalog Illus.*	
	W-T-13	Primadonna (Giebeler-Falk Doll Corp), c-1919	25, 30"		*Catalog Illus.*	
1157	W-T-14	Composition Walker, unmkd	23"		95	
	W-T-15	Composition Walker, unmkd	27"		95	
	W-T-15-1	Toddlers, compo/ cloth, c-1934				
	1a	Girl			45	
	1b	Boy			45	
	1c	Dutch Boy			45	
	1d	Puppy Dog			45	
	W-T-16	Walker, compo/sv, c-1948	22"		65	
1158	W-T-17	Schilling Talking Dolls, MP Hr, c-1949	22"	40	60	95
	W-T-17e	Schilling Talking Doll, glued-on MoHr Wg			NPA	
1159	W-T-18	Hard Plastic Walker, unmkd, 1950-1952	28½"	75	95	135
	W-T-19	Key-wind Walking-Talking Girl, plastic, unmkd, 1950-1952	25"	125	175	225
	WALT-1	Baby Belle, pm (German, Waltershausen), c-1906			*Catalog Illus.*	

MTCD Page	Key	Nomenclature	Size	Low	Price Avg.	High
	WAR DOLLS					
1160	WAR-1	Dolls Made by Refugee Artists:				
	1a	Moor (Russian artist Swieka)	15″		NPA	
	1b	Russian Poetess (Swieka)	13″		NPA	
	1c	African Baby, created by Piramonie			NPA	
	1d	Bretonne Peasant Girl (J. Tozan), c-1915	14″		NPA	
	WAR-2a-b	Delavan War Dolls (S.E. Delavan, Chicago), 1916-1921			NPA	
	WAR-3a-e	Dolls Made by Crippled French Soldiers, c-1918			NPA	
1162	WAR-4a-f	Dolls Made by Belgium Refugees (75 characters), c-1918			NPA	
	WAR-5	Dolls in the Service, compo, c-1943:				
	5a	Sailor	15″	65	90	125
	5b	Soldier	15″	65	90	125
	5c	W.A.V.E.	15″	65	90	125
	5d	W.A.C.	15″	65	90	125
	WARD, MONTGOMERY & CO.					
1163	WARD-1	Dew Drop, vinyl, c-1960	12″		25	
			16″		35	
	WARD-2	Wendy Ward (Uneeda), plastic/vinyl, c-1964	11″	15	22	25
	WARD-3	Suzie Steps, plastic/vinyl, walker mechanism, 1967-1968	21″		25	
1164	WARD-4	Baby Name Me, vinyl, c-1965	22″		35	
	WARD-5	Tammy Tears, with layette, 1967-1968	13″		25	
	WARD-6	Carol Brent, vinyl, c-1963	15″	20	35	45
	WARD-7	Hombre, vinyl, c-1971	12″		15	

MTCD Page	Key	Nomenclature	Size	Price Low	Avg.	High
1165	WARD-8	Otis O'Brien, vinyl/ cloth, c-1973	30"		25	
	WELL MADE DOLL CO.					
	WEL-1	Boy, compo/cloth, c-1919	14½"	*Catalog Illus.*		
	WELSCH					
	WEL-2	#200 Bisque-head, BJ compo body	20"	225	269	375
	WETZEL					
1166	WET-1	M. Wetzel Character Baby, compo/ cloth, c-1914			95	
	WHEELER & CO.					
	WHE-1	Little Miss Dot, with wardrobe, c-1913	9"		225	
	WHIMSIE, INC.					
	WHI-1	Wee Willie Winkie, bisq/plastic/felt/ lead feet	5"		25	
	WIGWAM CO.					
	WIG-1a	Backbone Dolls, compo/cloth		*Catalog Illus.*		
	1b-c	Structural Schematic of Backbone Doll, 1918		*Catalog Illus.*		
	WOLF, LOUIS & CO.					
1167	WOLF-1a	Baby Irene, bisq/ compo, c-1913		*Catalog Illus.*		
	1b	Little Jimmy, bisq/ compo, c-1913		*Catalog Illus.*		
	WOLF-2ab	Chubby, bisq, c-1915		*Catalog Illus.*		
	WOLF-3	Fairy Babe, bisq, c-1914		*Catalog Illus.*		
1168	WRI-1	Writing Rita, c-1963		45		

Z

MTCD Page	Key	Nomenclature	Size	Price Low	Avg.	High
	ZAIDEN, DAVID					
	ZAI-1	Zaiden Baby, A line developed at Colonial, c-1915		95	125	185
	ZAI-2	The Zaiden Doll, compo, c-1915		95	125	185

MTCD Page	Key	Nomenclature	Size	Low	Price Avg.	High
1169	ZAI-3	Boy's Head, only, compo, 1915-1918	6″		35	
	ZAI-4	Colonial "Next to Nature" Baby, c-1918	14″	95	125	185
			16½″	125	185	225
	ZAI-5	Next-To-Nature, Bent-limb Dolls, compo, c-1918	14″	95	125	185
			18″	125	185	265
			24″	185	265	295
			26″	265	295	325
	ZAI-6	Miss Colonial, c-1918			* 265	
	DEET DOLLS					
1173	DEET-1	Chubby Tubbies, foam-filled vinyl, (EEGEE) c-1974	16″		15 ea	
1174	DEET-2	Tossie Bean Bag, vinyl/bean bag body (EEGEE)	11½″		10 ea	
1175	DEET-3	Pirouette, cloth, (EEGEE), c-1974	36″		25	
	DEET-4	Karen, walking doll, (EEGEE)	19″		25	
1176	DEET-5	Caroline Kay, vinyl/plastic, (Playland), c-1961	30		NPA	

Index to the Twentieth Century Dolls Series

Just Me 582, 583
Just Rite 495
Jutta 113, 886

K

K 374, 498, 677, 693, 891, 913, 921, 1015, 1021
KB 913
KBK 289
KFS 664
K., Gbr. 111
K.H. 919, 922
K&H (in streamer) mark 921, 922
K and K Toy Co. (K&K) 117, 277, 783, 887-890
K(star)R 16, 226, 274-5, 549, 891-2, 895, 1100, 1107, 1115
K&W 634, 635
Kabibble, Abe 655
Kahler, Atha 919
Kahn, Albert 894
Kahn & Mossbacker 891
Kaizer Baby 16, 274, 275
Kallus, Joseph L. 120-134, 283, 493, 504, 622-625, 848, 965
Kammer & Reinhardt, 274-276, 501, 892, 1100
Kampes 893
Kampes, Louise R. 893
Kandi 710, 711, 717
Kangaroo, Captain 374, 375
Kanko-Walking Doll 894
Kansas City 893
Karena Ballerina 706, 707
Karo Princess 495
Kate 786
Kathe Kruse 11, 277-279, 368
Kathleen 535
Kathy 532, 533
Kathy Jo 1023, 1025
Katie 539
Katie Kachoo 863
Katnip 655
Katrina 1063
Kaulitz, Marion Bertha 894
Kay 279
Kaybee Doll & Toy Co. 913
Kaye, Sammy 329, 330
Kayo 988
Kay Sam Corp. 913, 914
Kaysam Corp. 498, 914, 1016
Keebler Co. 495
Keebler Elf 495
Keene, Carolyn 544
Kehagies 914
Kelley 937
Kellog Co. 30, 31, 495, 496, 714
Kelly 533, 937
Kelly, Emmett 347, 348, 1146, 1147
Ken 293, 294, 936, 937, 949
Kennedy, Cape 932
Kennedy, Caroline 239
Kennedy, Jacqueline 63, 239, 822, 1016
Kennedy, Pres. John F. 348, 349
Kenner Products Co. 896, 914-919, 1008
Kenny-Tok 1055, 1144, 1145
Kentucky Donkey 1102, 1103

Kerr & Hinz 919
Kerry 868, 869
Kestner, J. D. 280-283, 620, 621, 642, 643, 895, 896, 919-921
Ketcham, Hank 149, 150
Kevin 681
Kewpie 2, 120, 124, 283, 284, 310, 624, 625, 656, 888, 889, 980-982, 1069, 1115
Kewpie Kin 240
Kewpie-Type 884, 885
Kewty 587
Keystone Company 1007
Keywind 813, 879, 951, 1097, 1123, 1157
Kid, The 335
Kiddie Joy 81
Kiddie Kar Kid 1142
Kiddie Pal Baby 1051
Kiddie Pal Dolly 1051
Kiddles 942, 944
Killiblues 606
Kindergarten Girlie 1047
Kinemins 823
King of England 1006
King Features Syndicate 624, 663, 664, 669
King, Frank O. 11, 151, 665
King Kong 938, 1016
King Little 848
Kip 680-682, 1071
Kirget 605
Kirk, Jas. S. & Co. 798
Kiss Me 252, 710, 711
Kissing Pink 40
Kissy 260, 261
Kissy Baby 261
Kitchen, Dawn's 681
Kitten 59, 60, 62, 63, 938
Kitten, Littlest 543
Kitty Karry-All 1005
Kley & Hahn 921, 922
Knickerbocker Plastic Co. 142, 308, 349
Knickerbocker Toy Co., Inc. 653, 683, 685, 687, 689, 1005
Knievel, Robert (Evel) 1017
Knight, C. B. 780
Knight, Hillary 1013
Knitting Doll 778, 779
Knoch, Gebruder 111, 763
Knock-off 847, 851
Ko 692, 693
Ko-Ko 623
Koaster Kid 554
Kodak 31
Komikal Musical Klown 1055
Koppelsdorf, see Heubach
Korean 204, 205
Korn-Krisp 496
Koweeka 675
Krauss, Gebruder 111, 763
Krazy Kat 655
Kresge Co. 496
Krueger, Richard G. 957
Kruger 372
Kruse, Hannah 277-279, 370
Kruse, Kathe 11, 277-279, 368
Krypto 647
Khunlenz, Gebruder 111, 763
Kung Fu Grip 785

Kuryakin, Illya 1021
Kutie Kids 578, 579, 985
Kweenie 984

L

LB-12-H-197 871
LBJ 1016
LL-16-H-162 870
L6 1002
L.A. & S. 550, 555, 557-559
Ladies' Home Journal 887
Lady 690
Lady Bountiful 651
Lady Crimson 944
Lady Doll 511, 512
Lady Lace 944
Lady Lavendar 944
Lady Silver 944
Lakeside Ind. Inc. 663
Lakeside Toys 1017
Lamar Toy Co. Inc. 1033
Lamb 939
Lamb Chop 1017
Lambie-Pie 938
Lamour, Dorothy 255
Lamp 986, 988
Lancelot Lion 939, 944
Landon, Michael 1003, 1004
Lane, Ricky 1144, 1145
Langrock Bros. Co. 923
Lantz, Walter Prod. 671
Larry Lion 937, 939
Lastic Plastic, Inc. 236, 923, 1014, 1015, 1141
Latexture Prod. Inc. 930, 931
Latin Quarter 1162
Laughing Baby Peterkin 800
Laughing Dimples 812, 813
Laughing Face 1131, 1141
Laurel Doll Co. 924
Laurel and Hardy 349, 1017
Laurel, Stan 349, 1017
Laurie 548, 749
Laurie, Piper 1017
Lavable Grant Tient 759
Layette Baby 702
Lazy Dazy 871
Leapin' Leopard 938
Leather Dolls 925
Lee, Buddy 32, 33
Lee, H. D. Co. 32, 33
Lee, Jerri 358, 1018, 1019
Lee, Pinky 318, 349
Lee Riders 847
Lee Terri 358-361, 1018-1021
Lee, Terrl 1020, 1021
Lee, Tiny Terri 360, 1019
Leggy (Jill, Kate, Nan, Sue) 786
Lena the Cleaner 574, 575
Lenci 368, 371, 609, 896, 925, 926
Lennon, John 1003
Leopard 938
Leprechaun 505
Leslie 64
Lesney Products Corp. 936
Lettie Lane's Daisy 919
Lewis, Shari 350, 651, 1017
Libbey 346, 378
Liberty Belle 751
Liberty Boy 843
Liddle Biddle Peep 942

About the Author

Carol Gast Glassmire is the wife of a retired Navy chief. She says they have raised "six children, several foster children, seven ball teams, three swim teams, a softball league, and three sets of cheerleaders." They are now grandparents of six and empty-nesters, a condition which has led to still more life-style changes.

She free-lanced throughout the years of raising her family and was publisher/editor of a base military housing facility monthly newspaper for two years. She was employed for five years in civil service in Purchasing and Procurement for the Navy Department and has recently completed a manuscript for a book about her hilarious experiences in government service.

Plans for the future include more books plus a large motor home in which she and her husband, Ted, will tour the North American continent.